The Cooking of China

TIME LIFE BOOKS ®

The Cooking of China

by

Emily Hahn

and the Editors of

TIME-LIFE BOOKS

photographed by Michael Rougier

TIME-LIFE BOOKS, NEW YORK

TIME-LIFE BOOKS

FOUNDER: Henry R. Luce 1898-1967

Editor-in-Chief: Hedley Donovan
Chairman of the Board: Andrew Heiskell
President: James R. Shepley
Chairman, Executive Committee: James A. Linen
Group Vice President: Rhett Austell

Vice Chairman: Roy E. Larsen

MANAGING EDITOR: Jerry Korn
Assistant Managing Editors: David Maness,
Martin Mann, A. B. C. Whipple
Planning Director: Oliver E. Allen
Art Director: Sheldon Cotler
Chief of Research: Beatrice T. Dobie
Director of Photography: Melvin L. Scott
Senior Text Editor: Diana Hirsh
Assistant Art Director: Arnold C. Holeywell

PUBLISHER: Joan D. Manley
General Manager: John D. McSweeney
Business Manager: John Steven Maxwell
Sales Director: Carl G. Jaeger
Promotion Director: Paul R. Stewart
Public Relations Director: Nicholas Benton

FOODS OF THE WORLD

SERIES EDITOR: Richard L. Williams
EDITORIAL STAFF FOR THE COOKING OF CHINA:
Associate Editor: James Wyckoff
Picture Editor: Iris S. Friedlander
Designer: Albert Sherman
Staff Writers: Geraldine Schremp, Ethel Strainchamps,
Peter Yerkes
Chief Researcher: Helen Fennell
Researchers: Sarah Bennett, Malabar Brodeur, Marjorie Chester,
Val Chu, Helen Isaacs, Helen Lapham, Barbara Leach,
Susan Marcus, Jane Peterson, Diana Sweeney
Art Assistants: Elise Hilpert, Gloria duBouchet
Test Kitchen Chef: John W. Clancy
Test Kitchen Staff: Fifi Bergman, Sally Darr, Leola Spencer

EDITORIAL PRODUCTION
Production Editor: Douglas B. Graham
Assistant: Gennaro C. Esposito
Quality Director: Robert L. Young
Assistant: James J. Cox
Copy Staff: Rosalind Stubenberg (chief), Florence Keith
Picture Department: Dolores A. Littles, Barbara S. Simon

The text for the chapters of this book was written by Emily
Hahn, the recipe instructions by Michael Field, the picture es-
says and appendix material by members of the staff. Valuable
assistance was provided by the following individuals and depart-
ments of Time Inc.: Editorial Production, Norman Airey;
Library, Benjamin Lightman; Picture Collection, Doris O'Neil;
Photographic Laboratory, George Karas; TIME-LIFE News Service, Murray J. Gart.

THE AUTHOR: Emily Hahn left her native St. Louis to become the University of
Wisconsin's first woman graduate in engineering. Her unusual accomplishments
since then include living nearly a year with a pygmy tribe in Africa. Later she lived
in Shanghai, where she was interned by the Japanese in World War II. Among her
many books are *China to Me, The Soong Sisters* and *Animal Gardens*. She lives in England with her husband, Professor Charles Boxer.

THE CONSULTANTS: The principal consultant on the book was Mrs. Florence Lin
(*above, right, with Miss Hahn*), a native of Ningpo, near Shanghai. Mrs. Lin super-
vised the testing of recipes in the FOODS OF THE WORLD kitchen. Mrs. Grace Chu
(*below, left*) is author of *The Pleasures of Chinese Cooking*, and owns what is perhaps
the world's largest collection of chopsticks. She and Mrs. Lin have taught Chinese
cooking for years at the China Institute in New York.

THE PHOTOGRAPHER: Michael Rougier (*above, right*) first became acquainted with
the Orient as a LIFE photographer during the Korean War. His pictures have won
him many prizes, including the University of Missouri award for Photographer of
the Year. Now based in Los Angeles, he traveled to Taiwan and Hong Kong to
take pictures for this book. Pictures from mainland China were taken by the Swed-
ish journalist and photographer Ralph Herrmanns.

THE CONSULTING EDITOR: The late Michael Field was responsible for recipes and
food presentation for this entire series. One of America's top-ranking culinary experts, he conducted a cooking school in Manhattan and was a regular contributor
to leading magazines. His books include *Michael Field's Cooking School, Michael
Field's Culinary Classics and Improvisations* and *All Manner of Food.*

THE COVER: A spectacular fire pot holds a broth in which a colorful variety of foods
are cooked (*ten-varieties hot pot, Recipe Index*).

Contents

The Recipe Booklet that accompanies this volume has been designed for use in the kitchen. It contains all of the 63 recipes printed here plus 49 more. It also has a wipe-clean cover and a spiral binding so that it can either stand up or lie flat when open.

Introduction: The Cooking of the World's Oldest Civilization

I grew up in the Midwest with the firm conviction that it was wrong to take an interest in food. Why this should have happened to me, or me to it, in the city of St. Louis where French influence still exists, is just one of those things one can't explain. However, that is the way I was. I do not mean that I ate sparingly—on the contrary, I had a good appetite—but that it didn't matter what I ate as long as (a) it wasn't carrots, and (b) it was filling. In a shamefaced way I was fond of sweets, especially a stodgy German type of cake, but I felt that this preference was wrong and I didn't talk about it in public. It was anguish the first time I had a dinner date with a reasonably civilized man who didn't just give half a glance to the menu and then order steak or hamburger, but speculated *aloud* as to which dish on the list was likely to be best. He even asked the waiter's opinion, right out in the open.

This does not purport to be a piece of self-analysis, so we can cut it short and sum it up by saying that I was some kind of nut. And it was this nut, out of all possible people, who was chosen by Fate to go and live in prerevolution China.

It's amazing to think about. There was I, nourished on steak, pot roast, apple pie à la mode, banana split, and (on football days) waffles with a heathen mixture of sausages and syrup. There was I, suddenly face to face with the ancient, honorable and superlative cuisine of the world's oldest civilization. Inevitably the result of the confrontation was a complete transformation of one opinionated Midwesterner to whom all food, but especially Chinese food, suddenly became a brilliant revelation.

My ignorance of the Chinese people was nearly as complete as my ignorance of their food, but—among other things—I learned early how they felt about their cooking. Because I was unhampered by any earlier knowledge, I didn't waste time comparing that with this, this with that. I just ate, and as I ate I happily listened to my Chinese friends around me, talking of what they were eating, had eaten and were going to eat. How lengthy these conversations were, and how enjoyable! Most of the sessions took place in restaurants, for the Chinese did most of their entertaining there. Often the cook was invited in from the kitchen for discussion of some dish we were eating or planned to eat in the future, and even a newcomer like me could see that the cook loved these conversations. He was an artist, talking about his art to peers. He was a happy man.

They were golden days—part of the age before 1949 and the Communist revolution. I had left the country by then and was able to keep informed only through newspapers and rumors. Politics apart, I was often saddened at what was happening to old friends, but I didn't foresee what to me was an outrage, and when it arrived I could hardly believe it—that reformers should attack the art of cooking, in which lay some of their country's greatest genius. Chinese cooking had always been something understood and loved by all classes. It made something good and healthful of the most ordinary ingredients, and the poorest man, though he rarely had enough, could have something that tasted good when he did have food.

When the Red Guards appeared in the late 1960s, they attacked every symbol of what they regarded as bourgeois culture. Among the targets in Peking were the city's fine restaurants. According to news reports they started on the Chuan Chu Tah restaurant, described in a guidebook as late as 1960 as being famous for its Peking duck. Under direction from the Red Guards, "The revolutionary cooks and waiters smashed the old signboard, saying that this demonstrated their determination to wipe out all remnants of capitalistic exploitation and to eradicate all customs and habits inherited from the bourgeoisie." In order to serve the workers, peasants and soldiers better, the staff wrote austere new menus, "both cheap and tasty," which cost only half as much as the former meals. The new menus were then distributed to Peking's leading restaurants.

While the repositories of Chinese cooking have come under attack in some parts of the homeland, the cuisine has flourished undiminished outside of China, nurtured by custodians of its culinary secrets. Whatever I describe in the book, therefore, comes either from the old prerevolution days or from those people who got out and have set up new centers of cookery. I must warn you that whenever in the following pages I speak of Chinese cooking, I am speaking of the old dishes and methods. With this understood, we can proceed.

Anyone preparing Chinese food should keep in mind that to the Chinese, food is not only pleasurable but a good deal more. It is a truism that food is life, but with the Chinese it is also health and a symbol of other good things such as luck and prosperity. Heaven loves the man who eats well. At each meal a Chinese adds to his virtue, strengthening resistance to the ills of body and mind, curing ailments or, possibly, rendering himself capable of better work. He is also, of course, staving off death, but so are we all. We Westerners, more simply, eat because we like the taste, and a Chinese meal satisfies us because it is delicious, but we miss a lot if we do not know something about its other excellences.

Chinese food *is* delicious, and it is small wonder that people all over the world want to learn to prepare it. Cooking Chinese dishes demands unfamiliar but reasonably easy techniques. As in all cuisines, what a cook needs most is good will. Given this, with curiosity, patience, a few utensils and some special ingredients, you are in for a fascinating time. Once started, you are unlikely to give up the study of Chinese cooking.

—*Emily Hahn*

I

An Ancient and Honorable Art

Rice affected by the weather or turned [a man] must not eat, nor fish that is not sound, nor meat that is high. He must not eat anything discolored or that smells bad. He must not eat what is overcooked, nor what is undercooked, nor anything that is out of season. He must not eat what has been crookedly cut, nor any dish that lacks its proper seasoning. The meat that he eats must at the very most not be enough to make his breath smell of meat rather than of rice. As regards wine, no limit is laid down; but he must not be disorderly.

—*"THE ANALECTS OF CONFUCIUS" (BORN 551 B.C.)*

A scroll painting by the 12th Century Emperor Hui Tsung shows a party of scholars gathered in a garden to savor and discuss well-prepared dishes, drink numerous jars of wine, and enjoy the music, poetry and conversation of a literary banquet. Despite the passing of the centuries and in the face of political upheavals, many Chinese still feel that the appreciation of fine cooking is as rewarding as the appreciation of other arts.

After a reign of some 2,500 years, the powerful influence of Confucius on Chinese ways of life is certainly on the wane. Even in pre-Mao days, before World War II, when I taught school in Shanghai, Chinese youths resented him almost as violently as they do today. They hated his preaching, his insistence on the value of old age. At that time nobody had yet quarreled with his attitude toward food. On that point, they agreed with the Master that a man cannot be too serious about his eating. I was left in no doubt about this after my first meal in a Shanghai restaurant, to which I was taken as the guest of some Chinese friends.

For one thing, I was exasperated by the behavior of my host, who made what seemed to me a ridiculous fuss over giving the order. After all, I said to myself, we weren't celebrating anything, we were simply going to have lunch. Yet the host went into a long, incomprehensible (to me) discussion about the menu with the proprietor. With every minute that passed I grew more bored and hungry, wondering how people could possibly find that much to say about food. Long after the pro-

prietor had gone away with the order, I continued to feel indignant.

Then the first dish arrived—soup with sliced pork and Chinese vegetables —and I tasted it. I looked up in amazement, waiting for someone else to comment on its excellence, but nobody did. They spooned it up busily, and after a moment I followed their example. I was considering a second bowl when the waiter brought in a number of other dishes that he put on the table in a helter-skelter way, all together. One was steamed fish in black-bean sauce *(page 104)*, tender and juicy, full of different tastes of spice, and enriched by the sauce. There were spareribs of just the right crispness, and a dish of vegetables I did not recognize, crunchy and as fresh-colored as if they had not been cooked. I asked how this effect was attained, and was told that they had been "stir-fried," or cooked quickly in very hot oil. There was also chicken cooked in soy sauce *(page 85)*, and that completed what my host called a plain, simple little meal. It certainly showed me how much I did not know about Chinese food. I had come late to the realization, but I determined to make up for lost time.

Through the following years, pleasantly spent in various activities that included the fulfillment of this resolve, I think I gained a glimmering of why the Chinese have developed this genius for cooking. It has a lot to do with the antiquity of their civilization, which supplied the time—and, for the fortunate, the leisure—needed to evolve a cuisine, and the harsh conditions of their lives, which forced them to pay close attention to everything pertaining to food.

To begin to understand Chinese cooking, one must first understand the attitude toward their land that has conditioned the people of this oldest continuing civilization. The fact is that there are more Chinese than any other ethnic group on this planet, and feeding them is a monumental task. Thus, China is predominantly agricultural. The Chinese is never far from the land. He knows that his life and the lives of his family depend on soil, crops and weather. Whatever affects the harvest shows in his daily rice bowl. His is a direct confrontation with nature each day. This is a point of which Westerners are often ignorant, but it explains much about the life style of the Chinese.

The vast expanse of China has a far greater range of climates than the contiguous 48 states of the United States have. Subarctic conditions prevail in China's northernmost Manchurian reaches, where the ground stays frozen eight months of the year and the maximum annual rainfall is less than 20 inches, yet the southern provinces of Fukien, Kwangtung, Yunnan and Kwangsi enjoy year-round tropical temperatures and upwards of 80 inches of rain. China is very mountainous, with 60 per cent of its land rising at least 6,500 feet above sea level, an altitude that renders it unsuitable for cultivation. (Incidentally, this unevenness in topography puts the nation at a disadvantage, agriculturally speaking, compared with the United States [not counting Alaska]: Though both countries are roughly the same size and both are located in the Temperate Zone, only 11 per cent of China's 3,643,884 square miles can be cultivated, whereas 80 per cent of the United States' 3,022,387 square miles is arable.)

Such harsh conditions inevitably shaped the Chinese attitude toward food. Even the most sophisticated Chinese never forget the absolute *neces-*

sity of food. Since hunger and hardship are so much a part of the Chinese pattern, the avoidance, or at least propitiation, of these evils is an ever-present consideration. Indeed, even the spirits appreciate food and drink. A parent recently dead is regaled with bowls of food and cups of wine set out near his bier, a great feast made of attractive drawings on paper is burned at his burial so that he can give a party when he arrives in the next world, and for three years afterward, while his spirit still wanders close to home, he is offered his symbolic share of good things at family festivals. In the life of this world, the subject of food (always referred to in the abstract as "rice") is so overriding that a common greeting is, "Have you eaten rice yet?"

Where the need for food is so desperate, one might never expect fine cooking—a cuisine—to appear. And yet, it is possibly just because of the difficulties of life that the best Chinese cooking is superlative. The Chinese cook was forced to develop his art. The result has been a triumphant blending of inventiveness, flavor and economy. Cooking was no mere pastime nor merely the means to the end of filling stomachs. (Any cooking that aims at satisfying hunger alone produces the lowest level of cuisine. Chinese cooking, by contrast, was an activity in which the cook was totally engaged.) The eloquence of this art has survived war, famine, flood; it may even survive China herself.

I believe Chinese cuisine is better than any other in the world, and this is a view shared by many, including some who have long been devotees of French cooking. Today, Chinese cuisine is generally considered, along with the French, as one of the two greatest cuisines. For all that, it is simple, highly adaptable to the tastes of other countries, and, best of all, it can be prepared by anyone possessed of a little patience.

A well-prepared Chinese dish is expected to appeal to more senses than the one of taste. Its colors should be pleasing to the eye, the ingredients should be of uniform size, and it should be fragrant. There should be contrasting tastes and textures within the meal; if one dish is crisp, it should be offset by another that is smooth; a bland dish is paired with a spiced one. Always the effort is to create a balance.

This elegant cuisine evolved out of what were distinctly regional cooking styles. In earlier times, difficulties of transport and lack of means to preserve perishable foods caused each region and even subregion to develop a characteristic cookery that depended on locally available ingredients. As communications and methods of food preservation improved, the best recipes began to move beyond their native grounds. They were warmly welcomed, for the Chinese attach so much importance to food that they are open-minded about accepting good, new culinary ideas, regardless of origin. For example, no false sense of local pride prevented a cook in the northern province of Shantung—though proud of his local style —from adapting a dish from Fukien in the south, even though he did not understand, and would not learn, the dialect of his distant colleague.

Some Chinese still refer to the five early cooking styles of Peking, Honan, Szechwan, Canton and Fukien, but today it is more realistic to speak in terms of four more general schools of cooking *(see map, pages 12-13)*: northern (including Peking, Shantung and Honan); coastal (centered

Continued on page 14

11

The Sources of a Great Cuisine

On this map are shown four regions of China—the northern *(shown in purple)*, coastal *(mustard)*, inland *(orange)* and southern *(olive)*—that have contributed distinctive dishes from their local cooking styles to the national cuisine. In the north, Peking, the capital of China for many centuries, was the birthplace of such dishes as Peking duck *(page 166)*, reflecting the fact that the emperor and his courtiers recruited the best chefs in China and encouraged them to develop new dishes. Fukien province in the coastal region was almost inevitably the home of excellent fish dishes but in addition developed renowned soups, clear and savory. A Chinese gourmet has recalled meals at which hosts of this area, proud of their famous soups, have served three different kinds in a banquet of only 12 dishes—a proportion he found excessive. Canton, in the south, has perhaps the most varied cuisine in China, partly because of its abundant natural resources and partly because at the overthrow of the Ming Dynasty in 1644 many of the chefs of Peking's Imperial household fled to Canton. On their way south they acquired excellent recipes in each neighborhood, which they later introduced to the kitchens of Canton. The chefs of Szechwan, a province in the inland area, perhaps because of their penchant for more highly seasoned food, developed a distinctive dish called Szechwan duck *(page 52)*, whose mouth-tingling delight comes from liberal use of the Szechwan pepper that has given the region's dishes a fiery reputation.

on Fukien but including Shanghai); inland (Szechwan and Yunnan); and southern (the area around Canton).

In the northern school the staple food is not rice but wheat flour, from which are made many noodle dishes, steamed bread and dumplings. Barbecued meat and dishes cooked at table, such as the lamb preparation called Mongolian fire pot cooked in that region in a utensil of the same name *(Recipe Booklet)*, are popular. Northern food tends generally to be lighter than that of other provinces: a case in point is chicken velvet, a fine pulp of mashed chicken breast that becomes fluffy when cooked in bird's nest soup *(page 191)*. As the name implies, the texture of this dish is creamy, yet its fluffiness makes it seem as light as a meringue.

From Peking (which means northern capital) and its neighboring districts come noted dishes prepared with wine stock. Northern cooking includes both pungent sweet-and-sour dishes and more subtle, delicately seasoned foods. The use of garlic and scallions is also characteristic.

Probably the most famous of the northern delicacies is the celebrated Peking duck *(page 166)*. The fowl used for Peking duck must be a very

14

select fowl—incidentally, the ancestor of Long Island duckling. Traditionally, the duck's carcass is first made fairly airtight by tying up the neck opening, and then the skin is inflated away from the flesh until it is taut. Then it is roasted slowly until the thick, fat skin becomes crisp and golden in color. This crackled skin is the choice part of the dish, though the flesh beneath is also eaten. The skin, together with a piece of the meat, a spring onion and a thick, sweet *hoisin* sauce, is served as a sandwich, made either by folding over a pancake or with two flaps of steamed bread. The combined tastes and textures give an experience not to be forgotten—the crisp, green bite of onion and sweet plum sauce cutting the grease of the crackling (which might otherwise be cloyingly rich), while the pancake or bread holds all the parts together.

Honan, south of Peking, is celebrated for a dish that is known the world over as sweet-and-sour fish, made from carp caught in the Yellow River. There are several ways of preparing it, all equally notable. One of these is to deep-fry, first on a hot fire, then on a slow one, and then again on the hot, so that the outside is crisp and the inside soft. The

In central China, a rain-soaked farmer and his water buffalo strain to plow a flooded paddy—the first step in the age-old rice-farming cycle. Stalks from the last crop, stripped of their grain, have been set in bunches along the ridges of raised land; when they are fully dried, they will be used as fuel or fodder, or perhaps to make a rain cape such as the farmer wears.

sauce, made with wine and garlic and sugar and oil, gives a sweet but pungent flavor, and the crisp-soft combination is what makes the dish a special thing, a perfect combination of contrasting textures and flavors. Monkey head is another fine Honan dish; this is not really made of a monkey's head, but of mushrooms (vaguely resembling those agile animals), which are as prized as are truffles by the French. The imaginative title of this dish underscores the Chinese love of poetic and exotic titles for a variety of things—witness Bullsblood porcelain and Dragonwell tea.

Much of the north is bordered by Mongolia, where people eat a lot of mutton. After the invading Mongols conquered China and set up a dynasty that ruled from 1279 to 1368, a number of their dishes were adapted by the Chinese to suit their tastes. Lamb was introduced to northern cooks at that time, and it has remained a favorite in that region ever since; in other parts of China it is not, although the Cantonese do enjoy baby lamb. Mutton or lamb is the basis of the Mongolian fire pot, already mentioned. There is also the Mongolian grill, an indoor barbecue that I find delicious on a cold, wet day: Long, thin strips of mutton are roasted on a red-hot grill over an open charcoal fire. A lamb dish made in a more common Chinese fashion is jellied lamb *(page 47)*. This is boneless lamb simmered in a strong garlic and soy sauce, then left to cool and jell. It is rather like calf's-foot jelly, if you can imagine that steeped in garlic.

As the northern region gives way to the coastal area around Shanghai, wheat flour is replaced by rice as the staple. The cooks on the coast use more soy sauce and sugar, and specialize in salty and gravy-laden dishes. Fish and shellfish from the many rivers and the neighboring sea are, naturally, popular ingredients. There are gently spiced concoctions of meat, chicken, duck and seafood with, of course, lots of vegetables. In Shanghai and the rest of the coastal region the celebrated dishes include bird's nest soup and a wide range of seafood.

Fukien, which is farther south in the coastal area, produces the best soy sauce, and therefore its cuisine has a good deal of stewing in this sauce, or "red cooking" as it is called because of the color the sauce imparts. The soups are clear and light. The Fukienese excel at soft spring rolls *(page 131)*, which are thin dough wrappers stuffed with an extensive variety of mixtures of several meats and vegetables. The seafood is excellent. Fukien is also famous for its pork and chicken dishes made with sweet-tasting red fermented rice paste.

Turning west, we come to the inland region of Szechwan, Yunnan and their neighboring provinces. Now we are in the country of Szechwan pepper, called fagara. This piquant spice differs from the pepper we know; it has a peculiar delayed reaction, for at first it seems to have no taste at all. Then suddenly there it is, strong and hot. In fact, if enough is taken, it even makes the mouth numb for a little while. Used in cooking, this reaction is not so noticeable, but in any case the flavoring of Szechwan pepper is unmistakable. Inland cooking also makes much use of the fungus called "cloud ear," or "tree ear," as an ingredient. Chicken is seasoned and sealed in oiled paper before cooking. There is excellent ham in the western part of this area, but its most characteristic dishes are those notable for their vigor and zest—chicken with walnuts and hot pepper, diced pork with fish flavor, carp with hot bean sauce, steamed spicy Szechwan pork, and spiced ox tendon. They are all as wonderful to eat as they sound, but my favorite inland dish is Szechwan duck *(page 52)*, Peking duck's cousin. Spiced with pepper and deep-fried after steaming to remove the fat, it is redolent of unfamiliar and delicious flavors; the meat is so tender that it falls apart at a touch of the chopsticks. The experienced diner on Szechwan duck also eats the bones, which cooking should have made tender enough to chew and digest: Chinese say that the crunchiness of the bones is to them the chief appeal of the dish.

The Chinese delicacies Westerners know best—egg roll *(page 130)*, egg foo yung *(page 86)*, roast pork *(page 193)*—are from Canton, in the south. This is because the first Chinese to emigrate in large numbers came from there in the mid-19th Century. Although leaving the country was not easy at that time, the government at Peking was far off in the north and too weak to restrain resourceful southerners from slipping away to Southeast Asia, Europe and America. Foreigners were thus introduced to southern cooking, and for years afterward the Cantonese cuisine maintained top place in overseas Chinese restaurants. It is a colorful style, using lighter-colored soy sauce than do the other cuisines, which does not detract from the hues of the various foodstuffs. The southerners are famous for *dim sum:* steamed dumplings stuffed with meat or seafood, sweet paste or preserves.

Southern cooking is subtle and the least greasy of all the regional styles. The cooks excel in stir-frying. At its best, the cuisine tends to be more costly than the others because the cooks use highly concentrated chicken bouillon as the basis of their soups and general cooking. They like to use nuts and mushrooms in their dishes. They prepare many varieties of seafood and a lot of roasted or grilled pork and poultry. Steamed dishes, too, are featured, and the Cantonese claim to make the best shark's fin soup *(Recipe Booklet)* in China. They also make a wonderful turtle soup . . . but the list would be endless.

Common to the cooking styles of all regions is the important role played by fish—fresh-water or salt, finned or shelled, fresh or dried. In the West we depend primarily on meat for protein, with fowl and fish trailing behind, but the Chinese reverse this order. Since many kinds of fish and shellfish can be dried and preserved, there have never been the transportation difficulties with them that used to complicate the marketing of perishable ingredients. However, dried salted fish has so strong a flavor that it must be used sparingly—even, at times, as a condiment rather than a main ingredient—and dried shrimp and abalone serve as accents as well as complete dishes.

Perhaps Chinese cooking will never again be as it was when it reached its height during the Ching Dynasty (1644-1912), and maybe for our modern tastes this is just as well. One might say the same about French cooking, which is certainly not as it was early in the 19th Century. Yet neither French nor Chinese cooking is any the "less" for the comparison; it is simply different from the way it used to be.

In the old days in China there was more time, and consequently more care. The fantastic art of manners, of social exercise, unmatched in the

Continued on Page 20

This busy market, lining both sides of a bridge, was the wholly imaginary creation of an unknown artist who worked in the 12th or 13th Century. Nevertheless, its sharply delineated details accurately portray aspects of Chinese city life at that time and for many centuries thereafter. Even today, similar market scenes can be found in Chinese cities. The vast building in the background houses the town's military and civil officials. Amidst the noisy bustle there are charming human scenes, such as the man (center foreground) helping an elderly lady who has been knocked down by a porter.

East, was at its apogee. This elaborate style of living is gone, but stories told by elderly Chinese help to convey the flavor of life—and of dining—in Imperial China. I have combined several such accounts into the following description of a dinner party as it might have been given toward the end of the 19th Century by a noble I shall call Duke Wu.

Duke Wu, so our story goes, is an influential official at the court of the Dowager Empress in Peking. His home, a one-story building in a narrow, winding, walled street, seems inconspicuous when seen from the outside, but this is deceptive. Actually the duke's residence stretches on and on, past many courtyards: There are great reception rooms and any number of private apartments tucked in at unexpected spaces. Though it is very early in the day, all the bigger rooms seem to be full, even swarming, with shouting servants in the Wu livery, but this excitement is not due to a sudden uprising, nor is the house on fire. The clamor is merely due to the fact that Duke Wu has decided overnight to give an important dinner in honor of one of his kinsmen who has returned unexpectedly after seven years in the west country, where he has been governing a far-off province. The duke has instructed his major-domo to begin preparations. Hence the noise.

Noise is never strange in a Chinese house, but on this morning it is more than usually deafening. The major-domo is giving orders at the top of his voice, but many of his underlings interrupt him from time to time with comments of their own. The major-domo does not interpret such argument as a challenge to his authority: It is just the way Chinese do things. However, he never permits his decrees to be altered. Servants' complaints are only to be expected, and no one takes them seriously. Everybody knows that the house people are really highly gratified that their master is giving such a big party, for each of them will partake of the resulting glory.

In the duke's private study his secretary sits at a desk with his master's guest list at his elbow, writing out invitations. These are very handsome and elaborate, written in gold ink on thick red paper, containing beside the invitation itself details of date and time of day, and a list of all the other people who are being asked. When all the papers are ready he calls a messenger and sends him off to deliver them. All this has to be done as soon as possible, for the party date is not far off. (In Old China such elaborate parties were usually whipped up within a few days, differing from the Western custom of considerable advance notice.)

All the same, there is nothing slipshod or hasty about the preparations. In another room the host himself solemnly discusses the dinner with that all-important man, the head chef. Duke Wu is very proud of his chef Liang, for Liang's skill has made the Wu table famous in courtly circles. Indeed, he is so famous that the duke and his chef constantly fear that the Dowager Empress may summon Liang to the Palace and put him to work in her own kitchen. Liang would not like this any more than the duke would like losing him. For in the royal kitchens Liang would be one of many; in the house of Wu, he is alone in his glory.

Fortunately the summons has never come, and now master and chef discuss the coming occasion with a gravity that suits the subject. Like his Imperial ruler, Duke Wu maintains a staff of underchefs to help the head chef, all of them ready to take orders from Liang, and each with a specialty. One prepares fish and all meat but the roasts. Another cooks nothing but vegetables. Then there is the roast-meat man, and the man who prepares the sweet things, and one who cooks nothing but rice. All these experts must wait until Liang and the duke make their decisions; only then can they undertake the necessary shopping. Although both the duke and Liang know that there can be no final menu, simply because nobody can be sure what they will find at the market on that particular morning, they agree at last on a general outline. Liang gives the word, and in a great scamper of coolies, brought along to do the carrying, the chefs hurry off to the marketplace.

A huge, sprawling, bustling section of the city, it is still very much like a similar marketplace in the city of Kinsai, described six centuries earlier —in the days of Kubla Khan—by Marco Polo, the Venetian merchant and traveler, in his celebrated account of life in China.

Marco Polo wrote that more than 120,000 people brought produce to sell at the market every week, and his list of what could be bought is staggering. All sorts of game abounded, including deer of various kinds, hares and rabbits, partridges and pheasants and quail. Domestic fowl, especially ducks and geese, were remarkably cheap. Butchers cut and sold meat on the spot. At all seasons there was a great variety of fruits, vegetables and herbs. The famous traveler was especially struck by huge, pearlike fruit weighing up to 10 pounds apiece, with white, fragrant flesh. Peaches grown in China could be found there, as could grapes, imported and therefore expensive. From the sea 15 miles away came a constant supply of fresh fish, brought up the canal in boats or barges by the fishermen as soon as they were caught. Many shops in the same area sold things other than food—spices, drugs, trinkets and pearls. Even in Marco Polo's day rich people imported foreign grape wine; but rice wine, the drink of all classes in China, was of course far more popular. He describes wine shops near the markets, "which are continually brewing, and serve out fresh [wine] to their customers at a moderate price."

As they had been for many centuries prior to Duke Wu's banquet, transport and sale of fresh food were leading preoccupations of many merchants in China's big cities in the 19th Century. Food supplies were carried by boat, oxcart and pack horse, and on foot by coolies, who slung their loads at opposite ends of shoulder poles and hurried along at a special gait, half walk, half run. The farther the food had to come, the more it cost. It is said that the cause of the overthrow of Hsuan Tsung, a T'ang Dynasty emperor of the Eighth Century, was the price he paid for fresh litchis from Kwangtung. His favorite concubine, the notoriously extravagant Yang Kuei-fei, had an immoderate passion for this fruit, expecially the very best, which grew only in the southern provinces. Lesser mortals in Peking contented themselves with dried litchis, but that would not do for Yang Kuei-fei, so the Emperor arranged that during the litchi season she should have a supply of fresh ones every day, brought by relays of couriers on horseback. Such self-indulgence enraged the ordinarily quiet people until they rebelled and toppled the Emperor from his throne.

But we have forgotten Duke Wu's chefs, busily looking through the marketplace, each with an expert eye for his particular sort of food. The fish-and-meat man is busy demanding the best ham from Chinhua in Chiangnan and the choicest carp from Honan. He will probably buy shark's fin as well, for he has the three days needed to soak the fin before cooking it. (Today the fin is usually presoaked, then dried, before going on sale, so that one need soak it only overnight.) He passes up the dried abalone, or *pao yu* as it is called in China, for that needs even more soaking—four days—otherwise it is too tough. If the cook finds it possible to buy any special delicacies—such exotic items as bear's paw or that special cut of turtle meat called the skirt—he will pounce on them, whether or not his master has included them in his menu, knowing that they would add splendor to the party. Rarities like these are always good conversation pieces at a Chinese dinner.

Meanwhile, the vegetable chef is making a nuisance of himself by insisting that the cabbage he requires must be from Shantung, and the dessert chef, if he is lucky, will find a delicacy rare on Peking tables—bananas.

At last the shopping session is over: All the food has been either bought or ordered for delivery within a day's time. The coolies load themselves, and the cortege returns to the Wu house. Now comes the really busy time for the chefs, as they get everything ready for cooking. In China cooking itself usually takes very little time, but careful preparation is essential, and therefore demanding.

In the meantime, house servants are unpacking the best Wu porcelain and washing it, for porcelain too is important, and Duke Wu prides himself on his. It comes from Kiukiang in Kiangsi, where the clay is famous for its whiteness and smoothness. The dishes and bowls of Kiukiang come out of the kilns paper-thin and beautifully colored. Duke Wu's rice bowls are cunningly made in the "rice grain" pattern: That is, when held up to the light, scattered pieces of clear, translucent porcelain can be seen in the matrix. And the bowls are decorated with samples of his own calligraphy. Where Duke Wu's social position and wealth is evident—apart, of course, from the lavish food and wine and the porcelain—is in the dish covers of finely chased silver. The Wu guests are to eat with silver-and-ivory chopsticks, even though it must be admitted that such implements are much heavier and harder to manage than the ordinary bamboo chopsticks used by common people. This is the point of an incident in China's remarkable 18th Century novel *The Dream of the Red Chamber*, by Ts'ao Hsüeh-ch'in. The peasant woman Liu Lao-lao, eating in polite company for the first time in her life, is taken by surprise when she lifts her gold-and-ivory chopsticks, and because of their weight drops her pigeon's egg on the floor. This would not be an extraordinary breach of good manners, because even with light chopsticks it is something of a chore to eat a small bird's egg, such as a pigeon's or plover's, the way the Chinese serve them. Hard-boiled and peeled, their round, slippery surfaces offer no place where a novice can get a safe grip. A person who has mastered the art of eating a small egg whole with chopsticks—light or heavy—can justly claim to be an expert.

Though Duke Wu is giving a very special party and the porcelain and chopsticks are the finest available in China, the table settings for the

The arrival of either bird's nest or shark's fin soup *(opposite, top and bottom)* on his table would give the host at an elaborately formal Chinese banquet his proudest moment of the evening. The intricate preparation needed for these dishes, combined with the rarity of their main ingredients, lends them enormous prestige. The nests used are made by swiftlets that construct them with their own saliva; when cooked in chicken broth with the addition of the finely minced chicken breasts called "chicken velvet" *(pages 41, 191)*, they make a delicious soup. Shark's fin, sold in dried strips, has an unusual chewy consistency when cooked in stock with shredded mushroom and chicken. Both soups should be garnished with smoked ham.

guests are quite different from those that were in use in the West at the time. In place of the fine napery and lace and crystal and silver we would expect, Duke Wu's household offers bare tables made of the choicest wood inlaid with marble and mother-of-pearl. For that matter, until Chinese restaurateurs abroad learned the habits of Westerners, they did not use tablecloths for the good reason that people enjoying their food and serving themselves from dishes in the center of a table are apt to drop or dribble bits of food from time to time. Nobody minded this. It was permissible and even expected.

Before each chair at Duke Wu's banquet is the setting, as we would call it, of a few articles: a small dish, a pair of elegant chopsticks, a porcelain spoon, a bowl, a tiny wine cup without a handle, and a small container, perhaps divided into two compartments, for sauces. The decorations are modest. No flowers adorn the table: The space is needed for food. In fact, the space is already occupied by the first course, the cold dishes. These dishes in themselves are decorations, so beautifully are they arranged in patterns of color and shape with radishes and fruits carved to look like flowers and butterflies. There are no napkins as Westerners know them; at formal banquets the Chinese have always used hot, wet towels twisted decoratively to look like doughnuts or croissants. These are carried in on a tray and handed about several times in the course of a long meal by a servant who uses tongs to handle them, since they are really very hot. After the guests have wiped their faces and hands, the servant picks up the towels and carries them out. At Duke Wu's this evening there will be four separate rounds of towels, for the guests will sit very late at the feast.

If we were lucky enough to be among the guests we should find the sequence of courses puzzling. Duke Wu's dinner does not proceed along the lines with which we are familiar—soup first, then fish, then meat, and so on. Instead, on arrival the guests are shown into the drawing room and greeted by their host, and served with green tea flavored with rosebuds. To nibble as they sip they have their choice of lotus seeds, dragon's eyes (small fruit), dried litchis, honeyed dates, watermelon seeds, crystallized ginger root, almonds and walnuts. They also enjoy looking at tables laden with rare fruits that will be served after the feast: fresh litchis; Tientsin pears that are crunchy and juicy; pomelo, which is somewhat similar to our grapefruit; and Hami melon, very sweet and something like Spanish melon. In addition, an assortment of light and dainty *dim sum*, resembling cocktail food, is served, including steamed dumplings *(page 147)*.

Now everybody is asked to go in and take his place at one of the tables, to await the first dishes on what we would regard as an utterly overwhelming menu. Some of them are represented in this book with recipes. It is understood, since this is in Peking, that the wine will be Kaoliang, a strong, ginlike drink made from the *kaoliang,* or sorghum grain, grown on the neighboring farms. The cold dishes waiting on the table are: drunk chicken (fowl marinated in rice wine, *Recipe Booklet);* five-spiced Yellow River carp; pork kidney with sauce; preserved duck egg; marinated Chinese mushroom; chicken wing stuffed with ham, bamboo shoots and mushrooms; jellied lamb; and pickled celery cabbage.

Then comes the first of the newly cooked, or hot, dishes, an assortment of stir-fried foods: chicken with *hoisin* sauce and cashew nuts *(Recipe Booklet)*, fried pork with walnuts, chicken with pine nuts, fish fillet with snow peas, dried shrimp with cabbage, shredded spiced beef with fried transparent noodles *(page 53)* and shredded beef with oyster sauce.

The third course is a "heavy," or thick, soup of shark's fin, after which the dishes Chinese consider more substantial appear: fried squabs *(Recipe Booklet)*, braised sea cucumber, abalone braised in oyster sauce, chicken and ham in green paradise (a green vegetable supplying the heavenly foliage, *page 84)*, Peking duck *(page 166)*, roast suckling pig and braised shark's fin. These are followed by a light, clear soup, then by the whole chicken stuffed with bird's nest, and with it more *dim sum* and pork-stuffed steamed buns.

The fish course, signaling the end of the meal, is Honan tile fish, much like the famous carp from the same province, but lighter. It is intact, complete with head and tail. The vegetable with it is heart of white cabbage in a thick cream sauce. The servant is careful, as he puts the fish down, to place it as protocol demands, with the head pointing toward Duke Wu's kinsman, in whose honor the party is being given.

There are two desserts: a creamy walnut soup, served hot, and a cold Peking dust *(page 170)*, in which chestnut purée is sprinkled over a mound of whipped cream and surrounded with glazed pecans. And that is all, save for the fresh rare fruits that grace the drawing room and are now eaten to freshen tired mouths, along with cups of the banquet tea, brewed from the rare leaves called Iron Goddess of Mercy.

Did everybody really eat all these dishes? I don't think any one person could possibly have eaten heartily of each dish, but I'm quite sure that the guests showed their good manners by token sampling of most of the platters—avoiding only those that had troubled their digestions in the past. The method of serving made it easier for guests to pick and choose, for no one dish held the center of the stage as the turkey would at our Christmas or Thanksgiving dinner. Whatever was brought to the table was reverently uncovered, as much to show its arrangement and color as to present it to the diners—the Peking duck a golden brown, the vegetables clear green or red or white, and everything placed so as to form an attractive pattern. Each composition took its place in the center for as long as the guests concentrated on it. Afterward it was moved to the side and left ready for whoever wanted to go back to it for another taste, while the next dish was put in the middle.

The host, during the first course, and then the servants kept an eye on the wine cups so that they were never left unfilled. The guests grew merry and played drinking games, challenging each other to empty their cups at a single gulp. Laughter and noise filled the room, and drinking continued until the smiling servants brought in the dessert. After the final cup of tea, the party was over. Everyone said good night, complimenting the duke and thanking him for having given such a splendid dinner. Modestly he protested that it was but poor fare: inwardly, of course, he was pleased. He knew they had eaten a meal they would never forget—a dinner worthy of the House of Wu.

II

"Cooking Chinese" in Your Own Kitchen

Out in the garden in the moonlight, our servant is scraping a golden carp with so much vigor that the scales fly in every direction—perhaps they go as high as heaven. Those beautiful stars up there might be the scales of our fish.

— "BEFORE THE REPAST," AUTHOR UNKNOWN

Yun-li is a Chinese friend of mine who happens now to live in the West. She has done a good deal of traveling in her short life, and like most experienced travelers has learned to make herself at home wherever she is. In our house in England, she often gets a notion to go into the kitchen and try out some dish because she has a sudden hankering for it, or she thinks I will like it, or she has seen an ingredient in a shop window that gave her a new idea for cooking. Some people are mystified by Yun-li's urges, especially since they may develop at any hour of the day. But her behavior seems perfectly natural to me: That is the way people used to behave in China.

Not too long ago she came into my workroom early in the afternoon with a plate of fried potatoes doused in sauce of an unfamiliar, reddish-purple color. We sat down with the plate between us and tried out the dish. The potatoes were fried to just the right stage, not raw but not wilting, and the sauce, slightly gritty, was almost medicinally tart. I had never eaten anything quite like it, but potatoes are the best possible background to new tastes, being in themselves so neutral. I decided, after a couple of bites, that I liked the dish.

"What's this you've done them in?" I asked, chewing.

"Tamarind," she said. "I found it in an Indian place where they have

Scaling a fish with a cleaver, working at a stove and loading prepared dishes onto a tray, servants work in the outdoor kitchen at the resort home of a nobleman. Two woks, partially concealed, sit on the stove, one hidden by a stack of steamers, the other by a flat lid. Although the scene is from an 18th Century scroll, it could be duplicated except for the costumes in any open-air Chinese kitchen, for the tools and the pans have hardly changed since the artist depicted them.

all kinds of spices. Potatoes done this way are supposed to be very good for anemia." I am not anemic, but you never know, do you? So I finished my share of the potatoes, feeling all the healthier for them. And as I did I thought of the debt the West owes to people like Yun-li. For she and many other Chinese refugees—some of them celebrated chefs—are responsible for the astonishing speed with which knowledge of good Chinese cooking has come to the Western world in recent years. Chinese food used to be sadly misrepresented in America by "chop suey joints," but today the country can boast a large number of restaurants at which any Chinese gourmet would be pleased to eat. The great professionals have made their fortunes here with their remarkable repertories of dishes. But the Yun-li's have helped spread knowledge of how to cook a Chinese meal to the many Westerners who want to make these delicious dishes at home. They have stimulated the importing of standard Chinese utensils and ingredients —and more important, have shown how to use their traditional taste for experimentation in adapting our own utensils and supplies to the demands of Chinese cuisine.

Actually, Chinese cooking is often simple, even for beginners, provided you hold to a few firm rules. The first thing to remember is that preparation and cooking are separate procedures; all of the preliminaries— which in some instances are lengthy and exacting—must be completed before actual cooking begins. The second rule is that while the cooking is simple, it cannot wait while some ingredient is made ready for the pot. Chinese foods often must be cooked quickly and at very high temperatures. Since cooking times are so short, it is unwise to take your eye off the pot very long, for you must reduce the heat at the first sign of smoking, and you must be careful not to overcook. Each minute can be crucial in the preservation of the crispness that is a characteristic of good Chinese cooking, so it is essential to stick to the cooking time stated in the recipe.

If these two rules of advance preparation and precisely timed hot cooking are observed, you are well on your way to culinary triumphs, Chinese style. Although some of the ingredients may seem unfamiliar, you will soon be glad to make their acquaintance; if certain ones are unavailable, any number of Western foods occasionally can be used in their place *(page 198)* without significant loss. You do not have to adhere too faithfully to all the Chinese customs, for while Chinese cooking has an ancient tradition behind it, part of that tradition is exemplified by Yun-li's penchant for experimentation. The adaptation of recipes, ingredients and utensils to local demands is the Chinese way.

For Westerners, some of the delight of Chinese cooking is the insight it offers into a style of living different from ours. Over the millennia, the Chinese have developed a cuisine that in basic foodstuffs, preparation and techniques offers refreshing variations to those standard elsewhere.

For example the Chinese use oil in their cooking—usually vegetable oil— to a far greater extent than we do. With this oil, one can get the high temperatures needed to seal in the flavor and original color of the foods, and also to preserve the all-important crispness and vitamins of vegetables. "Sizzling hot oil is the marrying agent," says a Chinese cook. "It brings out the best qualities of each food to produce a new appearance and happy combination of flavors after the cooking ceremony is completed."

Cooking oil is all the more important since the Chinese seldom if ever use butter. They do not use many other dairy products either. In the past, cow's milk and its derivatives—butter, cream and cheese—were not a part of their diet at all, but today ice cream has become a favorite snack in many parts of the country. There have been other breachings of the gate as well—cream, for instance, is used in the rich dessert called Peking dust.

Vegetables rather than meat predominate. Though we in the West think highly of roast beef or thick steak, meat is a luxury to the Chinese and they prefer it in small quantities, usually pork rather than beef, and cut into small pieces and mixed with the vegetables.

For protein the Chinese depend heavily on the soybean, which has for this reason been called the cow of the East. Soybean oil, like peanut oil, is used for cooking. The beans, soaked, ground fine and strained, produce a fluid called soybean milk, which is a good substitute for cow's milk; doctors—even Western doctors—prescribe it for babies who cannot get mother's milk and are allergic to cow's milk. The soybean is also turned into bean curd, an exceptionally high-protein food known in China as "the meat without bones." (To make it, soybean milk is boiled, strained and curdled by adding a small amount of gypsum. Then the mixture is spooned out onto thin muslin, wrapped in pieces three by three by one and a half inches, and heavily weighted to squeeze out the moisture until the pieces are only about one half inch thick. The result is a smooth, mild, creamy cake with a fragile but slightly elastic texture something like firm custard.) Bean curd may be used in a variety of dishes, but it is delicate and must not be overcooked or else it will fall apart. It is inexpensive, which makes it doubly valuable in a poor country. The thickened curd skin is a food by itself, with a more concentrated flavor. Fermented bean curd tastes much like cheese. Then, of course, there are soy and mung-bean sprouts, which most of us know in Chinese dishes. In one form or another the soybean can be found in dishes eaten at every meal.

In spite of the great variety of dishes we find on any Chinese menu—fish, vegetable mixtures, meat, fowl and soups—you may have noticed that there are few sweet ones. This is because the Chinese do not go in much for confections and pastries, though children sometimes suck rock sugar. They prefer dishes with stimulating tastes—what the English call savories—such as dumplings and spring rolls. They eat savories, or sometimes dried fruits or biscuits, as between-meal snacks.

The few sweet dishes in the Chinese cuisine are usually encountered only at feasts, and then they are served most often as a diversion in the middle of the meal. This order may seem strange, but the Chinese system of arranging courses is different from ours. (To make things easier, the arrangement of courses in the Recipe Booklet approximates Western practice.) A meal in China need not begin with hors d'oeuvre. Duke Wu's banquet, for example, started with a selection, attractively arranged, of cold meats, fish and sliced or carved vegetables. There might be a soup near the beginning, but it is not the only one that is served at the feast. Soups play various parts in the symphony of a well-composed meal—not only is

Continued on page 32

Browning ingredients for a chicken-and-bean-curd dish, and stirring with chopsticks, the cook uses the intense fire of a brazier.

A Hong Kong Kitchen Long on Tradition

The cooks shown on these pages work in the fairly new home of a well-to-do Hong Kong family; nevertheless the kitchen equipment is in the direct line of ancient Chinese practice. Dominating the room is the red-tile coal-fed stove that runs along one wall, its counterlike top pierced with openings to hold various sizes of woks, the principal Chinese cooking pans. The cooks use a "stove on a stove" (*opposite*), which provides an easily regulated fire for broths or stews; in cold weather, these baked clay pots can be taken right to the dining table to keep food warm. By comparison with the innumerable gadgets found in many American kitchens, it is remarkable how few items this efficient kitchen holds. Its full complement of utensils is limited to little more than metal woks, clay pots, cleavers, chopsticks and round bamboo steamers. The steamers fit over woks (like the one shown in place at the far end of the stove) so that rising heat steams the food that they hold. There are also several different-sized cleavers (indispensable to Chinese cooks for cutting up and moving ingredients), a large mill for grinding rice and peanuts, and a chopping block. So important is the kitchen in the scheme of family life that a specialist was consulted to determine the most auspicious site for this room before the house was built; after that was settled, the rest of the house was designed around it. A further bow to tradition is the red paper placard hanging over the sink, with incense sticks below, asking the kitchen god's blessing on the home and family. While not everybody takes the deity seriously, his continued presence in many homes reflects the Chinese belief that the kitchen merits attention and respect as the source of family well-being.

Grinding rice into flour, one of the cooks uses a granite mill, which serves much the same purpose in Chinese kitchens as a large mortar and pestle. It is also used for such tasks as making peanut oil or bean paste.

Precisely mincing pork, the other cook uses a steel cleaver. Chinese cooks use these tools—clumsy or downright dangerous to some Western eyes—in place of knives even for very delicate operations. The chopping block is simply a cross section of a tree trunk.

there one as a light savory course, but clear soups are often used between courses as palate cleansers. Richer soups, like velvet corn, may, however, be served as a separate course.

As you begin to explore Chinese cooking, a few special implements can be very helpful. However, Chinese utensils are not absolutely necessary, despite the insistence of some enthusiasts. Even some of the Oriental women who have settled in America do very nicely without them, for quite acceptable substitutes are to be found in any American kitchen. But the Chinese utensils are useful, especially for the beginner, and fun as well. They are not expensive and they are easy to find, so it seems a pity not to try them out. In case the thought of a new set of pans worries you because they might take up a lot of room, relax: These utensils are so versatile that remarkably few are needed.

First in importance is the *wok* (rhymes with sock), which serves as both cooking pan and pot; the name in Cantonese means simply "cooking vessel." Its shape has remained unchanged for centuries. A wide cone rounded at the bottom, it has one or two handles. The wok's shape was originally dictated by the Chinese stove, which, like the wood-burning ranges once used in our kitchens, had an open top surface into which the round-bottomed wok with its flared-out sides fitted securely. Nowadays a metal collar or ring purchased with the wok adapts it neatly to any gas or electric range. The wok usually comes with a snugly fitting aluminum lid. In its classic form the vessel itself is made of iron, which keeps a steady, intense heat. However, very satisfactory woks are also sold in steel, stainless-steel and aluminum versions.

The wok is a wonderful addition to the kitchen: Any discussion of specific Chinese cooking methods will show clearly how practical it is. Its constant, even heat makes possible the very short cooking times so important in Chinese food. It is especially suitable for stir-frying, but there are few cooking methods for which it cannot be used, or ingredients that cannot be cooked in it, in either Chinese or Western style. For example, its smooth sides make it perfect for scrambling eggs or preparing omelets. But its particular success in Chinese stir-frying is due to its shape, since food is easily turned along the steeply sloping sides and evenly covered with oil as it falls back into the bottom. Remember, however, that the smaller the quantity of food stir-fried in a wok at one time the better; there should not be more than one pound of meat in your wok: If you have too many people for that amount, simply cook two lots.

Woks come in several sizes. For ordinary family cooking, one with a diameter of 12 to 14 inches is about right. An iron wok must be seasoned before its first use so that it will not rust, and also so that food will not stick to it. Before seasoning yours, wash it thoroughly inside and out with hot water and whatever detergent or soap you ordinarily use. Rinse it carefully, and then, after wiping it, heat it to dry off any excess water because the iron rusts easily: Even after seasoning, the wok must never be left wet. Wash, rinse and dry the cover in the same manner. Now put the wok over medium heat and wipe the surface with a small pad of paper toweling soaked with peanut or other vegetable oil until you are sure the entire surface is covered with oil. Repeat this process once or twice, until the paper remains clean after wiping: This shows that all dirt and impurities have been removed. Now the wok is ready for use. Keep potholders handy to grip the hot handles while you are cooking. To clean the wok after use, fill it with hot water and let it soak until all particles of food can be wiped off easily with a cloth. Do not use soap and do not scour with steel wool or use strong detergents; these will destroy the surface created by the seasoning process. Gentle rubbing with a cloth, brush or nylon scourer should be adequate. Always dry completely over the flame after cleaning, and do not be alarmed when the wok begins to blacken. It's supposed to.

If for some reason you cannot get a wok, all is not lost; you can still cook Chinese food. Chinese-American cooks suggest a heavy skillet as an alternative. They even declare that because it is flat-bottomed and easily exposed to the heat, the skillet has some advantages over the wok. If you do use such a skillet, take special care to turn the food continually while it is cooking, and thus cook it quickly and evenly.

Another Chinese utensil, the steamer, though not as essential or as versatile as the wok, can be adapted for many purposes. The Chinese make steamers in stacked sets that fit into each other, as many as five at a time, so that several different dishes can be steamed at once. Thus the cook saves time and fuel. Steamers look like baskets or like round, shallow bowls full of holes, and in China are often made of bamboo. The aluminum steamers widely available in America are quite as good, however, and probably easier to wash.

A resourceful cook can improvise perfectly good substitutes for the steamer; the plate-within-a-pot for instance, consists of a food-laden plate that is placed on a rack inside a large, heavy pot with some water in it. The plate ought to stand at least two inches above the level of the water. Cover the pot securely and boil. Instead of using a rack you can put the plate on a bowl, directly in the water; the water should reach no more than three quarters of the way up the sides of the bowl so that the boiling water cannot spill in.

While you can do without a steamer, the Chinese cleaver really is indispensable. Like the wok the cleaver is a splendid tool. It may look clumsy and heavy compared with the gleaming carbon-steel chopping knives so loved by French chefs, but it is even more versatile. Once you have mastered the cleaver you are bound to find how useful it truly is, and not only for cooking Chinese food. A cleaver performs almost every kind of cutting technique with ease, and besides is used for pounding and crushing, and even for scooping up on its blade otherwise unmanageable scraps of food *(see instructions on pages 38-41)*. It comes in two weights; heavy for cutting bones, and lighter for meats and vegetables. Both have wooden handles and broad blades about three inches across and eight inches long. Some cleavers are made of stainless steel, but most cooks prefer those that are made of tempered carbon steel, for they can be sharpened to a finer edge. Like your iron wok, the cleaver must be kept thoroughly dry or it will rust.

Partner to the cleaver is a chopping block, anywhere from four to six inches thick. An experienced chef plays on his chopping block as if he

A small brazier with a wok and chopsticks, used here to stir-fry vegetables, are the mainstays of the kitchen of a Communist Chinese family that can afford only minimal equipment. Much of Chinese cuisine is well adapted to poverty; stir-frying requires less cooking time, thus conserving expensive fuel.

Continued on page 36

Basic Kitchen Tools for Chinese Cookery

Over a period of at least four millennia, Chinese cooks have been refining their kitchen utensils to achieve a maximum of efficiency and usefulness. Illustrated on these pages are the principal implements. The most common cooking vessel is the wok (1). Traditionally, woks were made of cast iron, but today they also are made of other metals. Woks come in many sizes, ranging from 10 inches in diameter to the large sizes used in restaurants. Although the handle on the wok at lower right—shown with cooking chopsticks (2)—differs from those on the other two, all three woks are used in the same way. All are roughly conical and on Western stoves, a metal ring is placed over the burner to hold them securely in place; such a stand is seen supporting the wok at lower right. A very handy instrument for both Western and Oriental cooking is the Chinese cleaver (3), which comes in two types: a heavy chopper, and a thinner slicer and chopper (with a two-tone blade). Once Westerners get the knack of using a cleaver *(pages 38-41)* they may well prefer it to a knife for many tasks. A Chinese cook uses the cleaver on a chopping block (4) generally made from a cross section of a tree trunk. Bamboo steamers (5) hang on the wall and one sits on the wok at lower left. The brass strainers (6) drain deep-fried food; their bamboo handles prevent transmission of heat. The most unusual utensil is the Mongolian fire pot (7), a covered pot with a chimney rising through the center from a built-in brazier below. The brazier, heated by coals, keeps food hot or actually cooks some foods. The Chinese use ladles (8) and spatula (9) in the same way that Westerners do. However, one item rarely found in Western kitchens is the picture of the kitchen god watching over this display.

1 Wok
2 Cooking chopsticks
3 Cleavers
4 Chopping block
5 Bamboo steamers
6 Strainers
7 Mongolian fire pot
8 Ladles
9 Spatula

34

were performing on a musical instrument—which, in fact, is just what he is doing; next time you get a chance, try to listen to the chef at work in a Chinese restaurant. Rhythm is important, as it is in most physical work: When you become proficient you will be able to coordinate the effort of chopping so that everything—the cleaver, your hand holding the food, your whole body—works as one. Try to think of using the cleaver with the same economy of motion you would use in making golf or tennis strokes.

The size of the pieces the cook cuts with his cleaver depends on the kind of food he is working on. It is a rule in most Chinese cooking that all the pieces of food in a dish, vegetables and meat or fish, should be of roughly the same size and shape, not merely for esthetic reasons—though those matter too—but because only in that way can one be sure of uniform cooking. With a cleaver, food can be cubed, sliced, chopped, minced or shredded to any size.

The cleaver's broad blade is often used to carry cut-up food from chopping block to pot. A Western housewife might laugh at this idea and say that a plate surely would be better, but the aim in a Chinese kitchen is to keep things simple and quick. It saves another dish to use the cleaver as a carrying tool, and it saves the time that would be taken in getting— and cleaning—a plate. Anyone who watches a Chinese cook at work must be struck by the way he or she cleans up as he goes along. There is no trail of dirty pots and utensils. The cook keeps a clean damp cloth at hand and is continually wiping his cleaver or the table at which he is working. He completes each action as he does it, which is one reason he can produce elaborate meals in a tiny kitchen.

Two more tools just about complete the equipment you need. It is a good idea to have a large skimmer, preferably with a wooden or plastic handle, and a long pair of cooking chopsticks for handling the food. Once you can handle chopsticks *(page 44)* you will find them better than an ordinary metal fork when you are cooking in hot oil, for they do not conduct heat as metal does and they keep your hand a long way from the heat. In general chopsticks are extraordinarily useful; at a Chinese meal they are employed for eating everything but soup, for which porcelain spoons are provided. You can even cut tender meat with chopsticks and, if you are very adept, remove shreds that cling to a bone. The Chinese word for these tools is *kuai-tse*, which sounds like the word for "quick little boys," and that presumably is where we get our term, because in pidgin English a foreigner says "Chop, chop" when he means "Quick, quick!"—possibly a corruption of a Cantonese phrase, *kop, kop*, that means the same thing.

During the struggles of your earliest attempts to eat with chopsticks you may wonder why on earth the ancient Chinese did not spear his food with pointed sticks as our Western ancestors did—a practice that ultimately led to invention of the tined fork. The answer very likely lies in the vexatious and old shortage of fuel that has forced the Chinese to cut up food before it is cooked. Since everything is diced and shredded when it comes to the table, who needs knives and forks? Eating Chinese food with a fork is not unlike trying to spear a mouthful of peas. The lifting, shoveling action of chopsticks is much faster and much more satisfying.

The earliest chopsticks were probably made of bamboo. Some esthete then may have whittled himself a pair of fine hardwood chopsticks, and a later esthete, perhaps a Croesus, thought of using ivory. There were many trials of other cherished materials, amber and jade among them, but several centuries ago chopsticks made of silver and ivory were an accepted status symbol at any rich man's table. They were also on occasion a silent proof of his good faith. In those days a lord who wanted to rid himself of a number of enemies might polish them off all at once by inviting them to a fine dinner, one of whose dishes had been poisoned. Since it was believed that silver would turn black in the presence of poison, and that ivory in the same circumstances would fly to pieces, guests whose chopsticks remained whole and untarnished could be easy in their minds and eat their fill. One wonders how many people nearly died of heart attacks when they dug into egg dishes with their silver sticks and saw the silver blacken.

In a Chinese household wealthy enough to use ivory chopsticks, they are treated with great care. Ivory should not be subjected to extreme heat: Heat yellows and warps the material, so chopsticks of ivory must be carefully washed in lukewarm water and thoroughly dried. In more general use are inexpensive chopsticks of bamboo or wood that can be bought in bundles of pairs: 10 is the usual number when one buys bowls, spoons and teacups, since that is the maximum number of persons ordinarily seated at a single table at a Chinese banquet.

Chinese will tell you that they can guess many things about a person from the way he handles his chopsticks. If he places them across his rice bowl between bouts of eating, it indicates that he is a boatman, for this is considered a good omen in navigation. Usually, however, placing chopsticks across the rice bowl is simply the concluding gesture of the meal, signifying "dinner's over" or "I can't eat another bite." If the holder pushes the sticks against his stomach to even them up instead of tapping them on the table, chances are he is a coolie and is used to eating out of doors, squatting on the ground. The marital future of a baby girl can be foretold by the way she first picks up a set of chopsticks, for if they are grasped at the far end her husband will come from a distant province, but if they are seized near the eating end her husband may turn out to be the boy next door. To drop your chopsticks means bad luck. To find a pair of unequal length at your place at table means that you will miss a train, or boat, or plane.

With tools like these—or their American substitutes—you are ready to explore the principal cooking methods developed by the Chinese. Many of them resemble techniques familiar in the West but all involve nuances that give Chinese cooking its savory distinction. All are interesting and highly efficient, but the major ones include:

Stir-Frying: This is the most common method of cooking Chinese food. It requires meat and vegetables or other foods cut for uniform cooking. Once that advance preparation is completed, you put a little cooking oil into the wok, swirl it about, and heat over a high flame. Then place meat and tough vegetables in the wok, followed by others in descending

Continued on page 42

Using the Versatile Cleaver

Chinese cleavers may look like deadly weapons, but the Chinese have evolved a safe technique for handling them. Grasp the blade between thumb and forefinger just forward of the handle and let the remaining fingers fall naturally along the side of the blade. As shown on the facing page, hold the object to be cut with your fingers tucked under, and grip it with the fingertips. Cut carefully, with the flat of the blade held against the knuckles as a guide. Efficiency and safety are enhanced if the cleaver is lifted only a little. The cleaver performs a wide variety of operations. The illustrations on this and the following pages refer to specific ingredients, but these techniques can often be used for other foods.

The cleaver alone can easily prepare ingredients such as *(clockwise from top):* beef slices, shredded bamboo shoots, chicken velvet, minced ham, roll-cut carrots, sliced kidneys, diced ham and tenderized pork chop *(center)*.

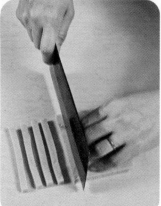

DICING HAM

1 Begin by cutting ham into strips as wide as the meat is thick, here, about ¼ inch.

2 Holding strips together, cut at right angles in the same ¼-inch width so that you get perfect cubes.

SHREDDING BAMBOO SHOOTS

1 Place shoot on one of its sides, slice, and stack as if to form a flight of stairs.

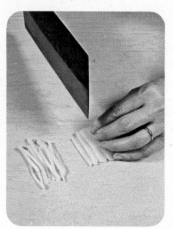

2 Cut in thin strips, parallel to the "steps." This unusual method of stacking keeps the vegetables from sliding.

SLICING BEEF

1 Cut a flank steak *with the grain* into long strips about 1½ inches wide.

2 Cut each strip *across the grain* into ¼-inch slices. Cutting across the grain gives meat more tenderness.

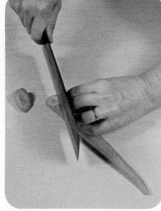

ROLL-CUTTING CARROTS

1 Make a diagonal slice straight down, roll carrot a quarter turn, slice again.

2 Repeat until all the carrot is used. Cut this way, carrot sections have greater surface area to absorb seasonings.

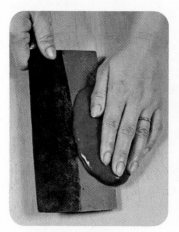

SLICING PORK KIDNEY

1 Holding the cleaver in a horizontal position, slice the kidney in half.

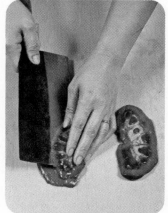

2 With cut surfaces up, slice about ¼ inch lower to remove the tough membrane from the meat.

3 Thinly slice each half with the cleaver almost parallel to the cutting board and the meat held firmly in your other hand. This method cleans the kidneys thoroughly so they can be cooked and eaten at once.

How to Work with the Flat, the Blunt Edge and the Handle of the Cleaver

PEELING GARLIC
Strike with flat of blade to loosen skin; peel; to crush, strike harder.

TENDERIZING MEAT
Pound both sides with blunt edge of blade, producing crosshatches.

GRINDING PEPPERCORNS
With a circular motion, crush peppercorns between handle and bowl.

MINCING MEAT
1 Cube meat; then chop into bits, keeping tip of blade pressed to cutting board.

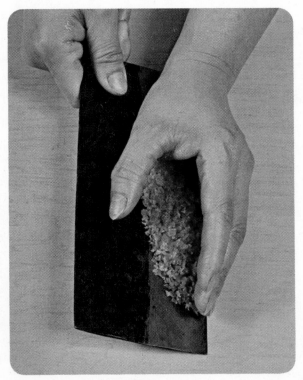

2 Once the meat is minced, it can be swept onto the blade with the left hand and carried to pan or plate.

The Many Uses of a Cleaver in Preparing a Purée Called Chicken Velvet

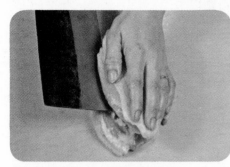

1 Lay a chicken breast on its side. Hold firmly and cut lengthwise along the curved breastbone.

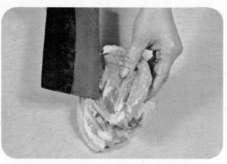

2 Working slowly, cut the meat from the bones, following the side of the breastbone and the outside of the ribs.

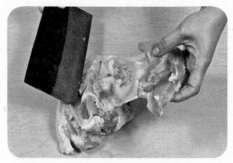

3 Pull meat off bones and away from skin, using the cleaver as needed to free it. Repeat on the other side.

4 Separate the small tubular cores of meat called the chicken fillets from the breast proper with your fingers.

5 Hold one end of the white tendon in each fillet and scrape the meat away, chopping it roughly into bits.

6 Holding the front of the main breast section, scrape meat from membrane with light strokes.

7 Combine shreds of meat from the breast with fillet and gently mince, following method shown on page 40.

8 As you mince, add, a little at a time, about 4 tablespoons of water. The meat will become fluffier.

9 Keep mincing until the meat is reduced almost to a paste. Finally, it will take on a puréed texture.

10 Use cleaver to fold mixture and transfer it to a bowl. To complete chicken velvet, combine the purée with cornstarch and salt, then egg whites —as described in the recipe for bird's nest soup *(page 191)*.

order of delicacy. The rapid coating with very hot oil seals in all the juices and flavor and also makes for quicker cooking. Add a little liquid such as stock, and whatever sauces and seasonings you wish. Stir-frying rarely takes more than five minutes. Because the wok retains heat so well it may be necessary to lower the heat to prevent smoking. The ease with which a flame can be adjusted makes gas generally more suitable for Chinese cooking than electricity (the coils of ranges retain their heat longer than do gas burners, despite flexible controls, but this disadvantage can be overcome if the wok is simply lifted off the burner to moderate the heat). Success in stir-frying depends very much on your knowledge of the textures and composition of the ingredients you are using and the order in which you introduce the different foods to the heat. Each food has its own cooking time, no more and no less; so it is of paramount importance to supply the right amount of heat for the right amount of time to secure best results. And you should eat stir-fried food as soon as it is ready, for it will get flabby and greasy if allowed to stand.

Steaming: Meat, fowl, dumplings, bread and, in some parts of China, rice, are steamed. "Direct steaming" is the usual method—rising vapor, from the pan directly on top of the heat, goes through the food on the perforated shelf or shelves stacked above. Cooking time depends on the ingredients used. For food that requires long steaming, the water may boil away before the cooking is finished, and should be replaced when necessary by more already-boiling water, carefully added so that it will not splash when poured into the pan.

Deep-Frying: This is done in several stages. In the preparation stage, the ingredients are usually cut into cubes. The pieces are coated with egg-flour batter or cornstarch, then plunged into hot oil a few at a time, to prevent the oil from cooling suddenly. The coating of batter plus high heat seals in juices in deep-frying. Sometimes the ingredients are marinated first in soy sauce and sherry (which takes the place of hard-to-find rice wine). The cooking stage is itself often divided into steps, sometimes two, sometimes more. The food is left in the oil only briefly the first time, long enough to turn a light golden color without burning. Then the oil is reheated and the food returned to it and cooked to a finish, when it should be crisp but cooked all the way through. Some cooks like to repeat the process of removing and cooking more than twice, asserting that this ensures the crispest possible foods. All deep-fried foods should be drained as soon as they are taken out of the oil. To cook a whole duck in this manner, season and steam the bird to reduce the fat; then when the oil on the bottom of the wok gets hot enough to move, immerse the bird and cook until crisp and brown. Beef or pork can also be deep-fried in the same way.

Shallow-Frying: This is a slower method of frying than stir-frying. A heavy skillet is used in this process instead of a wok, and the food is not stirred. It is used to cook meat dumplings and in the first stage of cooking soy-sauce beef.

Red Cooking: This method, a slower process than frying, has earned this name because the soy sauce in which the food is cooked darkens the food. It is a preferred method of preparing whole poultry, coarse-fleshed fish and large cuts of meat like shoulder of pork. The food is browned for a second in oil in a wok or immersed for a very short time in boiling water, then placed in a specified amount of sauce and cooked over low heat in a tightly covered wok—in other words, braised. The meat should be turned from time to time to prevent its sticking to the pot. The cook will always save the remaining gravy, add water and seasoning to it, and use it to cook other foods, removing some of that sauce in turn to be used elsewhere. The oftener it is used, the richer and more fully flavored the sauce becomes. A sauce of this sort can be kept going almost indefinitely, sometimes even for generations. The Chinese call such a preparation a master sauce.

Clear Simmering: This is a slow cooking in clear liquid, often broth. The Chinese use this delicate method for fish, chicken and clear soups.

Smoking: This is less a cooking method than a way of flavoring. Traditionally, brown sugar is burned in a tightly closed container insulated with foil so that the strong smoke flavors the food, which is placed on a rack within the pot.

Roasting: This method of cooking gave the 19th Century English essayist Charles Lamb the inspiration for a diverting and wholly untrue story, "A Dissertation on Roast Pig." For centuries, he wrote, the Chinese ate their meat raw. One day a swineherd's son, whose father had left him alone in the house with a newborn litter of pigs, began playing with fire and accidentally burned down the house with the piglets in it. The boy was horrified. Futilely pawing over the ashes, he happened to touch some of the charred meat and burned his fingers. He snatched his hand away and put his fingers into his mouth. To his astonishment his fingers tasted delicious. He touched the burnt meat again and tasted once more, and it was better than ever. By the time his father came back, the boy was eating hunks of the smoking meat. The swineherd in turn was horrified, as well he might be—nobody in his experience had ever before eaten burnt flesh—but the boy persuaded him to try some, and he too was immediately converted.

After that day, whenever the swineherd and his son got possession of a pig they put it indoors, burned down the house and had a feast. Of course, such a secret could not be kept very long. Inevitably the neighbors caught them in the act. These people too were shocked and disgusted, they too then experimented, they too found that the taste of roast pork was delightful. The practice spread wider and wider, until all over China houses were being burned down. At last some genius worked out a simpler, cheaper fashion of roasting pig, and ever since that day mankind has used the spit.

The mention of a spit is about the only factual part of this pleasant tale. The Chinese do indeed roast pork on a spit or some variation of one. But first they rub the meat with oil and then often marinate it for a while in a sauce containing soy, which gives it color. Then it is quickly seared over an open flame to crisp the skin, and roasted slowly—never lying in a pan, but hanging on hooks or resting on a rack—until it is done. A receptacle is placed beneath the roast to catch dripping juices. This method is excellent for any large cut of meat or whole fowl, and you almost never have to burn down a house to get good results.

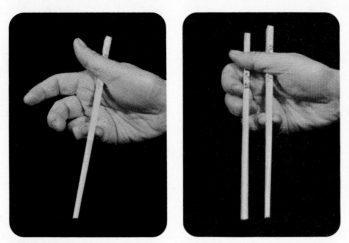

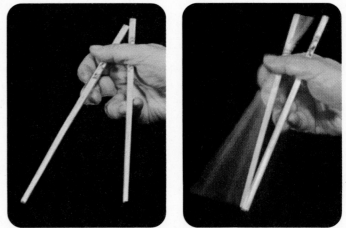

Holding one chopstick ⅔ of the way from its narrow (or round) end, cushion it in the curve of flesh between the thumb and forefinger and let it rest on the end of the little finger (1). Close the thumb over the chopstick to steady it; hold the second chopstick firmly between thumb and forefinger (2). Allow your middle finger to give the second chopstick support so that it is perfectly free to move, forming an angle with the first chopstick (3). Keep the tips even with one another at all times (4). The expert hand in these pictures is consultant Grace Chu's; she has found this technique an easy one for non-Chinese to master.

Hold chopsticks about an inch apart, at an angle to the food (5), and grasp pieces with the tips (6). Rice can be "shoveled" into your mouth from a lifted bowl. There is no one-and-only way to hold chopsticks, so shift this grip if necessary for comfort.

Stabbing at bean curd as if with a dagger, a four-year-old on a picnic near
Taipei, Taiwan, learns to use chopsticks under the amused smile of his mother.

Since the Chinese cuisine consists of thousands of dishes—some of which are but slight variations of others—it is enormously difficult to give precise English names to each dish. To make the names in this book as useful as possible, the title of the dish is given three ways: a phonetic rendering indicating approximately its pronunciation in Mandarin, the official language of China; in Chinese characters; and, finally, by an English name that usually emphasizes ingredients and methods of preparation, but may be a fanciful term by which the dish is commonly known.

Liang-pan-lu-sün
FRESH ASPARAGUS SALAD

涼拌蘆筍

1½ to 2 pounds of young, fresh asparagus, each stalk no more than ½ inch in diameter
4 teaspoons soy sauce
1 teaspoon sugar
2 teaspoons sesame-seed oil

PREPARE AHEAD: 1. Bend each asparagus stalk back until the tough root end snaps away. Discard the ends. Slice the remaining stalks in 1½-inch lengths, using the roll-cut method: that is, making a diagonal slice through one end of the stalk, then rolling the stalk a quarter turn and slicing again *(page 39)*. There should be about 3 cups of asparagus pieces.

2. Wash the asparagus under cold running water and parboil the pieces by dropping them into 2 quarts of rapidly boiling water for 1 minute. Drain at once, and run cold water over the asparagus to stop their cooking and set their color. Spread them on a double thickness of paper towels and pat them completely dry.

TO ASSEMBLE: In a small glass bowl, combine the soy sauce, sugar and sesame-seed oil, and mix until the sugar is completely dissolved. Add the asparagus. With a large spoon, toss to coat each asparagus piece thoroughly with the dressing. Chill slightly—no longer than 2 hours—before serving. As a separate salad course, this will serve 4. As part of a Chinese cold plate *(overleaf)* or full meal *(page 200)*, it will serve 6 to 8.

Wu-hsiang-niu-jou
BRAISED STAR ANISE BEEF

五香牛肉

2 pounds boneless beef shin
3 to 4 cups cold water
5 tablespoons soy sauce
2 tablespoons Chinese rice wine, or pale dry sherry
2 tablespoons sugar
4 slices peeled fresh ginger root, about 1 inch in diameter and ⅛ inch thick
1 whole star anise or 8 sections of star anise
1 tablespoon sesame-seed oil

Place the beef in a heavy 3- to 4-quart saucepan and pour in 3 to 4 cups of cold water—enough to just cover the meat. Bring to a boil over high heat and, as the scum begins to rise to the surface of the water, skim it carefully. Then stir in the soy sauce, wine, sugar, ginger and star anise, and partially cover the pan. Reduce the heat to moderate and cook the beef, adjusting the heat to keep the liquid at a simmer, for 2½ to 3 hours, or until it shows no resistance when pierced with the tip of a sharp knife. There should be about 1 cup of cooking liquid left in the pan. If there is more, remove the cover and increase the heat somewhat, and cook until the liquid is reduced. Add the sesame-seed oil and simmer slowly for another 10 minutes.

When the meat is done, transfer it to a carving board and, with a cleaver or sharp knife, cut it into the thinnest possible slices. Arrange them attractively in overlapping layers on a heated platter. Remove and discard the ginger and star anise, and pour the braising sauce over the beef.

Or you may, if you wish, serve the beef cold. In that event, let the unsliced beef cool in the sauce. Then refrigerate it until you are ready to serve it. Carve the beef into paper-thin slices and present it as part of the cold plate *(overleaf)*, or serve the beef as a separate dish with or without the braising sauce.

As a main course, this recipe will serve 4 to 6. As part of a cold plate or Chinese meal *(page 200)*, it will serve 8 to 10.

Tung-yang-jou 凍羊肉
JELLIED LAMB

This is a modernized version of a classic Chinese dish. The original recipe did not, of course, use packaged gelatin but fresh pork rind, chopped fine and cooked for hours until it turned to jelly.

PREPARE AHEAD: 1. With a cleaver or sharp knife, trim the lamb of any fat and cut the meat into 1-inch cubes.

2. Crush the garlic cloves, one at a time, by placing the flat of a cleaver, the side of a large knife blade or even a wooden kitchen mallet over a clove and giving it a sharp blow with your fist. Remove and discard the garlic peel.

3. In a heavy 1- to 2-quart saucepan, combine the lamb, salt, soy sauce, garlic, wine, star anise and enough cold water to cover the lamb pieces. Bring to a boil over high heat, skimming off any foam or scum as it rises to the surface. Then reduce the heat to low and simmer the lamb, partially covered, for about 1½ hours, or until the meat is soft enough to be shredded with chopsticks or a fork. Then remove and discard the garlic cloves and star anise, and, with a slotted spoon, transfer the cubes of lamb to a large mixing bowl, shred the cubes into tiny pieces and set the cooking liquid aside.

4. Pour the unflavored gelatin into ¼ cup of cold water and let it soften for about 5 minutes.

5. Stir the softened gelatin into the lamb's cooking liquid, bring to a boil and simmer, stirring constantly, a moment or two until the gelatin has completely dissolved. Turn off the heat and stir in the pieces of lamb. Pour the mixture into a 2½-by-5-inch loaf mold or 1-quart heatproof bowl. Refrigerate for at least 4 hours, or until it has set and is completely firm.

TO SERVE: Run a sharp knife around the inside of the mold to loosen the jellied lamb around the edges, and dip the bottom of the mold in hot water for a few seconds. Then wipe the outside of the mold completely dry, place a chilled serving plate upside down over the mold and, grasping both sides firmly, turn the plate and mold over. Rap the plate on a table, and the jellied lamb should slide easily out of the mold. If it does not, repeat the entire process. Cut the lamb into ½-inch slices and arrange these in a row down the center of a platter, overlapping them slightly. Serve chilled.

As a main course, this recipe will serve 3 or 4. As part of a Chinese meal *(page 200)* or combined with other foods on a cold plate *(overleaf)*, it will serve 6 to 8.

1 pound lean boneless lamb
4 large garlic cloves, unpeeled
1 teaspoon salt
2 teaspoons soy sauce
¼ cup Chinese rice wine, or pale dry sherry
1 whole star anise or 8 sections of star anise
1 envelope unflavored gelatin
¼ cup cold water

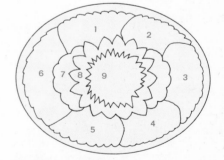

Foods on the cold plate *(overleaf)*:
1 Smithfield ham
2 Abalone
3 Star anise beef
4 Roast pork
5 White-cut chicken
6 Jellied lamb
7 Radish fans
8 Thousand-year eggs (quartered)
9 Asparagus salad

Learning the Knack of Neatly Shelling and Deveining Uncooked Shrimp

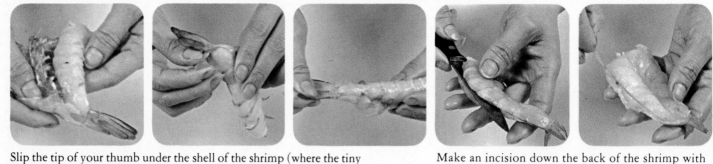

Slip the tip of your thumb under the shell of the shrimp (where the tiny legs are), and, working toward the tail, lift and peel off the shell. When you reach the tail, split the shell by cracking it with a fingernail. Then pull the shell gently to ease it off and leave the meat inside intact.

Make an incision down the back of the shrimp with a small, sharp knife and lift out the intestinal vein. The vein is sometimes black, sometimes white, and an occasional shrimp will have no vein at all.

Tricks That Ensure Successful Stir-Frying in a Wok or a Skillet

In a wok, both the flaring sides and the rounded bottom heat up, so the entire inside surface is used for cooking. To stir-fry food like the shrimp and peas here, lift and turn constantly. The handles get hot too; grasp one with a thickly folded towel to keep the wok steady. Any long-handled spoon will do, or try this Chinese spatula.

In a skillet the cooking takes place on the bottom of the pan, but a utensil like this one with sloped sides makes it possible to lift and turn food as easily as with a wok—and constant stirring cooks the food through evenly and amazingly fast. Keep a grip on the handle to prevent the pan from sliding around.

Ch'ao-hsia-jen
STIR-FRIED SHRIMP WITH PEAS

炒蝦仁

PREPARE AHEAD: 1. Shell the shrimp and, with a small, sharp knife, devein them by making a shallow incision down the back and lifting out the black or white intestinal vein with the point of the knife. Wash the shrimp under cold running water and pat them thoroughly dry with paper towels. Split each shrimp in half lengthwise, then cut each of the halves in two, crosswise.

2. Blanch the freshly shelled peas by dropping them into a quart of rapidly boiling water and letting them boil uncovered for 5 to 7 minutes, or until just tender when tasted. Then drain the peas into a large sieve or collander, and run cold water over them for a few seconds to stop their cooking and set their color. The frozen peas need only be thoroughly defrosted.

3. In a large mixing bowl, combine the shrimp and cornstarch, and toss them together with a spoon until each shrimp piece is lightly coated with cornstarch. Add the egg white, wine and salt, and stir them with the shrimp until they are thoroughly mixed together. Set the mixture aside for at least one hour.

4. Have the shrimp mixture, blanched peas, oil, scallions and ginger slices within easy reach.

TO COOK: Set a 12-inch wok or 10-inch skillet over high heat for 30 seconds. Pour in the 3 tablespoons of oil, swirl it about in the pan and heat for another 30 seconds, turning the heat down to moderate if the oil begins to smoke. Add the scallions and ginger slices, and stir-fry for 30 seconds to flavor the oil, then remove them with a slotted spoon and discard. Immediately drop the shrimp into the pan and stir-fry them for 2 minutes, or until they turn pink. Do not let the shrimp overcook. Then drop in the peas and stir-fry for about 1 minute to heat the peas through. Transfer the entire contents of the pan to a heated platter and serve at once. As a main course, this will serve 2 to 4. As part of a Chinese meal (page 200), it will serve 4 to 6.

1 pound raw shrimp in their shells (about 26 to 30 to the pound)

1 pound fresh peas, shelled, or 1 cup thoroughly defrosted frozen peas

2 teaspoons cornstarch

1 egg white

2 teaspoons Chinese rice wine, or pale dry sherry

1 teaspoon salt

3 tablespoons peanut oil, or flavorless vegetable oil

1 scallion, including the green top, cut into 2-inch lengths

3 slices peeled fresh ginger root, about 1 inch in diameter and ⅛ inch thick

T'ang-yen-hung-lo-po
MARINATED RADISH FANS

糖醃紅蘿蔔

PREPARE AHEAD: 1. With a small, sharp knife, cut away and discard the root and stalk ends of each radish. Wash them under cold running water. Then lay each radish on its side and make parallel cuts along its entire upper surface about 1/16 of an inch apart and 2/3 of the way down. Be careful not to cut all the way through the radish.

2. Pour 1 teaspoon of salt and 1 tablespoon of sugar into a 1-quart glass jar. Add the radishes, cover the jar and shake vigorously so that each radish is coated with the mixture. Marinate at room temperature for at least 6 hours or overnight.

TO SERVE: Pour off all the liquid that will have accumulated in the jar and remove the radishes. The radishes will now be soft and pliable, and can be spread out to form decorative fan shapes. These are used traditionally to garnish cold dishes or salads.

24 crisp red radishes, about 1 inch in diameter

1 teaspoon salt

1 tablespoon sugar

Hsiang-su-ya
SZECHWAN DUCK

香酥鴨

A 4- to 5-pound duck

2 tablespoons salt

1 tablespoon whole Szechwan
  peppercorns, crushed with a cleaver
  or with a pestle in a mortar

4 slices peeled fresh ginger root,
  about 1 inch in diameter and ¼
  inch thick

2 scallions, including the green tops,
  cut into 2-inch pieces

2 tablespoons soy sauce

1 teaspoon five-spice powder

3 cups peanut oil, or flavorless
  vegetable oil

Roasted salt and pepper, prepared
  according to recipe opposite

Steamed flower-roll buns, prepared
  according to recipe on page 149

PREPARE AHEAD: 1. Wash the duck thoroughly under cold running water, then pat it completely dry, inside and out, with paper towels. Place the duck on a table or chopping board, breast side up, and with the palms of both your hands press down hard on the breastbone to break it and flatten it.

2. In a small bowl, combine the salt, crushed peppercorns, scallions and ginger. With a large spoon or your hands, rub the seasonings together to release their flavors. Rub the duck inside and out with the mixture, finally pressing the ginger and scallions firmly against the skin and inside cavity of the duck to make them adhere. Place the duck on a platter and refrigerate it covered with aluminum foil or plastic wrap for at least 6 hours or overnight.

3. Before cooking, mix the soy sauce and five-spice powder thoroughly together in a small bowl, and rub it over the skin and inside the cavity of the duck.

4. Pour enough boiling water into the lower part of a steamer to come to within an inch of the cooking rack (or use a steamer substitute as described on page 56). Place the duck on its back on a deep, heatproof platter ½ inch smaller in diameter than the pot so that the steam can freely circulate around the duck. Place the platter on the rack, cover the pot securely and bring the water in the steamer to a rolling boil. Keeping the water at a continuous boil, steam the duck for 2 hours. Keep a kettle of water at a boil all the time the duck is steaming, and use this to replenish the water in the steamer as it boils away. Turn off the heat. Let the duck rest in the tightly covered steamer for 30 minutes, then turn the bird over on its breast. Re-cover the steamer and let the duck rest for 30 minutes longer. Transfer the duck from the steamer to a platter lined with a double thickness of paper towels. Brush off and discard the scallion pieces and ginger slices, and place the duck in a cool, airy place to dry for 3 hours or longer.

TO COOK: Pour 3 cups of oil into a 12-inch wok or heavy deep-fryer and heat it until a haze forms above it or it reaches a temperature of 375° on a deep-frying thermometer. With two large spoons, carefully lower the duck into the hot oil on its back and fry it for about 15 minutes. Keep the 375° temperature as constant as you can and move the duck about from time to time with chopsticks or two slotted spoons to prevent it from sticking to either the bottom or sides of the pan. Then turn the duck over on its breast and deep-fry it, moving it in the same fashion, for another 15 minutes.

When the duck is a deep golden brown on all sides, carefully transfer it to a chopping board. With a cleaver or large, sharp knife, cut off the wings, legs and thighs of the duck and chop them across the bone in 2-inch pieces. Then cut away and discard the backbone and chop the breast, bone and all, into 2-inch squares. Arrange the duck pieces attractively on a large heated platter and serve at once with roasted salt and pepper and steamed flower-roll buns.

As a main course this will serve 6. As part of a Chinese meal *(page 200)*, it will serve 8 to 10.

Hua-chiao-yen

花椒盐

ROASTED SALT AND PEPPER

Set a heavy 5- or 6-inch skillet over high heat, and pour in the salt and all the peppercorns. Turn the heat down to moderate and cook, stirring constantly, for 5 minutes, or until the mixture browns lightly. Be careful not to let it burn. Crush it to a fine powder with a mortar and pestle or wrap the mixture in wax paper and crush it with a kitchen mallet. Shake the crushed salt and pepper mixture through a fine sieve or strainer into a small bowl and serve it as a dip for Szechwan duck *(opposite)* or deep-fried phoenix-tailed shrimp *(Recipe Booklet)*.

To make about ¼ cup
5 tablespoons salt
1 tablespoon whole Szechwan peppercorns
½ teaspoon whole black peppercorns

Kan-shao-nu-jou-ssŭ

乾燒牛肉絲

STIR-FRIED FLANK STEAK WITH CELLOPHANE NOODLES

PREPARE AHEAD: 1. With a sharp knife or a pair of scissors, cut the cellophane noodles into 4-inch lengths, separating any noodles that cling together.

2. With a cleaver or sharp, heavy knife, trim off and discard the fat from the flank steak. To shred the steak, put it in the freezer for 30 minutes or so to firm the meat and make it easier to slice. Then lay the steak flat on a chopping board and slice the meat horizontally (with the grain) as thin as possible. Cut these slices into pieces 1½ to 2 inches long and ¼ inch wide.

3. In a small bowl combine the soy sauce, cornstarch and sugar. Add the shredded steak and toss it about in the bowl until it is well coated with the mixture.

4. Have the noodles, steak, oil, green pepper, ginger and cayenne pepper within easy reach.

TO COOK: Set a 12-inch wok or 10-inch skillet over high heat and pour in the 2 cups of oil. Heat the oil until it smokes, or it registers 450° on a deep-frying thermometer. Drop in half of the noodles and let them deep-fry for one second. As soon as they puff up, lift them out with a slotted spoon and spread them on a double thickness of paper towels to drain. Then fry the other half of the noodles. Pour off the oil and set it aside in a small mixing bowl.

Return the wok or skillet to the heat and return 1 tablespoon of the oil to the pan. Swirl it about in the pan and let it heat for 30 seconds, turning the heat down to moderate if the oil begins to smoke. Drop in the green pepper and stir-fry for 2 minutes until it begins to darken in color. With a slotted spoon, transfer the green pepper to a plate. Add another 2 tablespoons of oil to the pan and let it heat for 30 seconds. Add the ginger root, and stir it about for 1 or 2 seconds, then add the shredded flank steak and cayenne pepper, and stir-fry for 1 to 2 minutes, until the beef is lightly browned and any liquid which may have accumulated in the pan has completely evaporated. Return the green pepper to the pan and heat it through, stirring constantly.

To serve, place the beef and pepper mixture in the center of a large heated platter and arrange the fried cellophane noodles around the outside. As a main course, this will serve 2. As part of a Chinese meal *(page 200)*, it will serve 4.

Half of a 2-ounce package of cellophane noodles
½ pound flank steak
2 tablespoons soy sauce
1 teaspoon cornstarch
½ teaspoon sugar
2 cups peanut oil, or flavorless vegetable oil
1 green pepper, seeded, deribbed and shredded into strips 1½ to 2 inches long and ¼ inch wide
1 teaspoon finely shredded fresh ginger root
¼ to ½ teaspoon cayenne pepper, according to taste

To make about 2 dozen

1 slice fresh white bread
2 tablespoons cold chicken stock, fresh or canned, or cold water
1 pound uncooked shrimp in their shells
2 ounces fresh pork fat (¼ cup)
4 peeled and washed fresh water chestnuts, finely chopped, or 4 drained canned water chestnuts, finely chopped
1 teaspoon salt
½ teaspoon finely chopped, peeled fresh ginger root
1 egg yolk
1 egg white
3 cups peanut oil, or flavorless vegetable oil
Roasted salt and pepper, prepared according to the recipe on page 53

Cha-hsia-ch'iu
DEEP-FRIED SHRIMP BALLS

炸 蝦 球

PREPARE AHEAD: 1. Trim crust from the bread and tear bread into small pieces. Place them in a bowl and sprinkle with the stock or water.

2. Shell the shrimp. With a small, sharp knife, make a shallow incision down their backs and lift out the intestinal vein with the point of the knife. Wash the shrimp under cold water and pat them dry with paper towels. With a cleaver or sharp knife, chop the shrimp and pork fat together until they form a smooth paste.

3. In a bowl, combine the soaked bread, shrimp mixture, water chestnuts, salt, ginger and egg yolk, and mix thoroughly. Beat the egg white to a froth with a fork or whisk, and stir it into the shrimp mixture.

4. Have the shrimp mixture, a bowl of cold water, a baking pan lined with a double thickness of paper towels, and the oil within easy reach.

TO COOK: Preheat the oven to its lowest setting. Pour 3 cups of oil into a 12-inch wok or large deep-fat fryer and heat until a haze forms above it or it reaches 350° on a deep-frying thermometer. Take a handful of the shrimp mixture and squeeze your fingers into a fist, forcing the mixture up between your thumb and forefinger. When it forms a ball about the size of a walnut, use a spoon to scoop off the ball and drop it in the hot oil. Repeat until you have made 6 to 8 balls, dipping the spoon into the bowl of cold water each time to prevent sticking. Turn them with a Chinese strainer or slotted spoon to keep the balls apart as they fry. They should become golden in 2 to 3 minutes. Transfer the fried balls to the paper-lined baking pan to drain and keep warm in the oven while you fry the rest. Transfer the finished shrimp balls to a heated platter and serve with roasted salt and pepper dip. As an hors d'oeuvre or part of a Chinese meal (*page 200*), this will serve 6 to 8.

1 pound flank steak, trimmed of all fat
1 tablespoon Chinese rice wine, or pale dry sherry
3 tablespoons soy sauce
1 teaspoon sugar
2 teaspoons cornstarch
2 medium-sized green peppers, seeded, deribbed and cut into ½-inch squares
4 slices peeled fresh ginger root, about 1 inch in diameter and ⅛ inch thick
¼ cup peanut oil, or flavorless vegetable oil

Ching-chiao-ch'ao-niu-jou
PEPPER STEAK

青 椒 炒 牛 肉

PREPARE AHEAD: 1. With a cleaver or sharp knife, cut the flank steak lengthwise into strips 1½ inches wide, then crosswise into ¼-inch slices.

2. In a large bowl, mix the wine, soy sauce, sugar and cornstarch. Add the steak slices and toss with a large spoon to coat them thoroughly. The steak may be cooked at once, or marinated for as long as 6 hours.

3. Place the peppers, ginger root and oil within easy reach.

TO COOK: Set a 12-inch wok or 10-inch skillet over high heat for about 30 seconds. Pour in a tablespoon of the oil, swirl it about in the pan and heat for another 30 seconds, turning the heat down to moderate if the oil begins to smoke. Immediately add the pepper squares and stir-fry for 3 minutes, or until they are tender but still crisp. Scoop them out with a slotted spoon and reserve. Pour 3 more tablespoons of oil into the pan and heat almost to the smoking point. Add the ginger, stir for a few seconds, then drop in the steak mixture. Stir-fry over high heat for about 2 minutes, or until the meat shows no sign of pink. Discard the ginger. Add the pepper and cook for a minute, stirring, then transfer the contents of the pan to a heated platter and serve. As a main course, this will serve 2 to 4. As part of a Chinese meal (*page 200*), it will serve 4 to 6.

To form shrimp balls, scoop up a handful of the raw mixture and squeeze it up through your fist.

When the shrimp mixture forms a ball about the size of a walnut, lift it off with a spoon dipped in water.

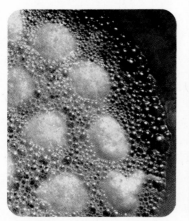

Immediately drop the balls into hot oil to deep-fry, turning the balls with a flat strainer to keep them apart.

Two or three minutes of deep-frying is all it takes to turn shrimp balls golden; they will float to the surface when they are done. Use a Chinese strainer, like the one shown, or a slotted spoon to transfer the shrimp to a paper-towel-lined pan to drain and keep warm while the rest are fried.

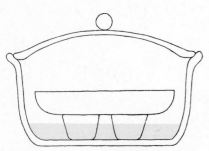

This cutaway view shows the construction of an improvised steamer: A plate is set, two inches above water, on two small, heatproof dishes set right side up in a large, tightly covered roasting pan. There must be enough space around the edge of the plate to allow the steam to rise and circulate freely.

½ cup glutinous rice
4 dried Chinese mushrooms, 1 to 1½ inches in diameter
1 pound lean boneless pork, finely ground
1 egg, lightly beaten
1 tablespoon soy sauce
1½ teaspoons salt
½ teaspoon sugar
1 teaspoon finely chopped, peeled fresh ginger root
6 canned water chestnuts, drained and finely chopped
1 scallion, including the green top, finely chopped

Pearl balls, shaped from a ground pork and water chestnut mixture, are rolled in rice until well coated. Arrange them for cooking in an aluminum steamer, set well apart on paper toweling to prevent the balls from sticking together.

Chen-chu-jou-wan 珍珠肉丸

PEARL BALLS

PREPARE AHEAD: 1. In a small bowl, cover the rice with 1 cup of cold water and soak for 2 hours. Then drain the rice through a sieve, spread it out on a cloth towel and let it dry.

2. In a small bowl, cover the mushrooms with ½ cup of warm water and let them soak for 30 minutes. Discard the water. With a cleaver or knife, cut away and discard the mushroom stems, and chop the caps fine.

3. Combine the pork, egg, soy sauce, salt and sugar in a mixing bowl. With your fingers or a large spoon, mix together until the ingredients are thoroughly blended. Then add the ginger, chopped mushrooms, water chestnuts and scallions, and mix thoroughly again. Scoop up about 2 tablespoons of the mixture and, with your hands, shape it into a ball 1 inch in diameter. Repeat this process with the remaining pork mixture, moistening your hands from time to time with a little cold water. Arrange the balls side by side on a strip of wax paper.

4. Roll one pork ball at a time in the rice, pressing down gently but firmly as you roll so that the rice grains adhere to the meat. Set the rice-coated balls back on wax paper.

TO COOK: Pour enough boiling water into the lower part of a steamer to come within an inch of the cooking rack (or use a steamer substitute as described above). Choose a heatproof plate approximately ½ inch smaller in diameter than the pot so that the steam can rise and circulate around the pork balls as they steam. Arrange the pork balls on it. Place the plate on the rack, bring the water in the steamer to a boil, and cover the pan tightly. Keeping the water at a continuous boil and replenishing it if it boils away, steam the pork balls for 30 minutes. Set the steaming plate on a large platter and serve at once. As a main course, this recipe will serve 4. As part of a Chinese meal (page 200), it will serve 6 to 8.

Finished pearl balls, shown here in a bamboo steamer, are so prickly looking they are sometimes called porcupine balls.

III

Secrets of Savor and Spice

*M*y new province is a land of bamboo groves:
Their shoots in spring fill the valleys and hills. . . .
I put the shoots in a great earthen pot
And heat them up along with boiling rice.
The purple nodules broken—like an old brocade;
The white skin opened—like new pearls.
Now every day I eat them recklessly. . . .   —"EATING BAMBOO SHOOTS," PO CHU-I, NINTH CENTURY

Whenever the mood strikes me to have friends in for a Chinese dinner and I begin to jot notes of what I will need, I find my thoughts straying to Duke Wu and his circle and the marvelous banquets they gave. My envy of those long-gone nobles grows as I make a mental reckoning of the skilled servants to whom they could entrust the innumerable details of shopping and preparation. My experience has been quite different.

The first time I ventured to go shopping in Shanghai—now so many years ago—I asked a friend if I couldn't go with her, because she knew her way around. Yelena was a White Russian, as refugees from the Russian Revolution of 1917 were called; she had been carried out of Russia as a small baby and grew up in China. In a hollow-cheeked, pale-blonde way she was beautiful, with slightly slanting eyes and high cheekbones. Like the other White Russians she was fluent in the local dialect, and hard necessity had taught her how to live on almost no money. We started out early and rode in rickshas to the marketplace.

Trotting in Yelena's footsteps I squeezed between crowded stalls,

Two Chinese children avidly sniff the delicious aroma of a bowl of sweet-and-sour pork. To illustrate the timelessness of Chinese cooking, a photograph of the dish—whose main ingredients are pork, green peppers, carrots, sugar and vinegar—was superimposed on a very old Chinese painting.

through a chaos of cabbages and pieces of raw pork and jars of spices and bundles of flattened ducks and tooth powder and dried fish and electric light bulbs and bags of rice. I was bewildered by the noise and the crowd generally, but Yelena knew exactly where she was going and led the way straight—or as straight as possible—to one particular stall behind which sat a hugely fat man, fanning himself. "He is my friend. I always go to him," she explained.

They greeted each other with enthusiasm, before Yelena set to work finding vegetables and sauces in his jumbled stock. They kept up a steady conversation about his wife and children while she added things to a growing pile on the table in front of him. At last she was satisfied, and at the same moment both fell silent. "How much?" asked Yelena after the pause. "For a friend, don't forget."

The old man named a price, and Yelena fell back as if stunned. "Well, how much you pay?" asked the fat man. Now it was his turn to be stunned at Yelena's suggestion. He gasped. Then he recovered enough to shave a few cents off his first figure, and she replied with a figure very slightly larger than her first one. It was a long-drawn-out ceremony that had been enacted many times before but could not be neglected. At last the two minds met on a compromise sum. Yelena took his grudging nod for consent, and counted out the money, in coins and dirty little paper notes. As we turned away with our purchases, Yelena picked up an egg from a basket on the counter. "You give me this cumshaw [tip], eh?" she said to her friend. He grinned and waved a hand in surrender.

On another occasion I did some shopping in the most inconvenient place one could imagine—during a houseboat party upriver. When our boat paused at a village to allow some relative of the pilot to disembark, a man came to the boat's side and held up some crabs—lively, big ones at that season, when they were supposed to be very good eating. I decided to take them home for dinner, and we struck a bargain. The man packed the crabs in a basket, tied it up and handed the basket over to me across the rail. I slung it into a corner of the cabin and rejoined the party on deck to admire the scene as we started back toward town: it was late afternoon, with a darkening purple haze over the country. All was very peaceful and quiet. Suddenly the pilot screamed, and we ran forward to find him kicking viciously with his bare feet at a crab that threatened his toes. The deck swarmed with my escaped crabs. Our voyage ended in a wild chase, as we rounded up the scuttling creatures.

While it is highly unlikely that any reader will have to endure shopping experiences like mine, it may be useful to offer some guidance on buying the ingredients called for in Chinese recipes. Let me say at once that it is getting easier every year to find at least some of the needed ingredients in gourmet shops, neighborhood groceries and supermarkets. Cans and boxes of prepared foods arrive in a steady stream from Hong Kong and Taiwan; American firms, too, supply quite good canned and frozen Chinese food. Choosing among these supplies is a bit tricky, however, for the selections may be unbalanced if we do not keep reminding ourselves, when planning Chinese dishes, to go light on proteins and carbohydrates and depend more on vegetables. (The photographs on pages 62 and 63 will help you recognize the most popular Chinese foods, and a list of ingredients and substitutions is in the Appendix.)

While canned foodstuffs are in fairly wide distribution, there are still many areas in the United States where finding fresh Chinese vegetables presents a problem. Fortunately some of our native produce makes equally good eating when it is prepared in the Chinese way, and the recipes in this book indicate acceptable American alternatives. Among the vegetables frequently called for in Chinese recipes, Chinese cabbage (or its close relative, *bok choy*) is becoming ever more available. If you should find it, do not buy it unless it is firm and crisp. If it were cooked in the Western manner, firmness and crispness would not matter much, but the Chinese never boil vegetables; they say that these ingredients already contain so much water that they should be stir-fried and then braised. These techniques may startle American cooks trained in the European tradition, but a little experimenting ought to convince skeptics of the virtue of the Chinese methods. Cooked the Chinese way, vegetables tend to be slightly underdone by our standards. However, they have more flavor and that slightly crunchy texture we usually associate only with fresh salad. They also retain their original fresh color. It is a nice change to eat green broccoli, for instance, rather than the mushy olive-drab version that boiling too often produces. Broccoli? Yes; this is one of many vegetables from the West that have been adopted by Chinese chefs. Many other vegetables such as asparagus, Brussels sprouts, carrots and spinach are surprisingly good when stir-fried and braised the Chinese way. And when so prepared, each offers a fresh experience in flavor, texture and appearance. What happens with this method is that after being turned in the hot oil the vegetable is braised in a little broth and salt.

If the supermarket you patronize has a sufficiently adventurous manager, your chances of finding fresh, typically Chinese vegetables are greater; you may, for instance, find Chinese mustard greens on occasion. These can be salted and pickled for later use in soup or with meat to add spice. Sometimes available are icicle radishes, those long white roots that are much larger than our little white ones, and also a number of unfamiliar things such as lotus root and snow peas, a variety tender enough to be cooked and eaten pods and all. Unfortunately, only those of us who are within shopping distance of a Chinatown market will be able to buy a variety of large, round, light-green melon called winter melon. Winter melon makes a special soup, sometimes served in the rind itself *(page 107)*. Watermelon, which the Chinese like as a refreshing tidbit after a meal, presents no problems, of course. Neither do celery, cabbage or garlic. On the other hand, Chinese parsley, or *cilantro*, has an entirely different flavor than the Western herb; it can be bought wherever there is a fairly large Chinese community. However, our own parsley makes an acceptable substitute as a green garnish.

Vegetables little known in Western cuisines but often found in Chinese recipes are ginger root, water chestnuts, bamboo shoots (or sprouts) and bean sprouts. All these can be bought canned, but if you can get them fresh they are better, especially ginger root, that hot, spicy vegetable most of us know simply as ginger, and eat in crystallized form or pre-

Basic Chinese Ingredients

Many Chinese ingredients—including some considered exotic in the West—are available in the Chinatowns of the United States. Listed below and shown on the next two pages are 30 of these foods.

 1 Scallions
 2 Chinese cabbage, or *bok choy*
 3 Celery cabbage
 4 Fresh ginger root
 5 Thousand-year eggs
 6 Fresh lotus root
 7 Egg-roll wrappers
 8 Bird's nest (two kinds)
 9 Winter melon
10 Fresh mung-bean sprouts
11 Fresh snow peas
12 Canned abalone
13 Fresh bean curd
14 Dried bean-curd skin
15 *Sao mai,* or meat-dumpling wrappers
16 *Wonton* wrappers
17 Dried rice stick noodles
18 Chinese sausages
19 Shark's fin (two kinds)
20 Cellophane noodles
21 Fresh egg noodles
22 Canned loquats
23 Canned ginkgo nuts
24 Canned litchis
25 Canned bamboo shoots
26 Canned water chestnuts
27 Canned kumquats
28 Preserved kumquats
29 Icicle radish
30 Chinese parsley *(cilantro)*

Continued on page 64

A nine-dish all-vegetable meal is eaten by Buddhists in the garden of West Forest Monastery in Hong Kong. Although Buddhist monks are vegetarians, like all Chinese they see no virtue in insipid meals. So they use a specialized cuisine in which the textures of meat, fowl and fish are ingeniously simulated with a variety of vegetables, mushrooms and bean curd.

served in syrup. The fresh, young ginger, which is tender enough to mince and use as the component of a dish instead of merely as seasoning, is available in shops only in the spring. Older, tougher ginger must be treated in a different way—it is too strong to eat, but just right for adding its flavor to the ingredients. It must therefore be sliced thin, added briefly while the dish is cooking, and removed before serving. Dried ground ginger will not do for this purpose because its form and flavor are not right. The powder cannot be manipulated as the fresh ginger slices can be, and the taste—even when used in minute quantities—is more pungent and pervasive. Peeled sliced ginger, packed in brine and available in cans, may be used as a fairly good substitute, but even in this form it lacks some of the flavor of the fresh root.

Another reason for caution in using ginger is the danger that its flavor will overpower the dish. In the Chinese cuisine the quantities of flavoring must always be carefully estimated, especially if you are cooking something that, like lamb, has a strong characteristic flavor of its own. (Lamb, indeed, does not really lend itself to most kinds of Chinese cooking because it defies the balance of flavors so prized by the Chinese.) But ginger used with reasonable care is invaluable, and it adds to the taste of many dishes. To ensure a regular supply of fresh ginger, you might try growing your own. This is not hard if you live near an Oriental grocery where you can buy a piece of good, healthy root. Plant the root either in the ground or a flowerpot, covered with four or five inches of firmly packed earth. If you are using a flowerpot, water once a week with one cupful of water, but if the root is planted in the ground, probably less water will be needed. When sprouts appear and the root is thriving, uncover it and break off a piece to use for cooking. Then replace the root and begin again. Your cooking piece can be stored by scraping off the skin and keeping the bit of root in the refrigerator, in a jar full of dry sherry for several months, or in an airtight plastic bag for two to three weeks.

Another ingredient—even more typically Chinese—that can be bought fresh in America is water chestnut, which the southern Chinese call *ma-ti* (horsehoof) because of its shape. The growing demand of Chinese markets for this edible bulb—which is what it really is—has led to its culture in Florida, where it does well and even grows larger than in its native China. It should have a subtle taste, fresh and almost sweet. It is good by itself, but in a dish its most desirable characteristic, I think, is the crispness that makes it a pleasure to crunch. Certain epicures may maintain that the Florida water chestnut is not very satisfactory because it tastes muddy, but the Florida water chestnuts I have bought are delicious.

Bamboo sprouts and bean sprouts, too, are on sale in cans, but you can easily grow bean sprouts at home. Soak one quarter cup of mung beans (a small green bean) in cold water overnight. After this you can either use a regular steamer or improvise a pot-within-a-pot *(as described in Chapter II)*. Place a perforated rack inside the steamer or pot and drape it with terry cloth or a kitchen towel so that you have a layer of dry towel about one half inch deep on the rack. Spread the soaked mung beans over the toweling in a single layer, not too close together. Cover them with an equal thickness of toweling, and then run water over the towel until both layers of cloth are well soaked through. Cover the container with a metal lid and leave for three to five days, watering three times a day with one cup of tap water. By the fourth day the sprouts should be nearly two inches tall. Remove them from the layers of toweling and rinse in a bowl of cold water, stirring to and fro until the husks separate and leave just the sprouts, ready for use in cooking. (They can also be stored for a week in cold water if you change the water every day.)

I have mentioned the lotus, a name that awakens echoes of Oriental poetry rather than physical hunger in the Western mind. But lotus root is an important food as well. Americans, particularly in the Southern states, are familiar with a different species of this water lily and its lovely pink or white blossoms. The botanical name, *Nelumbium nucifera,* implies it is nut-bearing, but it is not. What the early botanists described as nuts are the plant's seeds, spheres that may be as much as half an inch in diameter. These seeds are inside a pod—the fruit—that looks like a spouted watering can and is full of air cavities. The fruit keeps the lotus afloat in its watery habitat and is used for cooking, usually after it is sliced.

The lotus has long been known in China. It was in a lotus pond that, tradition tells us, the poet Li Po drowned after a drinking bout one moonlit night in 762 A.D. Lotus used to be cultivated in the moats and lakes of Peking's Forbidden City, where its beauty enhanced the setting of the Imperial palaces. It still grows plentifully in Peking's lakes. To Buddhists the plant has significance because Gautama Buddha, founder of the re-

Two chef's aides add engraved yams to the display of vegetables centering on a winter melon. Other foods enhanced by carving are (*front, left to right*): carrot god of longevity, carrot bird between cucumber flowers, carrot rose and yam chrysanthemums.

ligion, is often represented seated on a large lotus flower or holding one in his hand. It is said that after the Buddha achieved enlightenment, he thought of his fellow men as lotus buds in a lake, springing from mud and striving to attain the surface in order to blossom. Growing in mud yet undefiled, the lotus became a symbol of purity. Buddhist scholars teach that when you look down at the lotus from above, the petals represent spokes in the wheel of conduct. Expressing the symbolic connection with Buddha's divine birth, a chant of Buddhist priests contains the Sanskrit refrain *Om mane padme Hum*—"O the jewel in the lotus." Even among non-Buddhists the lotus with its many seeds represents fertility and is thought to give to those who eat it the promise of many children.

Apart from its mystical significance, the lotus is one of China's important sources of food and medicine. All of the plant—root, fruit, seeds and leaves—can be used. The flower stamens, dried, serve as an ingredient in cosmetics and as an astringent used for skin care. To Chinese physicians the seeds also have medicinal value as an aphrodisiac. These seeds can be boiled in soup, too—usually the sweet soup that is served at a big Chinese dinner somewhere in the middle of the meal or as the last course. The seeds are also eaten cooked or raw. The root, when cut straight across, has a pretty, lacy pattern and adds design as well as taste to many dishes. The leaves are employed to wrap around other portions of food—rice or meat, for instance. The root is also sometimes ground into a starchy paste that is used as we use arrowroot. Expensive and hard

to find in this country, the lotus-root thickener has given way to the low-cost and readily available cornstarch. Used with finesse, it thickens Chinese dishes to a manageable consistency without turning them pasty.

After my repeated explanations that Chinese dishes rest heavily on vegetables, it may come as no surprise to learn that the Chinese cuisine offers a special sort of cooking that simulates meat for the benefit of strictly vegetarian Buddhists, especially monks and nuns. These people sometimes need a change from their constant vegetable diet. Resourceful cooks have worked out methods to make dishes that look and feel like various sorts of the forbidden foods, though they are still, of course, vegetables. The chief ingredients of these dishes are bean curd and gluten, the elastic protein in wheat. In the opinion of Chef Wang Tsung-ting, who now supervises the kitchen of a well-known restaurant in New York, most of the dishes were invented by vegetable-weary Buddhist monks working in monastery kitchens. Chef Wang learned the special vegetarian technique from chefs in the Kung Teh Lin, the Shanghai restaurant that specialized in them—a place I knew well, because I used to order meals from it when I entertained Buddhists. "I was working in another restaurant, not vegetarian," said Chef Wang, "but quite often we would need several vegetarian dishes for a banquet, and then we invited a specialist from the Kung Teh Lin, or perhaps a cook from a monastery, to prepare them for us. I picked up the recipes that way, by watching and stealing their secrets. We chefs used to compete, to see which of us

Winter-melon soup supplies both flavorsome food and visual pleasure to these young women. Cooked inside the melon itself—on which is carved a dragon writhing in puffs of cloud—the soup is served with scooped-out pieces of melon.

Continued on page 70

67

From top right, scallion brushes, carrot and icicle-radish flowers, radish fans and bamboo-shoot trees surround a carved tomato rose.

BAMBOO-SHOOT TREES
With a sharp paring knife, trim shoots into triangular wedges. Make 4 or 5 V-shaped grooves lengthwise on two sides of the triangle. Slice into ⅛-inch-thick "tree-shaped" pieces.

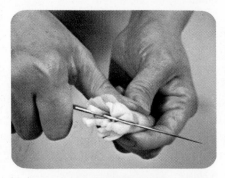

SCALLION BRUSHES
Trim root; cut off top, leaving 3 inches of firm stalk. Hold stalk firmly; make four crossing cuts 1 inch deep into one end. Repeat at other end. Place in ice water.

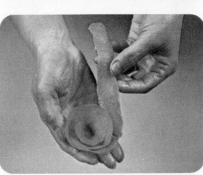

TOMATO ROSES
Peel a ripe, firm tomato to make a continuous strip of skin. Coil the strip, and in the palm of one hand spread the "petals" to form a rose shape with the other hand.

CARROT FLOWERS
Clean and peel the skin off a thick carrot. Cut V-shaped grooves lengthwise, spaced equally all around the carrot. Slice into ⅛-inch-thick pinwheels.

ICICLE RADISH FLOWERS
Peel and groove an icicle radish; trim one end into a cone. Using cone surface as guide, make very thin parings. Overlap ends of slice into flower cups. Refrigerate in ice water.

69

could best make nonmeat dishes that seemed to taste of meat, but the appearance and texture of the food were more important." Not long ago, Chef Wang was asked to furnish an eight-course, wholly vegetarian dinner for a New York association that was honoring a visiting Indian Buddhist monk, and he gave me the menu: vegetarian shrimp made from water chestnuts that could be carved to resemble real shrimp; sweet-and-sour spareribs made from lotus root; duck made from crisp bean-curd skin, colored and shaped to look like the bird's flesh; "eight-precious vegetarian dish" made of dates, chestnuts, ginkgo nuts, black mushrooms, radishes, lotus nuts, bamboo shoots and hair cabbage; chicken roll in *hoisin* sauce, the "chicken" made of soft soybean curd; mushrooms and heart of Chinese cabbage; sesame delight; sizzling rice-cake soup.

Chef Wang, as he prepared this meatless meal, had little trouble finding appropriate Chinese fruits in New York. A number of shops offer a good variety of preserved or even—in some cases—fresh fruits. Three species, canned, are widely available in supermarkets: the preserved kumquat, a little citrus like a doll's-house orange, very sweet but with a slightly tart overtone; the loquat, a fuzzy little yellow fruit that grows in clusters and is tart and juicy; and the litchi (which contributed to the downfall of an emperor), with a thin shell of strawberry red and deliciously juicy, sweet white flesh when it is fresh. (When dried the shell darkens to brown and the flesh shrivels; then it looks and even tastes like a prune.) Litchis canned in thin syrup—the form in which we usually get them—taste much like the fresh fruit, for the flesh is still resilient.

Despite the fact that many Chinese foods can be bought locally, do not pass up a chance to visit a real Chinatown market. You will enjoy the experience. These places are very much like those in China where I used to do my shopping, with plenty of raw and prepared meat and fowl hanging from steel hooks—pigs, Cantonese roast duck, smoked chicken, and squab cooked in soy sauce, ready to eat, its skin crackled and shiny. There are dried salted egg yolks, gnarled dried ginger root, dried squid and abalone, and scallops and sea cucumbers still soaking in water. Fish maws, or tripe, hang in great, fluffy golden bunches from the ceiling. There are jars of herbs—star anise, fennel, Chinese cinnamon, Szechwan pepper and sweet roots; there is sure to be ginseng, one species of which, a famous panacea, looks not at all impressive unprepared, merely a collection of little dried sticklike roots. It is enormously costly, nevertheless, for the Chinese think it a splendid medicine for a number of ailments, including impotence. Sometimes they put it into dishes as a preventive rather than a cure—like the tamarind potatoes my friend Yun-li prescribed to ward off anemia. Ginseng cooked with squab into soup, for example, is an expensive dish, but there are many Chinese who consider it worth the price. Another variety of the root, which grows in the United States, can be bought at drugstores, herbalist shops and food stores. As a matter of fact, America is now a major exporter of ginseng to Chinese communities abroad, a trade that goes back to 1784 when a merchant vessel carried a cargo of the herb from New York to Canton.

The Chinese market stocks mushrooms of many shapes and sorts, and jellyfish in solid pieces cut into strips, and dried shrimp and oysters. Buckets hold bean sprouts, soaking bean curd and shark's fin. There are seasonings and prepared sauces in jars and bottles. It is a whole new world of foods fascinating to see, but you need not feel that you must learn all about them, especially if you are a beginner: it is enough to get the general flavor and an idea of the variety of the cuisine.

Of course it is unnecessary to seek out special sources for many of the most basic Chinese foodstuffs. The Chinese like chicken, eggs and pork just as we do. Eggs, particularly, are important in their diet. Throughout the world the egg represents fertility and rebirth. To the Chinese it is a sign of good luck and happiness—the same thing really, for in their culture these are synonymous with fertility. The round, smooth shape of the egg is considered symbolic of a state of well-being, its lack of corners indicating tranquillity. Eggs are given as gifts when a child is born, always colored red because that is a lucky, happy color.

Chinese are very fond of eggs as food, and resourceful in using them. They make soups of them, scramble them or combine them with rice and ham. They steam eggs, smoke them, marinate them in tea, and make egg sheets—thin pancakes of pure egg. There are salted eggs and so-called thousand-year eggs. Nor do the Chinese confine themselves to chicken eggs. Duck eggs are also popular—the thousand-year egg should be a duck's—and the eggs of quail, squab, plover and goose are eaten with extra appreciation because they are less common.

In China chicken eggs are usually smaller than those we are used to because the fowl there have a harder time getting food. But ours suffice just as well; in fact, Chinese chefs in America feel that our eggs and fresh-killed chickens are superior in flavor to those of their native land.

Salted duck eggs are so very salty that they cannot be eaten in large quantity, and like salt fish they ought to be considered mainly as seasonings rather than substantial foods. However, the thousand-year eggs can be eaten as food. Of course they are not really that old—they are coated for only six to ten weeks in a particular kind of limey clay that preserves and colors them, and this is long enough for the desired effect. An egg is coated raw, but the chemicals that soak into the shell and meat from the surrounding clay make the whole thing firm in consistency with a smooth, creamy texture—if you have ever eaten a perfectly ripened avocado you will know what I mean. Unearthed and unshelled, a thousand-year egg should be translucent and brilliantly colored in blues and greens, the most vivid green being in the yolk—with the beautiful play of colors reminding you of a black opal. However it does not really taste eggy; it has a faintly fishy flavor. Thousand-year eggs are so rich that a few bites, about half of one egg, are usually enough at a party if you want to leave room for other courses, especially since they are usually served as cold food at the beginning of the meal.

There is not much difference in species between the meat and fowl eaten by Chinese and Westerners. Pigs are pigs, cows are cows, ducks and geese are much the same as ours—but there is one striking exception: the chickens of Chungking are weird and wonderful; they are white-skinned, light-fleshed and black-boned. Chungking is the only place where this unusual chicken is found, and the curious thing is that you can-

A Hong Kong market stall that specializes in eggs offers, among others, the following varieties: fresh *(right)*, salted *(lower left)*, "thousand-year" eggs *(upper left)* and salted egg yolks *(in the jar)*.

not tell whether or not it has black bones until after it is slaughtered. Although some experts claim to be able to tell by looking at the chicken's feet whether or not it has dark bones, this is strongly disputed by others, who insist that the fowl's external appearance gives not the slightest clue as to the color of its skeleton. Many Chinese consider the black-boned chicken to be especially nourishing, and it brings a premium price in the markets, even though its flesh and eggs—to the untutored eye—look remarkably similar to those of ordinary chickens.

The Chinese residents of Chungking must have been bored to death by us, the naïve Westerners, when we exclaimed over such odd-looking chicken bones. They themselves would never have been put off eating by a trifle like an unusual color in the food. Of all the peoples I have ever known the Chinese are the most adventurous in eating, the readiest to try anything new. Fortunately, considering how prone China is to famine, Chinese religions have very few dietary taboos. Indians suffer more because their caste system puts many foods outside the pale for them, and in times of famine Indians have been known to die of starvation rather than touch certain forbidden foods supplied by relief organizations.

A cooked-meat stall in Hong Kong sells *(top to bottom)* roast ducks, soy-sauce chicken and barbecued pork. These meats, freshly prepared daily, are sold by weight, and a customer may buy any quantity from a duck wing to a whole roast pig.

In China, on the other hand, all except a few strict vegetarians will eat whatever they know will not harm them. We Westerners have a saying that it must have been a very brave man who ate the first oyster. A Chinese might laugh politely at this joke but he would not really get the point. To him, anyone who refused to eat an oyster when he was hungry, even if he had never had one before, would be crazy.

In the same open-minded manner, a chef in China willingly adopts new methods regardless of where they come from, as long as people find the resulting dish pleasing and nutritious. Perhaps I should say that he *adapts* new methods, for a good cook is never satisfied with merely taking over ideas: he wants to improve on them. Thus the cuisine has amassed, and is still amassing, a great collection of recipes. A good example is the use today by Chinese of curry powder and so-called curry dishes. As we know, curried foods are Indian, but the Chinese, having sampled what can be done with the spice, have taken it over in their own ways. Without doubt, in the course of time they will evolve some dish with curry flavoring so Chinese that Indians will not recognize its origin.

Although there are many recipes in this book, there is nothing cut-and-

Continued on page 76

Chinese Seasoning: A Subtle and Varied Art

The primary purpose of condiments and spices in Chinese cookery is the accentuation, rather than the concealment, of natural flavors. Chinese chefs use relatively few condiments and spices (pictured opposite are some of the most popular) but they vary their combinations to achieve an almost endless chain of taste transformations that delight their countrymen and arouse mingled sensations of pleasure and bewilderment in foreigners. The bewilderment arises out of one basic difference between Chinese and Western cooking. The Chinese as a rule do not cook each item separately as Westerners do, for example in a fish, potato and spinach meal. Instead, the Chinese cook the fish with other ingredients such as bamboo shoots, dried mushrooms and minced smoked ham. This technique promotes an exchange of flavors, each ingredient acquiring flavors from the rest of the group and at the same time acting as a seasoning agent.

Among the best known of Chinese seasonings is soy sauce, which was mentioned in several Confucian classics as early as the Fifth Century B.C. Soybeans are also used to make other condiments, such as bean paste for preserving and flavoring meat, and *hoisin,* or vegetable, sauce, which is a sweet-and-spicy table dip for seafood and poultry. Beans are the basis of other seasonings such as the Cantonese specialty, fermented black beans, used to give zest to meat and fish dishes. And there is also the Chinese children's delight, sweet and velvety red-bean paste, used as filling for moon cakes, buns and many desserts. Another Cantonese specialty, oyster sauce, used both as a dip and a cooking condiment, intensifies the flavor of meat and seafood without imposing a taste of its own.

Among the spices are star anise, five-spice powder and Szechwan pepper. Star anise, with its distinctive licorice flavor, is used mostly with meat, poultry, game and fish braised in soy sauce. Five-spice powder, a finely ground mixture of anise seed, Szechwan pepper, fennel, cloves and cinnamon, is used in red-cooked and roasted meat and poultry; Szechwan pepper gives its special pungent flavor to many dishes from that province.

Dried foods, which must be soaked before they are used in cooking, often serve both as ingredient and condiment. Dried mushrooms, which are treasured for their bouquet, rank high on the list of dual-purpose ingredients but they vary in quality and flavor. The best mushrooms come from South China, where they are picked in the winter and dried by sun and air. A relative of the mushroom is the cloud ear—a dried black fungus —which looks like bits of charred leather but is nevertheless quite delicious, especially when cooked with dried tiger lily buds, also called "golden needles." Cloud ears and tiger lily buds are highly nutritious and inexpensive. Often used in desserts are such dried seeds and fruits as black and white sesame seeds; dried jujubes; lotus seeds; walnuts; longans, or dragon's eyes; and orange peel. Along with these dried plants, many other dried products are used as condiments and ingredients. The long list includes dried shrimp, baby fish, squid, scallops and ducks' gizzards.

CHINESE SAUCES AND CONDIMENTS
1 *Hoisin* sauce
2 Plum sauce
3 Oyster sauce
4 Soy sauce
5 Sesame-seed oil
6 Dried tiger lily buds
7 Dried Chinese mushrooms
8 Yellow-bean paste, or thick bean sauce
9 Star anise
10 Dried jujubes, or red dates
11 Fermented black beans
12 Rock candy
13 Five-spice powder
14 Red-bean paste
15 Cloud ears
16 Szechwan pepper
17 Dried shrimp
18 Black sesame seeds

With a delicate net two men on a lake near Hankow in central China harvest the seeds of a thick growth of lotus plants. In China the lotus is a sacred flower, a symbol of purity and a valuable food plant. The Chinese make use of all parts of this versatile plant—seed, stamen, leaf and root.

dried about what goes into any dish of the best Chinese cooking. In China as elsewhere, recipes are necessary to start out with, but expert cooks soon go their own ways and put their stamp on the dishes they produce. If you contrast Chinese recipes from different books that seem to be directions for the same dish, you are likely to find that they do not correspond in many details. There are more ways than one to cook even so simple a thing as boiled rice. While sweet-and-sour foods are always sauced with sugar and vinegar, and though there is another constant factor of soy sauce, from then on the cook is pretty much on his own. Many dishes call for fruit and vegetables, but what fruit, what vegetables? The answer is, whatever happens to be in season or available.

There are only a few basic seasonings in Chinese cooking, but the permutations and combinations of these will give many different flavors. Some substances, like ginger root, occasionally play the role of seasonings but at other times are ingredients in themselves. A brief listing and description of the principal sauces and seasonings is on page 74.

Although it is included in the listing, one Chinese seasoning—soy sauce —deserves special mention because it is probably the condiment best known to Westerners. Its manufacture is a complicated process, for it starts as a dough made of soy beans and wheat flour that is first allowed to ferment. Then salt and water are added, and the fermented liquid is placed in open earthenware urns, which are placed outdoors for several weeks while the sun's heat works on the mixture. It is said that the best

grades of soy sauce can take as much as six to seven years of aging to reach perfection, and that the making of a superb soy sauce requires "as much art in its preparation as good French wines." The predominant flavor is far from delicate—rather it is a pungent saltiness. Depending on the methods used, finished soy sauce has a considerable range of flavors and shades, and chefs select particular varieties to achieve desired effects of color and taste.

One of the seasonings not listed is M.S.G., which deserves a special word. Most of us know about the kitchen product called Ac'cent, tasteless in itself but recommended in advertisements for its property of waking up flavors of other ingredients in a dish. Ac'cent consists entirely of the chemical called monosodium glutamate (M.S.G.), which the Chinese have known for years as "taste powder." A lot of argument is heard about the ethics of using M.S.G. A really good Chinese chef considers it a questionable shortcut for giving taste to second-rate foodstuffs, but most Chinese cooks admit that its use in certain dishes is perfectly valid. The proprietor of an excellent Chinese restaurant in New York says that M.S.G. was used in large quantities in the chop suey joints of yesterday because at those places one got only the lowest quality of Chinese cooking at correspondingly low prices. This low-grade food required enormous reinforcement to make it palatable, and customers at such places ate a lot of M.S.G. without realizing it. Even now, this restaurateur continues, many Chinese restaurants in America still use far too much of the stuff, because the chefs have discovered that it is an easy way out, and because few customers know enough to object. He admits that a very little of it can enhance the flavor in certain dishes (especially ones that contain no meat or mushrooms)—all the more so if the ingredients are not in top condition. But this crusader for fine Chinese cooking insists no self-respecting chef in China would use even a small amount; to do so not only would be regarded as an admission of the inadequacy of his skill, but might also obscure the more subtle taste sensations of his dishes and reduce their variety.

To those with less idealistic views a case can be made for M.S.G., at least in restaurant cooking, because of the problems of catering for large numbers of diners and the inevitable delays between fire and table. If a restaurant proprietor could use the very best chicken stock in which to cook his food, M.S.G. would not be needed at all—but then the cost of the dishes would be so high that the restaurant might soon be priced out of business. M.S.G. becomes a compromise solution for the professional chef. As for its use in Chinese home cooking, the New York restaurateur is inflexible: there is absolutely no need for it.

Among other restaurant owners the subject is moot. Two of these gentlemen, both operating in San Francisco's Chinatown, talk bitterly about each other's use of M.S.G., one warning his Western clients that too much of it—and his rival, he declares, does use too much—destroys a man's virility. In counterattack, the second man accuses the first one of using cornstarch instead of good, honest lotus-root flour for thickening, while charging lotus-root prices. "Cornstarch makes you fat," he says warningly. (Both restaurants serve what seems to me excellent food.)

Clearly sauces and seasonings are of the greatest importance in Chinese cooking. Any self-respecting gourmet in China, discussing food and cooking as gourmets the world over like to do, lays considerable emphasis on these two subjects: while a *bon vivant* of the American West talks about the juiciness and tenderness of steaks served in his favorite eating place, a Chinese is more likely to lay stress on the trimmings. Mr. Wong, a Chinese gentleman I used to know in Shanghai, talked of very little but sauces and seasonings, though I remember that he did depart from the subject once. I was complaining that my cook, whose work he admired, was robbing me. "Never mind, never mind," he said urgently. "Keep him! Keep him no matter what he does, keep him. But if you are foolish enough to discharge him, send him to me."

One year Mr. Wong gave me a Christmas present of high value, a bottle of very special oyster sauce that had been made in his home village. It was a sauce, he told me, famous throughout the province for its delicate flavor. I realized that it was a choice gift. It was plainly up to me to give him something equally fine in return, preferably something American, but what? I worried about it for several days. What kind of sauce or pungent seasoning had America to offer? All I could think of was catsup or chili sauce, but I knew they would not do. In spite of what advertisements may say, there is no best or worst catsup—there is just catsup. Cucumber pickles? Cole slaw? No, they wouldn't do either. . . .

In the end I sent him a box of homemade fudge.

A small Hong Kong shop is packed to its ceiling with a wonderfully varied stock of dried foods that includes *(left of the aisle)* dried lotus seeds, beans, nuts, shrimp and *(right)* dried mushrooms, jujubes, heaps of squid, and dried oysters strung on bamboo loops. Lacking refrigeration, the Chinese have for centuries preserved foods by salting and drying them in the sun and wind.

Chao-ssŭ-chi-tou 炒四季豆
STIR-FRIED STRING BEANS AND WATER CHESTNUTS

To serve 4

1 pound fresh string beans
2 tablespoons peanut oil, or flavorless vegetable oil
1½ teaspoons salt
1 teaspoon sugar
10 water chestnuts, cut into ¼-inch slices
¼ cup chicken stock, fresh or canned
1 teaspoon cornstarch dissolved in 1 tablespoon chicken stock, fresh or canned

PREPARE AHEAD: 1. Snap off and discard the ends of the beans, and, with a small knife, remove any strings. Cut the beans into 2-inch pieces.

2. Have the beans, oil, salt, sugar, water chestnuts, chicken stock and cornstarch mixture within easy reach.

TO COOK: Set a 12-inch wok or 10-inch skillet over high heat for 30 seconds. Pour in the 2 tablespoons of oil, swirl it about in the pan and heat for another 30 seconds, turning the heat down to moderate if the oil begins to smoke. Drop in the string beans and stir-fry for 3 minutes. Add the salt, sugar and water chestnuts, and stir once or twice before pouring in the stock. Cover the pan and cook over moderate heat for 2 to 3 minutes until the beans are tender but still crisp. Now give the cornstarch mixture a stir to recombine it and add it to the pan. Cook, stirring, until the vegetables are coated with a light, clear glaze. Transfer the entire contents of the pan to a heated platter and serve at once.

Hsia-mi-pan-ch'in-ts'ai 蝦米拌芹菜
CELERY AND DRIED-SHRIMP SALAD

To serve 4 to 6

1 bunch celery
20 Chinese dried shrimp
1 tablespoon Chinese rice wine, or pale dry sherry
1 tablespoon warm water
1 teaspoon soy sauce
½ teaspoon salt
1 tablespoon sugar
1 tablespoon white vinegar
2 teaspoons sesame-seed oil

PREPARE AHEAD: 1. Wash the shrimp under cold running water. In a small bowl, combine them with the wine and 1 tablespoon of warm water. Let them marinate for 30 minutes. Drain, saving the marinade.

2. Remove and discard the leaves of the celery and any stringy stalks. Cut the stalks lengthwise in two, then crosswise into 1-inch pieces.

TO ASSEMBLE: In a large glass bowl, combine the reserved shrimp marinade, soy sauce, salt, sugar, vinegar and sesame-seed oil, and stir until the sugar dissolves. Add the shrimp and celery, and toss them about until they are coated with the dressing. Chill for 1 hour before serving.

La-pai-ts'au 辣白菜
STIR-FRIED SPICED CABBAGE

To serve 4

1 pound Chinese cabbage, celery cabbage or *bok choy,* or substitute green cabbage
2 tablespoons sugar
2 tablespoons white vinegar
1 tablespoon soy sauce
1 teaspoon salt
¼ teaspoon cayenne pepper
1 tablespoon peanut oil, or flavorless vegetable oil

PREPARE AHEAD: 1. With a cleaver or sharp knife, trim the top leaves of the cabbage and the root ends. Separate the stalks and wash them under cold running water. Cut each stalk, leaves and all, into 1-by-1½-inch pieces. If you are substituting green cabbage, separate the leaves and wash in cold water. Then cut the leaves into 1-by-1½-inch pieces.

2. In a small bowl, combine the sugar, vinegar, soy sauce, salt and cayenne pepper, and mix thoroughly. Have the oil within easy reach.

TO COOK: Set a 12-inch wok or 10-inch skillet over high heat for about 30 seconds. Pour in the oil, swirl it about in the pan and heat for another 30 seconds, then turn the heat down to moderate. Immediately add the cabbage and stir-fry for 2 to 3 minutes. Make sure all the cabbage is coated with the oil. Remove the pan from the heat and stir in the soy-vinegar mixture. Transfer the cabbage to a platter and let it cool to lukewarm before serving. Or, if you prefer, serve it chilled.

Chao-hsüeh-tou 炒雪豆 To serve 4

STIR-FRIED SNOW PEAS WITH CHINESE MUSHROOMS AND BAMBOO SHOOTS

PREPARE AHEAD: 1. In a small bowl, cover the mushrooms with ½ cup of warm water and let them soak for 30 minutes. Remove them with a slotted spoon. With a cleaver or sharp knife, cut away and discard the tough stems of the mushrooms and cut each cap into quarters. Strain the soaking water through a fine sieve and reserve 2 tablespoons of it.

2. Snap off the tips of the fresh snow peas and remove the strings from the pea pods.

3. Have the above ingredients, and the oil, bamboo shoots, salt and sugar within easy reach.

TO COOK: Set a 12-inch wok or 10-inch skillet over high heat for 30 seconds. Pour in the 2 tablespoons of oil, swirl it about in the pan and heat for another 30 seconds, turning the heat down to moderate if the oil begins to smoke. Immediately drop in the mushrooms and bamboo shoots, and stir-fry for 2 minutes. Add the snow peas, salt and sugar, and then 2 tablespoons of the reserved mushroom-soaking water. Cook, stirring constantly at high heat, for about 2 minutes, or until the water evaporates. Transfer the contents of the pan to a heated platter and serve at once.

6 dried Chinese mushrooms, 1 to 1½ inches in diameter
1 pound fresh snow peas (thoroughly defrosted frozen snow peas will do, but they will not have the crispness of the fresh ones)
½ cup canned bamboo shoots, sliced ⅛ inch thick and cut into 1-by-1-inch triangular tree-shaped pieces *(page 69)*
1½ teaspoons salt
½ teaspoon sugar
2 tablespoons peanut oil, or flavorless vegetable oil

These crisp dishes are *(top to bottom)*: string beans and water chestnuts, celery and dried-shrimp salad, snow peas and bamboo shoots.

To serve 4 to 6

1 pound fresh lotus root
1 tablespoon soy sauce
1 tablespoon white vinegar
1 tablespoon sugar
2 teaspoons sesame-seed oil
½ teaspoon salt

T'ang-ts'u-ou-pien
FRESH LOTUS ROOT SALAD

糖醋藕片

PREPARE AHEAD: 1. Wash the fresh lotus root under cold running water and, with a sharp knife, peel off the skin. Trim off and discard both ends of the root.

2. With a cleaver or sharp knife, cut the lotus root into ⅛-inch-thick slices, dropping the slices as you proceed into a saucepan of cold water to prevent them from discoloring. Drain off the cold water and pour 3 to 4 cups of boiling water over the lotus root slices to cover them completely. Let them soak for 5 minutes. Drain the slices again, rinse them thoroughly under cold running water and then pat the slices completely dry with paper towels.

3. In a small mixing bowl, combine the soy sauce, vinegar, sugar, sesame-seed oil and salt, and stir them together until the sugar and salt are dissolved.

TO ASSEMBLE: Arrange the slices of lotus root, overlapping them in concentric circles on a serving plate. Pour the soy sauce-vinegar dressing evenly over the slices. Chill the salad in the refrigerator for at least 1 hour before serving.

Lacy slices of lotus root, tastefully arranged on a platter, then seasoned with sweet-and-sour dressing, make an inviting summer salad.

Cha-yeh-tan

茶葉蛋

TEA LEAF EGGS

TO COOK: In a 1½- to 2-quart saucepan, cover the eggs with 2 cups of cold water, bring to a simmer and cook uncovered for 20 minutes. Leave the eggs in the water until they are cool enough to handle, then pour off the water and tap the eggs gently all over with the back of the spoon until the shells are covered with a network of fine cracks. Now return the eggs to the saucepan, pour in 2 cups of cold water, add the salt, soy sauce, star anise and tea. Bring to a boil over high heat, then reduce the heat to its lowest point, cover the pan and simmer for 2 to 3 hours. Check from time to time and if the liquid is cooking away, add enough boiling water to keep the eggs constantly covered. Turn off the heat and leave the eggs in the liquid at room temperature for at least 8 hours.

TO SERVE: Just before serving the eggs, remove their shells carefully. The whites should be marbled with fine, dark lines. Cut the eggs in halves or quarters and arrange them on a plate. Tea leaf eggs are usually served as an hors d'oeuvre, or they may be part of a Chinese cold plate combined with various meats and salads.

6 eggs
1 tablespoon salt
2 tablespoons soy sauce
1 whole star anise or 8 sections star anise
2 teaspoons black tea (or substitute 2 tea bags)

Liang-pan-huang-kua

涼拌黄瓜

CUCUMBER SALAD WITH SPICY DRESSING

Peel the cucumbers and cut them lengthwise in two. With a small spoon, scrape the seeds out of each half, leaving hollow boatlike shells. Cut the cucumbers crosswise into ¼-inch slices. In a small glass or porcelain bowl, combine the soy sauce, vinegar, sugar, sesame-seed oil, Tabasco and salt, and mix well. Add the cucumber. With a large spoon, toss to coat each slice thoroughly with the dressing. Chill slightly before serving. As a separate salad, this will serve 3 or 4. As a cold side dish at a Chinese meal, it will serve 4 to 6.

2 medium cucumbers
1 teaspoon soy sauce
1 tablespoon white vinegar
1 tablespoon sugar
2 teaspoons sesame-seed oil
¼ teaspoon Tabasco
½ teaspoon salt

H'sün-tan

燻蛋

SMOKED EGGS

TO COOK: In a 1½- to 2-quart saucepan, cover the eggs with 2 cups of cold water, bring to a boil over high heat, reduce the heat and simmer uncovered for 4 minutes. Remove the eggs with a slotted spoon, plunge them immediately into a bowl of cold water and let them remain there for at least 5 minutes. This will stop their cooking and keep the yolks somewhat soft, as they should be. Carefully shell the eggs and place them side by side in a shallow dish just large enough to hold them in one layer. In a small bowl combine the soy sauce, sesame-seed oil, liquid smoke, sugar and salt. Pour the mixture over the eggs and let them marinate at room temperature for 2 to 3 hours, turning them over every 30 minutes to keep them well moistened with the marinade.

TO SERVE: Just before serving, cut the eggs in half and arrange them on an attractive plate. Smoked eggs may be served separately as an hors d'oeuvre, or they may be part of a Chinese cold plate served with various meats and salads.

6 eggs
2 tablespoons soy sauce
1 teaspoon sesame-seed oil
½ teaspoon bottled liquid smoke
1 teaspoon sugar
½ teaspoon salt

The boiled white-cut chicken *(left)* is served with ham and broccoli. Braised soy-sauce chicken is served alone or with its sauce.

A 4-pound roasting chicken,
   preferably freshly killed
3 slices cooked Smithfield ham, ⅛ inch
   thick, cut into 2-by-1-inch pieces
A 2-pound bunch broccoli
2 quarts chicken stock, fresh or
   canned, or 2 quarts cold water, or
   a combination of both
1 scallion, including the green top,
   cut into 2-inch pieces
4 slices peeled fresh ginger root, about
   1 inch in diameter and ⅛ inch thick
¼ teaspoon salt
1 teaspoon cornstarch dissolved in 1
   tablespoon cold water

Yu-lang-chi 玉蘭雞

WHITE-CUT CHICKEN AND HAM IN GREEN PARADISE

PREPARE AHEAD: 1. Wash the chicken inside and out under cold running water. Dry the chicken thoroughly with paper towels.

2. Cut off the broccoli flowerettes. Peel the stalks by cutting ⅛ inch deep into the skin and stripping it as if you were peeling an onion. Slice the stalks diagonally into 1-inch pieces, discarding the woody ends.

3. Have the chicken, ham, broccoli, chicken stock (or water), scallion, ginger and cornstarch mixture within easy reach.

TO COOK: In a heavy flameproof casserole or pot just large enough to hold the chicken snugly, bring the stock or water to a boil. Add the scal-

84

lions and ginger, and place the chicken in the pot. The liquid should cover the chicken; add more boiling stock or water if it doesn't. Bring to a boil again, cover the pan, reduce the heat to low and simmer for 15 minutes. Then turn off the heat and let the chicken cool in the covered pot for 2 hours. The residual heat in the pot will cook the chicken through.

Transfer the chicken to a chopping board. (Reserve stock.) With a cleaver or knife, cut off wings and legs, and split the chicken in half lengthwise cutting through the breast and back bones. Cut the meat from the bones, leaving the skin in place. Then cut the meat into pieces about 2 inches long, 1 inch wide and ½ inch thick. Arrange the chicken and ham in alternating overlapped layers on a heated platter and cover with foil.

Pour 2 cups of the reserved stock into a 3-quart saucepan. Bring to a boil and drop in the broccoli. Return to a boil, turn off the heat, let it rest uncovered for 3 minutes, then remove the broccoli and arrange it around the chicken and ham. Or garnish the meat with only the flowerettes and serve the stems separately.

In a small saucepan, combine ½ cup of the stock with salt and bring to a boil. Give the cornstarch mixture a stir to recombine it and add it to the stock. When the stock thickens slightly and becomes clear, pour it over the chicken and ham. Serve at once. As a main course, this will serve 4 to 6. As part of a Chinese meal *(page 200)*, it will serve 8 to 10.

Chiang-yu-chi　　　醬　油　雞
BRAISED SOY SAUCE CHICKEN

PREPARE AHEAD: 1. Wash the chicken inside and out under cold running water. Dry the chicken thoroughly with paper towels.

2. Have the water, soy sauce, wine, ginger, anise, rock candy (or sugar) and sesame-seed oil within easy reach.

TO COOK: In a heavy pot just large enough to hold the chicken snugly, bring the water, soy sauce, wine, ginger and star anise to a boil, then add the chicken. The liquid should reach halfway up the side of the chicken. Bring to a boil again, reduce the heat to moderate and cook covered for 20 minutes. With 2 large spoons, turn the chicken over. Stir the rock candy or sugar into the sauce and baste the chicken thoroughly. Simmer 20 minutes longer, basting frequently. Turn off the heat, cover the pot and let the chicken cook for 2 to 3 hours.

Transfer the chicken to a chopping board and brush it with sesame-seed oil. Remove the wings and legs with a cleaver or sharp knife and split the chicken in half lengthwise by cutting through its breastbone and backbone. Lay the halves skin side up on the board and chop them crosswise, bones and all, into 1-by-3-inch pieces, reconstructing the pieces in approximately their original shape in the center of a platter as you proceed. Chop the wings and legs similarly, and place them, reconstructed, around the breasts. Moisten the chicken with ¼ cup of the sauce in which it cooked and serve at room temperature. As a main course, this will serve 4 to 6. As part of a Chinese meal *(page 200)*, it will serve 8 to 10.

NOTE: The sauce in which the chicken cooks is known in China as a master sauce and it is stored in a covered jar for use in red-cooked dishes. It will keep for 2 weeks in the refrigerator, indefinitely in the freezer.

A 4½- to 5-pound roasting chicken, preferably freshly killed
2 cups cold water
2 cups soy sauce
¼ cup Chinese rice wine, or pale dry sherry
5 slices peeled, fresh ginger root about 1 inch in diameter and ⅛ inch thick
1 whole star anise, or 8 sections star anise
¼ cup rock candy broken into small pieces, or substitute 2 tablespoons granulated sugar
1 teaspoon sesame-seed oil

To serve 6

½ cup fresh or canned bean sprouts
3 to 4 medium fresh mushrooms, cut
    into ¼-inch dice (about ½ cup)
½ pound raw shrimp in their shells
¼ cup peanut oil, or flavorless
    vegetable oil
3 eggs

FOO YUNG SAUCE

¾ cup chicken stock, fresh or canned
1 tablespoon soy sauce
½ teaspoon salt
1 tablespoon cornstarch dissolved in
    2 tablespoons cold chicken stock,
    fresh or canned, or cold water

Hsia-jen-ch'ao-tan

蝦仁炒蛋

SHRIMP EGG FOO YUNG

PREPARE AHEAD: 1. Rinse fresh bean sprouts in a pot of cold water and discard any husks that float to the surface. Drain and pat them dry. To crisp canned sprouts, rinse them under running water and refrigerate them in a bowl of cold water for 2 hours. Drain and pat them dry.

2. Shell the shrimp. With a small, sharp knife, make a shallow incision down their backs and lift out the intestinal vein. Wash the shrimp under cold water, pat them dry and cut them into ¼-inch dice.

3. Have the bean sprouts, shrimp, mushrooms, eggs and oil, and the stock, soy sauce, salt and cornstarch mixture within easy reach.

TO COOK: In a small saucepan, bring the stock to a boil. Add the soy sauce, salt and cornstarch mixture. Reduce the heat and cook for 2 minutes until the sauce is thick and clear. Keep warm over low heat.

Set a 12-inch wok or 8-inch skillet over high heat for 30 seconds. Pour in 1 tablespoon of oil, swirl it about in the pan and heat for another 30 seconds, turning the heat down if the oil begins to smoke. Add the shrimp and stir-fry for 1 minute, or until they are firm and light pink. Transfer them to a plate. Break the eggs into a bowl and beat them with a fork or whisk until they are well combined. Add the shrimp, bean sprouts and mushrooms. Set the pan again over high heat for 30 seconds. Add 1 tablespoon oil, swirl it about in the pan, reduce the heat to low, then pour in about ¼ cup of the egg mixture. Let it cook undisturbed for 1 minute, or until lightly browned. Turn the pancake over and cook for another minute. Transfer the pancake to a heatproof platter and cover with foil to keep warm. Following the same procedure, make 5 more pancakes with the remaining egg mixture. Add about 1 teaspoon of oil to the pan for each new pancake and stack them on the platter as you proceed. Serve with sauce poured over each pancake. Although not classic, some Chinese cooks garnish this dish with green peas.

ROAST PORK EGG FOO YUNG: Substitute ½ cup of diced roast pork for the cooked shrimp, but otherwise follow this recipe precisely.

To make about 16 slices

THE FILLING

½ pound boneless pork shoulder,
    finely ground
2 teaspoons soy sauce
1 teaspoon cornstarch
1 tablespoon Chinese rice wine, or
    pale dry sherry
1 teaspoon salt
1 egg, lightly beaten

THE EGG PANCAKES

4 eggs
2 teaspoons peanut oil, or flavorless
    vegetable oil

Tan-chuan

蛋捲

ROLLED EGG PANCAKE WITH PORK FILLING

PREPARE AHEAD: 1. In a small bowl, combine the pork, soy sauce, cornstarch, wine, salt and beaten egg, and mix them thoroughly together.

2. Beat the 4 eggs with a fork or whisk just enough to combine them.

3. Have the pork mixture, beaten eggs and oil within easy reach.

TO COOK: Set a 12-inch wok or 8-inch skillet over moderate heat for about 30 seconds. With a pastry brush or paper towel, brush the bottom of the pan with 1 teaspoon of oil. Pour in half the beaten eggs. Lower the heat at once and—working quickly but carefully—tip the pan from side to side until a thin, round pancake about 8 inches in diameter forms. Immediately pour any uncooked egg on the surface of the pancake back into the bowl. As soon as the pancake is firm enough to handle—no more than 30 seconds—lift it up with your fingers or a spatula and transfer it to a plate. In similar fashion, make another pancake, transferring it to a second plate when it is done. Reserve any uncooked egg. Spread

Clockwise from upper right, eggs prepared in various traditional ways—thousand-year egg, red eggs, smoked egg and tea-leaf eggs—surround two popular dishes, rolled egg pancakes with pork filling and egg foo yung garnished with peas.

half of the pork filling over each pancake. Roll them tightly, jelly-roll fashion, and seal the edges with a little reserved uncooked egg. Press the edges together firmly to make them adhere.

Pour boiling water into the steamer to come within an inch of the rack (or use a steamer substitute, page 56). Lay the pancakes on a heatproof platter ½ inch smaller than the diameter of the pot. Set this on the rack; cover the pot. Keeping the water at a slow boil, steam the pancakes for 20 minutes. Remove the platter from the steamer. Cut the rolls diagonally into ½-inch slices and serve hot. Or refrigerate the whole rolls, and serve them cold. (Peas may be used as garnish, but are not classic.)

IV

A Reverence for Good Food

Decapitation is a gruesome affair but I am condemned to die that way. . . . Be sure not to forget to eat dried bean curd with fried peanuts. The two give you the taste of the best ham. —CHIN SHENG-TAN'S INSTRUCTIONS TO HIS SON IN HIS WILL, 17TH CENTURY

After the autumn harvest Chinese villagers, such as the group pictured in this 17th Century woodcut, traditionally have offered thanks to effigies of the god of agriculture. The deity, portrayed holding a grain stalk, is honored with prayers, incense and candles, and presented with gifts of rice, wheat and other cereals.

It was during the Japanese occupation of Hong Kong in 1941. Mei-mei looked ruefully at the dock, littered with the belongings she planned to take with her. Standing there impassively, the Japanese customs officer waited for her to pick them up again after his rough examination. I was seeing her off for Kwangchowan, from where she meant to escape into Free China, as many Chinese already had done. Small and slender, she was dressed for business, in peasant blue instead of her usual pretty dress, and her baby was strapped to her back. Until the customs official played such havoc with her belongings she had carried them neatly packed in two of those bags that look like sausages. Now they lay exposed for all to see—a wok, a couple of saucepans, baby clothes, a large jar of bean curd, a bolt of cloth, a piece of ham, a tin of jam, a wad of knitting, some paper-wrapped slices of spiced sausage, half-empty medicine bottles, her husband's best shirt and a yard of buckram.

We had begun to gather them up and repack when I realized that Mei-mei was crying. Until the last minute she had been stoical, but the treatment at customs was just too much. To cheer her up I said, "That'll teach you to be so Cantonese, Mei-mei," and sure enough she laughed at what was an old joke between us. As a Cantonese, Mei-mei had always prided herself on being stingier than anybody. "Stingy" was her word: I preferred the politer "thrifty." Certainly she was a great hoarder and I had often expostulated with her about keeping so much useless stuff. The buckram was a case in point—why carry it into China when she had no immediate use for it? But Mei-mei said that there was bound to be a time some day when she would need it for something or other, and if she didn't take it she would have to buy another piece. As it was, she added, times were hard—"Everything going out, nothing coming in."

That was life as Mei-mei knew it, an unremitting procession of needs that must somehow be satisfied in the most economical way possible. One moved from one period of want to the next as best one could, scraping and saving and managing. Yet in prewar days Mei-mei had not been poor. I even doubt if she had ever in her life gone hungry, but in her Chinese heart the tradition of thrift was stronger than experience. Chinese can be generous, they can spend a good deal on hobbies or whatever interests them, but they make sure to get value for what they spend.

Getting the best you can get out of what you have is a fundamental tenet of the Chinese philosophy—though when I say "philosophy" I do not mean that they are much given to metaphysical speculation. As practical people they take the earth's bounty as it comes. Food must be treated with respect and to be sure it always has been so treated. Nearly 4,000 years ago, about 2000 B.C., a sage named I Ya is said to have written a treatise on cookery, and to this day he is a kind of patron saint for all Chinese chefs. Some of Confucius' precepts have to do with the preparation and eating of food. One legend says that he left his wife because her cooking never met his high standards.

Even the great majority of poor people, who have always counted themselves lucky if they had enough plain rice or noodles to fill their stomachs, share the same attitude toward food. The difference between classes is one of wealth, not philosophy. Most people live marginally the year around, through perilous stretches when a handful or two of rice makes the difference between life and death. I remember how even their scraps of food were treated with reverence and prepared with all possible care.

Side by side with those whose first concern has always been to secure the bare essentials of life are the most fortunate ones who have pursued, and written extensively about, the most exotic recipes, the rarest ingredients, the subtlest seasonings. We have to search long and hard through English literature to find anything even approximating so deep an absorption in cooking. I doubt if Shakespeare would have felt at home in the kitchen, but among the stars of Chinese literature are many who have enjoyed spending time in this fashion. There are too many to list here completely, but among them are Madame Wu of Kiangsu, who wrote and published a cookbook at the end of the 12th Century, and Su Tung-po, the 11th Century poet whose life Lin Yutang has related in *The Gay Genius*. Su loved to cook, and left to posterity a beautifully simple recipe of his own for braised pork. The modern recipe for red-cooked shoulder of pork *(Recipe Booklet)* is very similar. He also prepared fish by a method often used today—rubbing it with salt and stuffing it with Chinese cabbage heart, then shallow-frying it with scallions in a little oil. He directed that when the fish was browned you should add raw ginger and pickled turnip sauce with a dash of wine, and at the very end when it was just right and ready to come off the fire, he suggested the addition of a few slices of orange peel. In exile, presumably for slandering the emperor, Su Tung-po found solace in a local cinnamon wine, and sometimes experimented with brewing wines of his own invention.

In the 14th Century, Yiu-shan Cheng-yao produced a volume that was not so much a cookbook as a health book, telling what effect different foods have on the body. My little friend Yung-li with her tamarind potatoes was following his example: So much Chinese lore deals with the subject that it is sometimes hard to discern the line between cooking and medicine. Li Li-weng, a 17th Century poet, wrote at length of food and cooking in his *Arts of Living,* and the Emperor Chien Lung, fourth ruler in the Manchu Dynasty, wrote an *Ode to Tea* in the 18th Century. But it was probably the writer Yuan Mei (1715-1797) who had the most to say about food. As an old man he finished a cookbook—*Shih Tan,* or *The Menu* —he had been compiling for years. To gather material he talked about food endlessly. He experimented; he sent his cook around to other men's houses to learn how to make any new dish he might have enjoyed as a guest. Cooking was his hobby: He did it for enjoyment, but he also felt that he was setting a good example. He felt that excellence in cooking was a moral virtue. I like his introduction to *Shih Tan* because in its scope and in its very platitudes it is typical of the Chinese outlook. "Everything has its own original constitution, just as each man has certain natural characteristics. If a man's natural abilities are of a low order, Confucius and Mencius themselves would teach him to no purpose. And if an article of food is in itself bad, not even I Ya could flavor it."

To us this may seem high-flown. Cooking is cooking, we might say, and character is character, different things altogether. Why mix them? But there *is* a moral excellence in good cooking, and few people would not feel a glow of virtue when serving a dish one knows to be just right. Besides, to the Chinese there is no difference between physical and mental health, and we have seen how closely they relate health and eating. "To cure an illness, one must first know the origin of the illness. One must know what the person has eaten before the proper medicine can be prescribed," says a manual on eating that makes clear the intimate association between eating and health. We are left in no doubt that the illness referred to is not merely or necessarily a stomach ailment. It can be a lung complaint or a fever in the brain. No matter: All is related to food.

This is logical to the Chinese. To them all knowledge is one thing, and cannot be chopped into pieces and pigeonholed under different labels such as Character, Cooking and Health. Naturally, therefore, a professional chef is a master of one of life's most important activities.

In the old days the chef's craft was highly specialized. That is to say, he was expected to polish and improve his art as long as there was strength in his body. He was a dedicated man, and his apprentice too was dedicated. It was a solemn thing to be a cook's apprentice, but once you had been accepted and approved by some master your life was settled.

To learn the art thoroughly as a professional, it was formerly considered necessary to serve a long apprenticeship. Chef Wang, whom we met in a previous chapter, is a product of the older discipline, but he mourns that nobody really gets a decent training nowadays. His own kitchen education began when he was barely 14. A raw country boy just arrived in Shanghai, he was taken on as apprentice by Su, the head chef of the famous Great China restaurant in the city. It was good to start so young, he thinks; for one reason, a chef must keep everything—recipes, methods, quantities—in his head, and young people have better memories than old ones. Wang at that time was only one among 22 young hopefuls at the restaurant who for two years did only scullery work—scrubbing floors, cleaning out woks and washing chopsticks and cleavers. But once in a while as a special treat he was sent out to fetch some plain comestible—a bag of onions or a bunch of cabbage—that had run short. These humble errands furnished his only contact with foodstuffs until at last Chef Su gave him a slightly higher job: Wang was allowed to cut his first vegetable. Thus the chef indicated that he felt the boy had learned a certain amount of humility and patience and understanding—he was becoming a cook. Thereafter Wang cut meat and vegetables every day, and sometimes made bean curd or did some very plain cooking.

Six years went by while he went through early training, and the number of apprentices dwindled, some through weakness, others being fired for stupidity or laziness. Wang got no regular salary during this time, but he was given a percentage of the pooled tips. It was the custom, and was not as bad as it sounds, for the restaurant was responsible for his board and lodging, and the tips took care of clothing and incidental expenses. When he entered the fourth year, he began receiving a set wage—one bag, or 33⅓ pounds, of rice per month. (Chef Su's salary was three bags.) Wang was now accepted as a star pupil. But even though he had attained the dignity of a salary he was not allowed to feel that his education was finished. The next step was to learn to cook with flour, and in time he could produce masterly pancakes, dumpling skins and various kinds of buns and savories. Then came the cold dishes and the art of carving vegetables into decorative shapes. Finally he studied the making of complicated banquet dishes such as Peking duck.

The results of this training can be seen nowadays when Chef Wang occasionally indulges in a competition traditional among Chinese lovers of good food. Recently, for instance, he was challenged to reproduce a memorable Chinese banquet that had been served in Hong Kong years earlier, and he took the dare. He is proud to say that he turned out dishes exactly like the originals—as exactly, that is to say, as one chef can reproduce another's work—and the banquet was right in every detail except for only one vegetable that he could not find anywhere in New York.

Another well-known chef now in New York, Liu Hai-yin, comes from Szechwan, where the training of young cooks must have been just as long and demanding as it was in Shanghai. The restaurant with which Chef Liu became associated speedily won fame among the Chinese expatriates of the city, not only for its excellent food but because the customers found pleasure in discussing the philosophy of cooking with the chef. Chef Liu maintains that Chinese cooking is like traditional Chinese medicine in that there are no systematic rules for either science. In China a doctor does not depend on X-rays or cardiograms, but feels the patient's pulse and forehead, then gives him whatever medicine seems to suit the case. He works from instinct—and so does the Chinese cook. Chef Liu, like Chef Wang, never uses written recipes.

Another chef, Sou Chan, is something of a rarity among Chinese chefs in America because he had no formal training as an apprentice before emigrating from his native Canton. In 1928, as a boy, he came to America and worked in Seattle washing dishes in a Chinese restaurant. Then he moved by slow degrees across the country to New York, working his way up to the status of waiter as he went and picking up basic cooking knowledge. Like other chefs he speaks of cooking as an art, and he knows —as all cooks know—that love must go into it. "Even if you're only cooking a scrambled egg, you must take a real interest in making something special out of it. You think about every step from the time you crack the egg—how much do you mash the yolk? How hot is the pan? What is the best seasoning to bring out the egg's flavor?"

Dedication of this nature explains why the cuisine of China achieved its superb quality. Chinese chefs and their public have a far wider vision of food than do most of us in the West. It is not only that the chefs undergo—or used to undergo—a rigorous training: For that matter the apprentice system of France is strikingly similar to China's. But I doubt if even the French carry appreciation of food to the lengths of Chinese gourmets— devotees who are fanatic in their approach to cooking and who make up elaborate games connected with it. The banquet challenge to Chef Wang was such a game. Another is hunting rare dishes. Gourmets seek these dishes as a kind of social activity; eating clubs try out new restaurants and their members urge their own cooks to do more and more research so that they can give memorable banquets. To such people the triumph of finding something new comes to mean more than eating it: The game is a means of status-seeking. Professor Chen, the painter and amateur cook who brought Chef Liu to America, once satirized this kind of hunt by drawing up a list of eight delicacies without which, he soberly claimed, no banquet of ancient times was worth eating—deer's tail, ape's lips, unborn baby jaguar, camel's hump, bear's paw, elephant's trunk, fish tail and monkey head. His object was to ridicule the rare-dish snob, but it is almost impossible to exaggerate some of the foibles and excesses of genuine hunters of the exotic in Chinese food.

A distinguished amateur cook but no snob is Dr. F. T. Cheng, formerly Chinese Ambassador to the Court of St. James's and possessor of many imposing honors and titles. Dr. Cheng is fond of discussing food, and often writes of it. In his book *Musings of a Chinese Gourmet* he says that food in China "stirs the imagination of her thinkers, sharpens the wit of her scholars, enhances the talents of those who work by the hand, and enlivens the spirit of the people. . . . In it the Chinese find something that makes life worth living." Dr. Cheng says Chinese consider their cooking an art, because it involves complicated processes and is of an infinite variety. Whether or not this agrees with your particular concept of art, it is true that Chinese cooks and philosophers of food never tire of repeating

A familiar scene along the Hong Kong waterfront, fish dry in the sun on bamboo mats. The Chinese often preserve their foods by sun-drying not only because it is economical and effective, but because in the process more concentrated flavors are created. The worker in the picture spends all day turning thousands of fish of the species known as Malabar crevalle, which sell as a cheap staple food.

Continued on page 100

The Life of a Fishing Family
in a Floating Village

In the British colony of Hong Kong, populated predominantly by Chinese, 80,000 people work, play, eat, sleep, bear children and die on bobbing fleets of junks and sampans. Most of these boat people are fishermen who, after their work is done, cluster in mooring places that make up floating settlements in several picturesque harbors. Others operate water taxis, floating restaurants and cruising stores. Although half of the 9,400 fishing junks have modern auxiliary diesel engines, all retain the traditional painted eyes on the prows so that, as the fishermen believe, the junks can scan the sea. Pictured here and on the following pages is the life of a typical fishing family whose junk, like thousands of others, is moored at Aberdeen *(left)*, a bustling port on the south shore of Hong Kong.

After a day's fishing, the family sits on the deck of their junk to enjoy a four-dish dinner of carp, chicken, pork and vegetables, with rice.

Every day the family sails out to cast its huge net at different fishing grounds near Hong Kong. The net, attached to the junk, is

lowered into the water by the men in the little dinghy. Then they thrust poles into the water to drive the fish into the net.

Cooking on a single brazier, the mother and daughter prepare the meal. To save fuel, the carp and the chicken will be steamed.

Despite its humble way of life, this family realizes enough from its daily catch to afford a variety of other foods to supplement their catch of salt-water fish. So the daughters often shop (*left*) on land for things like fresh-water carp. Chinese generally consider that fish and shrimp from fresh water have a more delicate flavor and a more tender texture than those from the ocean. Later, the girls purchase pork, poultry and green vegetables and take them back to their floating home.

Their marketing on land done, the girls go home in a sampan, maneuvering through the crowded harbor with a skill acquired in childhood.

rules of cookery, and their admonitions sometimes sound like directions for a minuet.

For instance, Dr. and Mrs. Lee Su Jan, in their book *The Fine Art of Chinese Cooking,* list standards by which the details of a meal should be judged, and because this list represents exactly what is *different* about Chinese cooking, I reproduce it. Lee says that a good Chinese dish exhibits:

Purity: the equivalent of the Western idea of clarity and concentration, as in rich, clear chicken stock. Weak, insipid or muddy broths and gravies do not qualify.

Sweetness: not sugar-sweetness, but that indefinable quality which we refer to when we speak of sweet air or sweet water.

Smoothness: the quality that is usually achieved by the proper use of cornstarch. Anything lumpy or bumpy, any pastiness in a sauce will disqualify a dish.

Youth and Tenderness: the qualities of young vegetables. Tough, overgrown or mushy vegetables are to be avoided.

Texture: the dish should have one or more of several textures—crispness, tenderness, smoothness, softness. The textures to be avoided are sogginess, stringiness or mushiness. Texture is a matter of integrity. If a dish is supposed to be crisp, let it be crisp; if it is to be tender, let it melt in your mouth.

Color: also a matter of integrity. If the vegetables are cooked properly they will be clear green, not olive green. A sauce should have some character; it should be a rich brown, or light and clear in tone. A rich, pure broth has a clear, golden hue.

In another passage Dr. Lee sums up much of the philosophy behind Chinese cuisine: "Harmony, contrast and accent are the three principles of the culinary art. The art of Chinese cooking lies in the selection, blending and harmonizing of texture, color, aroma and taste. . . . The Chinese feast is a study in contrast; sweets are played against salts, smoothness against crunchiness, large foods against miniature ones, hot foods against cold ones." He goes on to explain the third esthetic principle of accent, but it is what he says of contrast that I find most interesting.

Contrast, or dynamic balance, is something often mentioned by the Chinese. They not only respect it, they insist on it—in cooking to be sure, and in all other aspects of life. In so doing they are echoing one tenet of Taoism, the religion that until the Communist takeover held a place among the Chinese as important as Confucianism and Buddhism. Taoists—the word "Tao" means "Way," or "Way of Nature"—see a duality in the universe, a division in its power, with one half working against the other, not in hostility but for the sake of harmonious existence. These two halves are known as Yin and Yang. The symbol for Yin and Yang is a circle containing two interlocked shapes, one black and one white. "Yin and Yang: In Chinese philosophy and religion two principles, one negative, dark and feminine (Yin), and one positive, bright and masculine (Yang). . . ."—so says an unabridged dictionary in a definition that is good as far as it goes. There are any number of further examples, such as motion versus stillness, all of which show that in Taoism everything is supposed to have its opposite so that the balance of the universe remains undisturbed. For Taoism teaches that without this equilibrium, life might well grind to a halt. So, while the furniture arrangements of a formal room have the same number of chairs on each side of a room, this is countered by gardens that retain the random asymmetrical lines of nature. While scrolls of calligraphy hanging on the walls will be balanced on either side of the room, the calligraphy itself has irregular lines that relieve the formality of the scrolls' placement. Abstract qualities, too, should balance; so, the true gentleman keeps his emotions temperate and even.

At this point, just when the Westerner thinks that he has begun to understand the theory of Taoistic balance, the interpreters start throwing monkey wrenches into the system. For instance, the *Chinese Primer of Eating and Drinking* says that moderation in eating and drinking keeps the equilibrium. However, the writer then goes on to warn that foods with opposing properties should not be mixed in one dish. By "properties" he does not mean such qualities as crispness and sweetness, but those in the Yin-Yang sense of dark-light, moving-still, masculine-feminine. Some ingredients, he explains, are either Yin or Yang. On the assumption that ordinary nonexperts cannot be expected to know which is which, he gives a few detailed warnings, directing us to avoid certain combinations in our meals. Beef and pork should not be eaten together, he says. Other incompatible mixtures are lamb's liver and pepper (which causes heart trouble), rabbit with ginger (likely to bring on cholera), beef and chestnut, quail and pork, shrimp and pork, shrimp and sugar, scallions and honey, and many more. Some of the partnerships he mentions, such as scallions and honey, do not sound tempting in any case.

The trouble with these sets of rules is that each derives from the theories of one man, and I have heard far too many experts in the field lay down their own laws to take them very seriously. Each expert has clear and logical explanations for his decisions, so how can one be sure of any? Taking advice on Yin and Yang is rather like going to a doctor. Your particular adviser may differ on all points from the expert across the street; all you can do is have faith. Of course, Yin-Yang strictures on ingredients, or rather on combinations of ingredients, are not meant to discourage cooks, and fortunately they almost never have that effect. For the great asset of Chinese food is the cook's adaptability, and as the only rigid thing about Chinese cooking is a cook's particular interpretation of Yin and Yang, there is still plenty of room for invention.

Moreover, cooks by their very nature are competitive: They love to try new combinations that will arouse the envy of their peers, and Chef Wang only recently invented a new dish, shrimp with apples, which has become very popular in the restaurant whose kitchen he supervises. In addition to the spur of competition, Chinese cooks are moved to invent by sheer necessity—though this fact does not detract at all from their genius. A cook who cannot afford to lose any opportunity to rearrange ingredients will dare to try combinations that would never occur to Westerners. A chef may lack some ingredient necessary to the dish he has been planning; in such case he simply transforms whatever he finds at hand into something pleasant, if different. One day in wartime Hong Kong, when my cook had no meat or fowl or fish for the meal, he refused to give up. He simply created a delicious dish of lettuce, cabbage

Catching fat grass carp with their hands, farmers south of Taipei harvest fish they have raised as a crop. This area has over 200 fish farms and plentiful water. At harvest, they drain the ponds, gather the fish with nets and select the big ones, leaving the younger fish for another harvest.

leaves and rice, and depended for his effect on the seasonings. I would probably have starved on a prolonged diet of lettuce, but after that meal, at least, I did not feel hungry.

The circumstances that have made Chinese cooks so inventive have made it natural, too, that every Chinese should be a farmer at heart: The growing of food seems instinctive with him. The Chinese is pledged to the land, shackled to it. Given a tiny plot of land in the most unlikely place, even in the middle of a city, a Chinese will keep chickens and—if it can possibly be squeezed in—a vegetable garden. I first visited Nanking, then the capital of China, in 1935. Though it was one of the biggest cities in the nation, with a population of a million, the large spaces between houses were planted with growing vegetables and interspersed with rich piles of manure for fertilizer. These scenes were repeated all the way downtown to the city center, up to the very walls of the government buildings.

Nobody in the government objected—the largest and most flourishing of the gardens probably belonged to high officials within the walls. The Chinese green thumb was even more vividly evident when Hong Kong was occupied by Japanese troops during World War II. For a century before the war the colony had been run by British officials who forested the land, and then protected the newly planted trees from fuel-seekers so strictly that from an airplane one could see at a glance where the British territories gave way to China. The Britishers carefully preserved woods, and shrubbery abruptly disappeared at the border; on the Chinese side all was bare. Inside Hong Kong landlords forbade all tenants to grow vegetables in their backyards or keep livestock on the premises, for Westerners objected to the smell of manure, and flies would have been attracted by pigs and poultry. Chinese residents had to curb their agricultural passions until the Japanese came and imprisoned the Westerners. Then the old regulations were void. Famine threatened, and literally overnight the city was transformed. Every Chinese who could lay claim to a scrap of land, even if it was no larger than a handkerchief, began to cultivate it. People in apartment houses requisitioned the ornamental concrete flowerpots that decorated their outside staircases and put them to use as tiny vegetable plots. This agricultural activity was by no means confined to peasants: Bankers, lawyers, doctors and art dealers were all in it together. Soon crops were growing on every hand, and chickens roamed the streets.

That a varied and subtle cuisine should have developed in a country with such a history of hardship, poverty and famine is a wonder, but it is no mystery if we remember that mankind always does its best when it is up against trouble and forced to use ingenuity. It stands to reason that if the Chinese had not been among the most resourceful people on our planet they would have died out long ago. When I read about new calamities and natural catastrophes besetting China today, I think of Ting-ling.

She was a pretty young widow I used to know in Hong Kong, who supported her five children with a flower shop she ran in the middle of town. I used to see her with her flock at the movies on Sunday, and once I came upon a school party picnicking in the woods, with Ting-ling handing out plates of ice cream and looking like one of the schoolgirls herself. Then the war came and all the stores shut down. The flower shop's windows were boarded up. It was several days after the British surrendered before it became possible to buy food once more, not from the closed stores but in the streets, where some enterprising shopkeepers set up stalls and conducted their trade in the open air. I was there, one among hundreds trying to find supplies, when I saw Ting-ling again. Dressed in worn jeans and looking much older, she carried a sack on her back, slung to one of those head straps that coolie women use for heavy loads. There were the children too, carrying smaller loads, clustering about her as the group moved from stall to stall. Ting-ling chaffered and haggled and argued, laughing when it seemed politic, promising the stallkeepers to pay later.

I said, "Hello, Ting-ling, how are you getting on?"

Ting-ling straightened up. "Well, we aren't starving," she said emphatically. She and her children moved on, looking for food.

Tou-shih-cheng-hsien-yü 豆豉蒸鮮魚
STEAMED SEA BASS WITH FERMENTED BLACK BEANS

A 1½-pound sea bass, cleaned but with head and tail left on (or substitute any other firm white fish)

1 teaspoon salt

2 teaspoons fermented black beans

1 tablespoon soy sauce

1 tablespoon Chinese rice wine, or pale dry sherry

1 tablespoon finely shredded, peeled fresh ginger root

1 scallion, including the green top, cut into 2-inch lengths

1 tablespoon peanut oil, or flavorless vegetable oil

½ teaspoon sugar

PREPARE AHEAD: 1. Wash the bass under cold running water and pat it dry inside and out with paper towels. With a sharp knife, lightly score the fish by making diagonal cuts ¼ inch deep at ½-inch intervals on both sides. Then sprinkle the fish, inside and out, with the salt.

2. With a cleaver or knife, coarsely chop the fermented beans, then combine them in a bowl with the soy sauce, wine, oil and sugar. Mix well.

3. Lay the fish on a heatproof platter ½ inch smaller in diameter than the pot you plan to steam it in. Pour the bowl of seasonings over the fish, and arrange the pieces of ginger and scallion on top.

TO COOK: Pour enough boiling water into the lower part of a steamer to come within an inch of the cooking rack (or use a steamer substitute as described on page 56). Bring the water in the steamer to a rolling boil and place the platter of fish on the rack. Cover the pot securely. Keep the water in the steamer at a continuous boil and replenish it if it boils away. Steam the fish for about 15 minutes, or until it is firm to the touch. Serve at once on its own steaming platter placed on top of a serving dish. As a main course, this will serve 3 or 4. As part of a Chinese meal *(page 200)*, it will serve 4 to 6.

Tung-yü 凍魚
JELLIED FISH

A 1½-pound whiting, pike or sea bass, cleaned and with the head and tail removed (or substitute any other firm white fish)

1 tablespoon salt

2 tablespoons Chinese rice wine, or pale dry sherry

4 slices peeled fresh ginger root about 1 inch in diameter and ⅛ inch thick

1 scallion, including the green top, cut into 2-inch pieces

Fresh Chinese parsley sprigs *(cilantro)*, or substitute flat-leaf Italian parsley

PREPARE AHEAD: 1. Wash the fish under cold running water and pat it dry with paper towels. To flavor and partially cure the fish, sprinkle it with salt, inside and out, and refrigerate for at least 4 hours.

TO COOK: Pour enough boiling water into the lower part of a steamer to come to within an inch of the cooking rack (or use a steamer substitute as described on page 56). Lay the fish on a deep heatproof platter ½ inch smaller than the diameter of the pot. Pour the wine over the fish, and scatter the ginger and scallions on top. Bring the water in the steamer to a rolling boil, place the fish on the rack and cover the pot. Keeping the water at a continuous boil, steam the fish for 15 minutes, or until it is quite firm to the touch. Remove the platter of fish from the steamer, discard the scallions and ginger, and, with a slotted spatula, transfer the fish to a cutting board or a large plate. Reserve the juices in the platter.

With a small, sharp knife, skin the fish by making a small slit at the base of the tail and peeling off the skin from tail to head. Carefully turn the fish over and skin the other side similarly. Now cut the top layer of the fish crosswise into 1-inch sections without cutting through the backbone. Detach them from the bone with the spatula and place the pieces of fish in a soup plate about 6 inches in diameter and 2 inches deep. Then lift out the backbone of the fish in one piece, discard it and divide the bottom layer of fish into similar portions. Pour the reserved juices over the fish and refrigerate for 4 hours, or until it jells. Garnish with fresh parsley. As part of a cold platter *(page 47)*, this will serve 4 to 6.

Arranged for beauty and flavor, sea bass on a plate inside a bamboo steamer rack are ready to cook. During the brief steaming the garnish of crisscrossed scallions, fermented black beans and ginger will suffuse the tender flesh with its subtly balanced flavors.

1 For squirrel fish, remove head, fillet—leave tail on.

2 Score the flesh with deep, crisscrossing cuts.

3 Coat fish—flesh side and skin—with dusting of flour.

4 Then deep-fry the fish and head until golden brown.

5 Serve the fish piping hot, with the head in its original place; generously cover with sweet-and-sour sauce.

To serve 4 to 6

2 dried Chinese mushrooms, 1 to 1½ inches in diameter

¼ cup freshly shelled peas, or substitute thoroughly defrosted frozen peas

A 2-pound sea bass, cleaned, but with head and tail left on, or substitute pike, carp, red snapper or another firm white fish

3 cups plus 2 additional tablespoons peanut oil, or flavorless vegetable oil

½ cup flour

1 small onion, cut into ¼-inch-thick slices

1 small carrot, scraped and roll-cut into 1-inch wedges (pages 38-39)

4 peeled and washed fresh water chestnuts or drained canned water chestnuts, cut into ½-inch dice

1 teaspoon finely chopped garlic

1 teaspoon salt

¼ cup white vinegar

¼ cup sugar

1 teaspoon Chinese rice wine, or pale dry sherry

1 teaspoon soy sauce

2 tablespoons tomato catsup

½ cup chicken stock, fresh or canned

1 tablespoon cornstarch, dissolved in 2 tablespoons cold chicken stock, fresh or canned, or cold water

Sung-shu-yü

松鼠魚

SQUIRREL FISH

This is called squirrel fish because the body curls as it is deep-fried—and, when arranged on a plate with the head, the fish is said to look like a squirrel. This recipe uses catsup as a substitute for Chinese crab-apple candy, which has a sweet-sour taste like catsup, but needs lengthy soaking.

PREPARE AHEAD: 1. In a small bowl, cover the mushrooms with ½ cup of warm water and let them soak for 30 minutes. Discard the water. Cut away and discard the stems, and cut each cap into quarters.

2. Blanch the fresh peas and carrot wedges in a quart of boiling water for 7 to 10 minutes, or until tender. Drain, run cold water over them.

3. Wash the bass under cold running water and pat it dry inside and out with paper towels. With a cleaver or heavy, sharp knife, remove the head at the point where it joins the body. Turn the head upside down and, with a few sharp blows of a cleaver or heavy knife, break the head bone in the middle. Then, with the palm of your hand, press down firmly on the top of the head to flatten it. Lay the fish on its side and split it in half, cutting along the backbone, but do not remove the tail. Lift out the backbone, severing it at the base of the tail. Score the flesh side of each fillet with crisscrossing diagonal cuts an inch apart and almost down to the skin. The bass should be 2 separate fillets joined at the tail.

4. Have the above ingredients, oil, flour, onion, water chestnuts, garlic, salt, vinegar, sugar, wine, soy sauce, catsup, stock and cornstarch mixture at hand.

TO COOK: Preheat the oven to 250°. Pour 3 cups of oil into a 12-inch wok or a large deep-fryer and heat the oil until a haze forms above it or it reaches 375° on a deep-frying thermometer. Sprinkle the flour over a piece of wax paper and press the scored sides of the fish into it. Then coat the skin sides. Hold the fish by the tail, shake it to remove any excess flour and lower it into the hot oil. Flour the head and add it to the pan. Deep-fry the fish for 5 to 8 minutes until the body and head are golden brown. Lift the fish out of the oil and drain on a double thickness of paper towels. Place the fish, skin side down, on a heated platter and set the head in its original position. Keep the fish warm in the oven.

Set a 12-inch wok or 10-inch skillet over high heat for 30 seconds. Pour in 2 tablespoons of oil, swirl it about in the pan and heat for 30 seconds, turning the heat down if the oil smokes. Add the mushrooms, peas, carrot, onion, water chestnuts and garlic, and stir-fry for 3 minutes. Add the salt, then the vinegar, sugar, wine, soy sauce, catsup and stock, and bring to a boil. Stir the cornstarch mixture and add it. Cook, stirring, until the vegetables are glazed. Pour over the fish and serve at once.

Hün-t'un-t'ang　　　　　　　　　　　餛飩湯
WONTON SOUP

This is not the wonton soup you may have come upon in restaurants. The Chinese call this "soup wonton" and serve it as a substantial lunch. The serving of wontons in each portion makes this a full-meal soup.

PREPARE AHEAD: 1. To make the filling: In a large bowl, combine the pork, soy sauce, ginger and salt, and, using a spoon or your hands, mix them thoroughly. Then mix in the spinach.

2. To assemble the *wontons:* Place 1 teaspoon or so of the filling just below the center of each wrapper. Fold one side over the filling and tuck its edge under the filling. Then, with a finger dipped in water, moisten the exposed sides of the wrapper and roll up the filled cylinder, leaving ½ inch of wrapper unrolled at the top. Now take the two ends of the cylinder in the fingers of both hands and pull them down beneath the roll until the ends meet and overlap slightly. Pinch the ends firmly together. As each *wonton* is finished, place it on a plate and cover with a dry towel.

TO COOK: In a 4- to 5-quart saucepan, bring 2 quarts of water to a boil and drop in the *wontons.* Return to a boil, reduce the heat to moderate and cook uncovered for 5 minutes, or until tender but still a little resistant to the bite. Drain the *wontons* through a colander. Pour the stock into the pan and bring to a boil, add the watercress or spinach and the *wontons,* and return again to a boil. Serve at once.

To serve 4 to 6

THE WONTONS
1 recipe *wonton* wrappers, prepared according to directions on page 128, or ½ pound ready-made *wonton* wrappers, or 1 pound ready-made egg-roll wrappers cut into 3½-inch squares
¾ pound lean boneless pork, finely ground
4 teaspoons soy sauce
¾ teaspoon finely chopped, peeled fresh ginger root
¾ teaspoon salt
¾ pound fresh spinach, cooked, drained, squeezed dry and finely chopped, or 1 ten-ounce package chopped frozen spinach, defrosted, squeezed dry and chopped again (6 tablespoons after chopping)

THE SOUP
6 cups chicken stock, fresh or canned
1 cup loosely packed fresh watercress leaves, or 1 cup fresh spinach leaves, torn into very small pieces

Tung-kua-t'ang　　　　　　　　　　冬瓜湯
WINTER MELON SOUP

PREPARE AHEAD: 1. In a small bowl, cover the mushrooms with ½ cup of warm water and soak them for 30 minutes. Discard the water. Cut away the stems of the mushrooms.

2. Peel the melon, and discard the inner seeds and stringy fibers. Cut the melon pulp into ¼-inch slices, then cut the slices into 1- to 1½-inch pieces.

3. Have the mushrooms, melon, stock and ham within easy reach.

TO COOK: In a 2- to 3-quart heavy saucepan, combine the chicken stock, melon and mushrooms, and bring to a boil. Reduce the heat to low, cover the pan and simmer for 15 minutes. To serve, ladle the soup into a tureen or serving bowl and stir in the pieces of ham.

To serve 4

6 small dried Chinese mushrooms, ½ to 1 inch in diameter
1 pound of winter melon
3 cups chicken stock, fresh or canned
A ⅛-inch-thick slice cooked Smithfield ham, cut into 1- to 1½-inch pieces

To serve 4

2 large fresh ears of corn, shucked,
    or substitute an 8¾-ounce can of
    creamed corn
2 egg whites
2 tablespoons milk
3 cups chicken stock, fresh or canned
1 teaspoon salt
1 tablespoon cornstarch dissolved in
    2 tablespoons cold chicken stock,
    fresh or canned, or cold water
A ⅛-inch-thick slice cooked
    Smithfield ham, finely chopped
    (about ¼ cup)

Su-mi-t'ang   粟米湯   蟹肉粟米湯
VELVET CORN SOUP

This is a modernized version of a classic recipe. The original dish was made with field corn (not sweet table corn), available and succulent for only a few days at the height of the summer, and thus considered a great treat. Though corn may not seem a "Chinese vegetable," it was brought to China by Spanish and Portuguese explorers, and has been grown there for more than 400 years.

PREPARE AHEAD: 1. With a cleaver or sharp knife, slice the kernels of fresh corn from their cobs into a bowl, making sure not to cut too deeply into the cob or to lose any of the milky corn juices.

2. In a small bowl, beat the egg whites with a fork until frothy. Then beat in the 2 tablespoons of milk.

3. Have the corn, egg white mixture, chicken stock, salt, cornstarch mixture and chopped ham within easy reach.

TO COOK: In a 2-quart saucepan, bring the chicken stock to a boil over high heat. Add the corn and salt, and, stirring constantly, bring to a boil again. Give the cornstarch mixture a quick stir to recombine it and pour it into the soup. Cook, stirring constantly, until the soup has thickened and become clear. Then turn off the heat and immediately pour in the egg white mixture, stirring only once. Quickly pour the hot soup into a tureen or individual bowls and sprinkle with the chopped ham.

VARIATION: Velvet corn soup may be made with crabmeat. Increase the stock to 1 quart and add ½ pound of fresh crabmeat or a 7½-ounce can of crabmeat, carefully picked over, with the corn. Omit the ham.

To serve 4 to 6

4 dried Chinese mushrooms, 1 to 1½
    inches in diameter
2 squares, 3 inches each, fresh Chinese
    bean curd, about ½ inch thick
½ cup canned bamboo shoots
¼ pound boneless pork
1 quart chicken stock, fresh or canned
1 teaspoon salt
1 tablespoon soy sauce
¼ teaspoon ground white pepper
2 tablespoons white vinegar
2 tablespoons cornstarch mixed with
    3 tablespoons cold water
1 egg, lightly beaten
2 teaspoons sesame-seed oil
1 scallion, including the green top,
    finely chopped

Suan-la-t'ang   酸辣湯
SOUR-AND-HOT SOUP

PREPARE AHEAD: 1. In a small bowl, cover the mushrooms with ½ cup of warm water and let them soak for 30 minutes. Discard the water. With a cleaver or knife, cut away and discard the tough stems of the mushrooms, and shred the caps by placing one at a time on a chopping board. Cut them horizontally into paper-thin slices, and then into thin strips.

2. Drain the pieces of bamboo shoot and bean curd, and rinse them in cold water. Shred them as fine as the mushrooms.

3. With a cleaver or sharp knife, trim the pork of all fat. Then shred it, too, by slicing the meat as thin as possible and cutting the slices into narrow strips about 1½ to 2 inches long.

4. Have the above ingredients, stock, salt, soy sauce, pepper, vinegar, cornstarch mixture, egg, sesame-seed oil and scallions within easy reach.

TO COOK: Combine in a heavy 3-quart saucepan the stock, salt, soy sauce, mushrooms, bamboo shoots and pork. Bring to a boil over high heat, then immediately reduce the heat to low, cover the pan and simmer for 3 minutes. Drop in the bean curd, and the pepper and vinegar. Bring to a boil again. Give the cornstarch mixture a stir to recombine it and pour it into the soup. Stir for a few seconds until the soup thickens, then slowly pour in the beaten egg, stirring gently all the while. Remove the soup from the heat and ladle it into a tureen or serving bowl. Stir in the sesame-seed oil and sprinkle the top with scallions. Serve at once.

Four popular Chinese soups that are simple to prepare *(pages 107, 108)* are, clockwise from the top: clear and delicate winter melon soup, creamy but light velvet corn soup, *wonton* soup garnished with spinach, and piquant sour-and-hot soup with shredded pork.

一耘

時雨既巳潤良
苗日維新去草
如去惡務令盡
陳根涅蟠任瀆
鼻膝行生浪紋
眷惟有虞氏德
盛感鳥耘

V

Oriental Staff of Life

Mounting on high I begin to realize the smallness of man's domain;
Gazing into distance I begin to know the vanity of the carnal world.
I turn my head and hurry home—back to the court and market,
A single grain of rice falling—into the great barn. —PO CHU-I, 772-846 A.D.

Many of our common turns of speech deal with bread: earning one's daily bread, eating the bitter bread of sorrow, bread and circuses, man does not live by bread alone. In these phrases we really mean far more than bread; we mean food in general and the wherewithal to buy it. When I was younger, we used to call money "dough," and today the slang for man's earnings is "bread." All of which simply means that bread is the staple food of the West, the fundamental necessity. On the other side of the world the word "rice" has exactly the same significance.

Half the globe's population depends on rice, so Easterners naturally refer to it just as we refer to bread, but when a Chinese tells you that he works for his daily rice he may be telling the literal truth. Chef Wang, when he said that his salary as an apprentice used to be a bag of rice a month, meant exactly what he said. He used that rice much as if it had been money, giving some to his parents and no doubt selling the rest, since he was adequately fed at the restaurant. Incidentally, a bag of rice a month—33⅓ pounds—would hardly have been enough for a hungry boy. During the Second World War the Japanese in occupied China paid the coolies pressed into labor a catty and a quarter of rice per day—about a pound and a third—and the coolies grumbled that this was not enough

One of a set of delicately hand-colored woodprints, this scene shows farmers weeding a small rice paddy "as if purging evil," in the words of the accompanying 13th Century poem. Two men irrigate the land with a bucket, and a small boy plays his pipe from the back of one of the farm animals, a water buffalo. Some other prints in the series depict the full cycle of rice cultivation; they appear on pages 118-119.

to keep them going at their hard jobs. You and I, however, could not swallow that much rice in a day, at least not without practice, for it is a very bulky food for those who are not used to it.

An even more powerful barrier to the regular consumption of rice by Westerners is the enormous strength of eating habits. Those of us who live in big towns can see around us the proof of this: the more foreign students live among us, the more restaurants spring up to take care of their special needs. In the years right after World War II there were so few Indian restaurants in New York City that any visiting Indian could name every one of them: today eating places serving curry and other Indian dishes are all over the place. But many of the foreign students can, when put to it, exist on our food because they have been broken in to it through lengthy residence among us. Such was not the case with some unfortunate students of mine in Shanghai when I first went to live there and innocently entertained a few of them every week at lunch in my apartment. Naturally I served food in the Western style: I would not have dared to try anything Chinese. But I thought there was plenty to eat (even though I rarely included rice) and it came as a considerable shock when I learned that most of the boys got ready for my lunches by first eating a hearty meal at home. Without rice, they simply did not feel as if they had eaten.

There are about 7,000 different forms of this grain, but all of them (with the exception of wild rice, which is part of a separate botanical family) are a kind of grass the botanists call *Oryza sativa*. During the centuries of its cultivation by man, changes in the size and shape of the grain have developed; even the environmental requirements have altered for many of these changed forms. Today the commonest sort, paddy rice, is grown in water. But a quite different mountain or upland rice is cultivated by farmers, inside China and out, who live in hilly country where the water supply is limited. Upland rice resembles the other varieties in that it does best in a warm, humid climate. In China, rice fanciers distinguish among many kinds of rice—long-speared and short-speared, long-grain and pointed-grain, round-top and flat-top grains, among others. Even the colors vary: Westerners think of all rice as white, but there are also ivory, red, semiviolet, brown and dappled black varieties. A 17th Century Chinese treatise, *The Growing of Grain*, mentions an exotic type called "fragrant rice," noting that it is a special sort enjoyed by aristocrats. But the writer severely comments that "with a small yield and lacking in nutritious value, this variety deserves no recommendation."

For purposes of discussion, rice can be classified in three divisions: the oval, rather starchy short grain, which seems to be losing ground to long-grain rice even though it has an excellent flavor and when cooked has the soft and moist texture that Chinese like; a long-grain, less starchy variety sometimes called Patna rice (though it is also grown widely outside India), preferred for general daily use and which epicures insist is the very best because the texture remains firm after cooking; and glutinous, or sticky, rice, which molds easily into fancy shapes—sticky rice is used only occasionally by the Chinese and then for sweets such as the eight-treasure rice pudding *(page 172)*. The Japanese, on the other hand, regularly use glutinous rice with pickled radish and fish for some meals, and some-

Taking their main meal of the day, a family of Taiwan rice farmers serve themselves from large bowls of vegetables. The bulk of the meal is rice, and a small boy *(foreground)* is filling his bowl from an enormous tub of this Oriental staple.

times on special occasions for decorative effects. I have seen rice models of Mount Fuji complete with vegetable coloring to show the green slopes and ash-white peak. I was expected to eat one of these in spite of the fact that it was stone cold and tended to stick in the throat. The more sophisticated American food shops carry all of these varieties.

The Chinese claim that rice was first used in their country nearly 5,000 years ago. At that time, according to the legend, the Emperor Shen Nung held a ceremony each year at the beginning of the planting season. He himself would plant rice seeds of the first and best quality, while his sons walked after him and planted four other varieties of the same grain. Thus the season was declared open and the population was free to follow the royal family's example. No doubt some such ritual was actually followed, but Shen Nung—if he really existed—cannot be awarded the honor of introducing rice to mankind; the Indians did that. For thousands of years, from well before the alleged dates of Shen Nung's reign, they had been growing and eating a wild grass called *newaree,* the ancestor of the rice plant we know.

As man became more mobile, travelers carried rice seeds far afield, and the grain spread through China and on to other countries of the Far and Middle East, reaching Egypt by the Fourth Century B.C. In due course the Saracens brought it on to Spain, from where it spread throughout Europe. Italy began growing rice in the 15th Century, and it became so popular there that in some districts it nearly displaced pasta. Slowly it moved north to the British Isles, but it was not a common article of diet when the English first colonized America. In the middle of the 17th Century some Virginians tried to grow rice but failed, no doubt because the settlers sowed it on dry farming land. For years after the crop died off it was firmly believed that rice would not live in America, and nobody tried again to grow it there until the 1690s. Then a ship, Liverpool-bound from Madagascar, put into Charleston, South Carolina, for repairs. The city fathers went aboard to pay a social call, and one of them, on learning that part of the cargo was unhulled rice, obtained a small bag of the grain for an experiment. He planted it in swampy land where it flourished so well that the yield was almost enough to feed the whole colony. After this triumph the Americans imported shipload after shipload of seed rice.

Today the United States devotes some two million acres to rice culture and produces over eight billion pounds of the grain a year. This is far more than the country eats, for on the average an American consumes seven pounds a year, whereas a Chinese eats at least a pound a day and a Japanese about half as much. Among the principal rice-growing states— California, Texas, Louisiana, Arkansas, Mississippi and Missouri—California leads in productivity with 5,000 pounds per acre, though the world average is only 1,450. Most of this American production dates back to World War II, when imports from the Far East ceased. American botanists promptly developed an all-purpose grain that would do well here, and for a while a tremendous amount of rice was grown in the States. The crop level has fallen off somewhat, but there is still a preponderance of the American type of grain in United States shops, and old China hands complain that with this standardization a lot of the fun has gone out of cooking rice.

When used in its natural form, rice is especially nutritious. Just under the husk is a brownish skin of bran containing protein, minerals and vitamins. Unfortunately, the whole grain does not keep as well as white, or polished, rice. Moreover, it takes much longer to cook than white rice. Then, too, there is an ancient esthetic preference for white rice that is too strong to battle. No less a person than Confucius insisted that his rice be as white as possible. For these reasons, most rice has been marketed in the polished form. In Confucius' time—and for that matter until the machine age—rice-eaters milled their grain by hand to rid it of its brown color. They pounded the rice in a mortar with a pestle, a very inefficient process but one that did not succeed in removing all the nutrient value present in the skin. After the invention of the milling machine, milled rice turned out all too white and pretty, mere globules of pure carbohydrate, and in those countries where rice was the principal food, people began to suffer from a vitamin shortage that causes the disease called beriberi. When the cause of the disease was understood, dietitians suggested adding vitamin B to the milled rice, a practice now fairly widespread. If you are worried about your protein and vitamins and still want to eat white rice, the "precooked" (or converted) brands widely sold in Western markets can solve the problem, for this rice is parboiled before packaging, which preserves valuable constituents of the whole grain. But precooked rice is expensive, and some Chinese cooks think little of its texture and flavor.

The impact of the machine on rice goes beyond milling. In California,

favors to come in the New Year. A whole day of the New Year is devoted to the celebration of its first planting, five millennia ago.

Paradoxically, only under circumstances of dire poverty will a Chinese eat rice and nothing else. It should always be combined with a portion, however small, of vegetables and—if it can be afforded—a portion of meat. On the other hand, as the proverb has it, a meal without rice is like a beautiful girl with only one eye. Hence my hungry Shanghai students' sad experience. No matter how lavish the prospective meal, one of the self-deprecating phrases uttered by polite Cantonese hosts when their guests are taking their seats at table is, "There's not much *sung*" (the other cooked food that goes with rice), "but take your fill of rice." The saying was reversed during the rice shortage in wartime Hong Kong to read: "there's not much rice, but take your fill of *sung*." There was sadly bitter humor in the comment, for *sung*, too, was in extremely short supply.

At a meeting some time ago of a New York society devoted to Chinese culture, one of the speakers gave a long and—it must be admitted—boring talk on China's internal politics as he supposed them to be today. Almost everyone was half asleep when at last he came to a stop and the chairman said the customary thing: "Are there any questions?" For a while it seemed that nobody was going to avail himself of the chance; silence prevailed. Then in the back row an American woman stood up and said, "I have a question. How do you boil rice?"

Although it was not the ideal moment for such a discussion, she had hit on a topic that has never really been satisfactorily settled, and possibly never will be. It is amazing how many theories exist as to the really correct way to carry out this apparently simple operation—and how many methods, for that matter, turn out well.

We all know about the absorbent qualities of rice: given the right conditions it will readily soak up whatever liquid it is cooking in, from milk to oil. In Chinese cooking the medium used is water, and it gets into the rice either through boiling or steaming.

For a yield of 3 cups, use 1 cup of rice to 1¾ cups of cold water, but if the recipe is doubled the proportion of water to rice should be slightly less than doubled. For example, for 2 cups of rice, use 3 cups of water—not 3½. First rinse the rice by pouring it into a 2-quart saucepan and adding enough cold water to cover it. Give the rice a thorough stir, then pour off the rinse water, add 1¾ cups of fresh cold water and bring to a boil over high heat. Boil for 2 to 3 minutes until craterlike holes begin to form on the surface of the rice. When these are clearly visible through the steam, cover, reduce heat and cook for 20 minutes. Remove the pan from the heat, allowing the rice to remain in the covered pot, to relax, as the Chinese say, for 10 minutes. This period is vital for properly cooked rice, for it is then that any remaining water is absorbed and steaming completes the cooking. Then the rice should be briskly stirred to loosen the grains before serving. One cup of long-grain rice will yield 3 cups of cooked rice; this is more than the yield from the same amount of the shorter-grain variety. After cooking, rice may be kept warm until it is served by placing the still-covered pot in a heated oven. Cold cooked rice will keep for a few days in a covered container in the refrigerator.

Continued on page 120

Farmers in the northern part of Taiwan laboriously
harvest the terraces of a rice field that follow the contours
of a hillside. In the background at left, two men work
a hand-operated thresher. After threshing, the rice will
be carried to the area in the lower foreground to dry.

Prints and poems, centuries old, that describe the unvarying toil of rice farming

1 PLOWING

"By the eastern bank he plows in the rain;
Wood pigeons sing, urging on the plow.
Green fields are dark in the springtime dawn;
The black ox's shoulders turn red with the strain."

2 SOWING THE SEEDLINGS

"Now we enter the fields to sow and plant,
Walking backward, our hand throwing out the seed.
Next morning when we view the level fields,
Green tips will have emerged in wind and rain . . ."

5 THRESHING

"At frost time the weather is fine;
In brisk winds the tree leaves fall.
Now is the time to thresh the rice,
The flails making a wild noise."

6 POUNDING THAT HUSKS AND POLISHES THE RICE

"Delicate, bright the moon rises above the wall;
Rustling, whispering, the wind blows down the leaves.
And in the villages at this time
The sounds of pestles echo and resound."

TRANSPLANTING SEEDLINGS

"The new sprouts have just topped the water:
A vast expanse of even, blue-green carpeting.
In the clear morning, let us pluck and wash them,
Father and son striving together to pull them up."

4 REAPING

"When the farmers reap and gather,
Their sickles hurry on the work. . . .
Children come and carry off the sheaves,
Chill winds biting through their little coats . . ."

SIFTING THE RICE

From thatched eaves, the sound of mortar and pestle;
By bamboo huts, finely they sift the rice. . . .
The farmers' work has not been slight:
Well may they congratulate each other as they eat their fill! . . ."

8 STORING IN THE GRANARY

"Now it's cold, the oxen are in the pen;
At year's end the rice is brought to the granary.
The farmers, finally enjoying a moment of leisure,
Rest below the eaves, sunning their backs . . ."

Then there is the rice-cooker method, which many people prefer. The most popular and foolproof way of cooking rice is to use a rice cooker made either in Japan or Taiwan and now on sale in good appliance shops in large cities all over the States. If you have occasion to cook rice often and in large amounts these steamers, which come in two- to six-cup sizes, should be in your kitchen. The methods of using Japanese and Taiwanese models differ slightly: instructions come with each. Some experts prefer the Japanese variety because of its convenient arrangement for keeping the rice warm between cooking and serving, but the Taiwanese kind produces a better texture of rice.

(For additional information on how to cook rice, see FOODS OF THE WORLD *Supplement Number One.*)

In China, boiled or steamed rice is served plain and piping hot throughout the meal or sometimes only at the end of dinner. Chinese take a mouthful of plain rice, then a separate mouthful of flavored food. While they sometimes spoon the sauce of a flavored dish over their plain rice, they never douse it with soy sauce as do many Americans. But there are many other ways to use it, especially fried rice *(page 124)*. This is cold cooked rice with beaten egg added, stir-fried in oil and served as a separate dish. Many tasty variations on this dish can be made by adding pork, shrimp, fish or other ingredients. Rice can also be combined with other foodstuffs—especially vegetables—while it is cooking, so that the heat of the rice cooks the rest of the food. Sizzling rice is made of the crusts of rice that sometimes stick to the bottom of the wok after boiling. Some say that the discovery of this dish was accidental: an apprentice overcooked a pot of rice, tasted the nearly scorched residue and found it good. The rice crusts are deep-fried, and should then be served immediately—so hot that when they are dropped into soup or are doused with sauce they sizzle.

A Chinese dish usually made with rice, though barley or millet will answer the same purpose, is congee *(page 125)*, a thick gruel or porridge suitable for invalids and babies. Having a neutral taste itself, it will respond to almost any flavoring—sugar, salt or ham. I have had it for breakfast, as the Chinese eat it on cold mornings with tiny salted shrimp, salted vegetables or meat, and even peanuts.

In the north of China, where the weather is colder, the conditions are more suitable for wheat-growing than for rice paddies. So northerners depend mainly on wheat for their everyday starch. However, northern Chinese eat rice, when it is available, as readily as their compatriots in the south. When the wheat crop fails or when its price is too high, other cereals take its place—barley, millet, buckwheat, corn and sorghum. Millet, cheaper than wheat, is usually available in sufficient quantities, and though not so nutritious it serves as an adequate substitute.

Bread is not unknown to the Chinese, but they usually eat wheat as *mien* (noodles), or as a pastry made of wheat flour, soybeans and perhaps a dash of rice flour. Westerners are bound to notice, when they first encounter Chinese noodles or one of the many varieties of dumplings, that these dishes are very similar to Italian noodles and ravioli. Sometimes Chinese, half jokingly, will claim that this is because Marco Polo carried home to Venice the secret of pasta-making. To this allegation Italians, of

120

course, retort that Marco, on the contrary, taught it to the Chinese. But neither claim stands up: the Italians were using pasta for years before Marco Polo's return, and the noodle has been a basic of Chinese cuisine for thousands of years. However, both Chinese and Italians agree that noodles should be eaten with sauce.

Chinese noodles come in a wide range of shapes, from flat ribbons to very thin, delicate strings, and they are always very long because they are a symbol of longevity; they are served at birthday parties as we serve birthday cake. Many Chinese make their own *mien* at home, from wheat, rice, corn and even peas. However, ordinary egg noodles bought at the supermarket are perfectly good substitutes. Many varieties are available in Chinese markets and most Chinese housewives buy rather than make them.

The way to cook noodles depends upon what you intend to use them for —a basic like rice to provide solid substance, or as a special dish for a snack. (The noodle snack is much enjoyed by southern Chinese.) For the first purpose noodles are usually parboiled by slowly adding them to salted boiling water. Vigorous boiling should continue for 5 minutes, until the noodles are tender but not mushy—noodles should hardly ever be mushy. But for the fried or stewed snack, noodles should boil only 3 or 4 minutes and should not be soft all the way through when taken out of the water. Then they are thoroughly drained and rinsed free of starch. Noodles can be used in various soups, or as the base for a number of delicious stir-fried mixtures of chicken, shredded ham, or anything else that you think might be good. Dried shrimps are so savory that a few can flavor a whole bowl of noodles. The same is true of salted egg.

In the south, wheat is used mainly as the wrapping or skin for dumplings, familiar to habituées of Chinese restaurants as *wonton*. Ready-made *wonton* wrappers can be bought at Chinese specialty stores but are not hard to make at home; the constituents are wheat flour and egg with water *(page 128)*. To fill the dumplings you can use meat or seafood minced with vegetables, or a vegetable mixture alone. Boiled in soup, shallow-fried, steamed or braised, dumplings provide richly delicious accents; after being cooked they will keep for several days in the refrigerator. In the north, where dumplings are equally popular, they like to dip them in vinegar sauce. In the south a whole meal is sometimes made of different kinds of *wonton* which go well with mustard sauce and even with a sweet-and-sour dressing. For wheat-eaters like ourselves these dumplings are more satisfying than are the rice dishes, and the great number of tastes and textures—crisp bits of vegetable here and there in the filling, or the smoothness of finely minced meat—make *wonton* very tempting.

Spring rolls and egg rolls are made in much the same way as *wonton*, though their shape resembles small German pancakes rather than *wonton*. The distinction between the two forms of roll is that the spring roll is made by quickly pressing a ball of dough into a hot skillet to produce a very thin pancake. For egg rolls the dough is rolled flat; the resulting flap of thin, tough pastry is wrapped around a filling of minced meat or seafood and liberal quantities of chopped vegetable, with plenty of savory seasoning, and then fried. Spring rolls are difficult and messy to make; the Chinese usually buy them already made. A more elaborate

Thick bunches of noodles, each looking like a hopeless tangle of fragile wires, dry in the sun outside a noodle factory near Shanghai. This is the last stage in the preparation of these noodles—unusual to Western eyes but quite common in China—that are sometimes called "cellophane" noodles because of their transparency. Those seen here are made out of mung-bean starch paste; wheat is a more generally used base for Chinese noodles.

form of pastry is the mandarin pancake *(page 172)*, or Peking doily, which is used to wrap the crackling and scallions in Peking duck, among other foods. This envelope is made of flour and boiling water and oil, kneaded and rolled out and cooked slowly. It is more tender than the spring-roll skin, and has a delicious smell when hot, something like that of our fresh-baked bread.

One more cereal is important in Chinese cuisine, or, at any rate, in the Tibetan, which comes within our scope since for long periods in the past, Tibet alternated between independence of and domination by China and is today once more under Chinese rule. The principal food of that mountainous land is *tsampa*, a kind of gruel of flour made of barley, Tibet's chief grain, and water, usually mixed with tea made with yak butter. The only garnish most Tibetans get with their *tsampa* nowadays are some of the hardy vegetables that can grow in Tibet's lofty altitude and difficult climate—turnips, cauliflower, beets and carrots. But formerly the gruel was enlivened by an occasional shred of dried yak meat. In easier days, those who could afford imported food ate in the Chinese style, with an occasional departure into Indian dishes, but today everybody eats *tsampa*. According to reports coming out of Tibet, the poor people can no longer

even put yak-butter tea into their *tsampa* but merely roast their small allowance of barley and mix it with water to make a thin broth.

Rice, millet, barley, noodles, bread—these are the farinaceous foods that, eaten alone, are foolers, deceiving the hungry into thinking they are satisfied. Without them people accustomed to a starch-rich menu feel hungry no matter what other food they get. Moreover, it must be the kind of starch they are used to. Although rice is one of the bulkiest of starches, it is digested very quickly, which explains why Westerners unaccustomed to the Chinese diet feel hungry soon after a Chinese meal, regardless of how much they have eaten. This attitude toward Chinese food must be ingrained at a very early age, as witness the following story.

"You know, there must be something in that old platitude about Chinese food going right through you," a young father told me. "Yesterday we tried out that Chinatown restaurant you recommended, and we took Betsy with us. She's six. She never had any Chinese food in her life before, but she was crazy about it—waded into it like a veteran, until I thought she'd burst. Honestly she ate up everything on the table, but on the way home, I give you my word, she stopped short after we'd walked only two blocks and said, 'I'm hungry!'"

Huo-t'ui-tan-ch'ao-fan
火腿蛋炒飯
HAM AND EGG FRIED RICE

To serve 3 to 4

½ cup shelled, fresh peas, or
   substitute thoroughly defrosted
   frozen peas
3 tablespoons peanut oil, or flavorless
   vegetable oil
2 eggs, lightly beaten
3 cups Chinese boiled rice, prepared
   according to the directions
   opposite
1 teaspoon salt
2 ounces boiled ham, sliced ¼ inch
   thick and cut into ¼-inch dice
   (about ½ cup)
1 scallion, including the green top,
   finely chopped

PREPARE AHEAD: 1. Blanch fresh peas by dropping them into 4 cups of boiling water and letting them boil uncovered for 5 to 10 minutes, or until tender. Then drain and run cold water over them to stop their cooking and set their color. Frozen peas need only be thoroughly defrosted.

2. Have the peas, oil, eggs, rice, salt, ham and scallions handy.

TO COOK: Set a 12-inch wok or 10-inch skillet over high heat for 30 seconds. Pour in 1 tablespoon of oil, swirl it about in the pan and immediately reduce the heat to moderate. Pour in the beaten eggs. They will form a film on the bottom of the pan almost at once. Immediately lift this film gently with a fork and push it to the back of the pan so that the still-liquid eggs can spread across the bottom of the pan to cook. As soon as the eggs are set, but before they become dry or begin to brown, transfer them to a small bowl and break them up with a fork. Pour the remaining 2 tablespoons of oil into the pan, swirl it around and heat it for 30 seconds. Add the rice and stir-fry for 2 to 3 minutes until all the grains are coated with oil. Add the salt, then the peas and ham, and stir-fry for 20 seconds. Return the eggs to the pan, add the scallions and cook only long enough to heat the eggs through. Serve at once.

Hsia-jen-ch'ao mi-fên
蝦仁炒米粉
STIR-FRIED RICE STICK NOODLES WITH SHRIMP AND VEGETABLES

⅓ pound rice stick noodles
½ pound celery cabbage
1 pound uncooked shrimp (30-36 to
   the pound)
4 tablespoons peanut oil, or flavorless
   vegetable oil
1 tablespoon Chinese rice wine, or
   pale dry sherry
1 teaspoon salt
½ teaspoon salt
½ teaspoon sugar
1 tablespoon soy sauce
½ cup chicken stock, fresh or canned

PREPARE AHEAD: 1. In a large bowl, cover the rice stick noodles with cold water. Soak for 5 minutes then drain thoroughly in a colander.

2. With a cleaver or sharp knife, trim off any wilted top leaves of the cabbage and the root ends. Separate the stalks, wash them thoroughly and slice each stalk lengthwise into ⅛-inch-wide strips.

3. Shell the shrimp, and, with a small, sharp knife, make a shallow incision down the back and lift out the black or white intestinal vein. Wash the shrimp, dry with paper towels and cut each in half lengthwise.

4. Have the above ingredients, the oil, wine, salt, sugar, soy sauce and chicken stock within easy reach.

TO COOK: Set a 12-inch wok or 10-inch skillet over high heat for 30 seconds. Pour in 2 tablespoons of oil, swirl it about in the pan and heat for another 30 seconds, turning the heat down to moderate if the oil begins to smoke. Add the shrimp and stir-fry for 1 minute, or until they turn pink. Add ½ teaspoon salt and the wine, stir once or twice, then transfer the contents of the pan to a plate and set aside. Pour 2 more tablespoons of oil into the pan, heat it for 30 seconds and in it, stir-fry the cabbage for 2 minutes. Then add the salt, sugar and noodles, and cook, stirring, for 1 minute. Pour in the soy sauce and stock, and boil briskly for 3 minutes, or until the liquid has evaporated. Return the shrimp to the pan and, stirring constantly, cook for 30 seconds. Transfer the entire contents of the pan to a heated platter and serve at once. As a main course, this will serve 2 to 4.

T'ang-mien
湯麵
CHINESE NOODLE SOUP

To serve 4 to 6

PREPARE AHEAD: 1. In a small bowl, cover the mushrooms with ½ cup of warm water and let them soak for 30 minutes. Discard the water. With a cleaver or sharp knife, cut away and discard the tough stems of the mushrooms, and cut the caps in half.

2. Have the mushrooms, noodles, chicken stock, bamboo shoots, watercress, salt, chicken, pork and ham within easy reach.

TO COOK: In a 3- or 4-quart pot, bring 2 quarts of water to a boil over high heat. Drop in the noodles and boil them vigorously, uncovered, for 2 minutes, stirring occasionally. Drain the noodles through a large sieve and run cold water over them to stop their cooking. Now bring the stock to a boil in the same pot, add the mushrooms, bamboo shoots, watercress, salt and noodles, and reduce the heat to low. Simmer, uncovered, for about 2 minutes. To serve, lift the noodles and vegetables out of the simmering soup with a bamboo strainer or slotted spoon, and transfer them to a large tureen or serving bowl. Arrange the chicken, pork and ham on top of them. Pour in the soup stock down one side of the bowl so as not to disturb the arrangement. Serve at once.

4 dried Chinese mushrooms, 1 to 1½ inches in diameter
½ cup cooked chicken, sliced ⅛ inch thick and cut into 1-inch squares
½ cup roast pork, prepared according to the recipe on page 193, sliced ⅛ inch thick
½ cup Smithfield ham, sliced ⅛ inch thick and cut into 1-inch squares
¼ cup thinly sliced canned bamboo shoots
½ cup loosely packed watercress leaves
½ pound fresh Chinese egg noodles, or substitute narrow Italian egg noodles such as *tagliarini*
1 teaspoon salt
4 cups chicken stock, fresh or canned

Pai-fan
白飯
CHINESE BOILED RICE

To serve 4

Rinse the rice by pouring it into a heavy 2-quart saucepan, adding enough cold water to cover it completely and giving the rice a thorough stir. Drain the rice, add the 1¾ cups of fresh cold water and bring the rice to a boil over high heat. If you have any reason to think the rice you are using is old—and, therefore, very dry—add another ¼ cup of water. Boil for 2 to 3 minutes, or until craterlike holes appear in the surface of the rice. Then cover the pan tightly, reduce the heat to low and cook for 20 minutes. Turn off the heat but do not uncover the pan. Let the rice rest for 10 minutes. Now remove the cover and fluff the rice with chopsticks or a fork. Serve the rice at once while it is still hot. If the rice must wait, keep it in a covered heatproof serving bowl in a preheated 250° oven. To reheat any leftover rice, place it in a colander and set the colander into 1 inch of water boiling in a large pot. Cover the pot and steam for 5 to 10 minutes—depending on how much rice you have.

1 cup long-grain white rice
1¾ cups cold water

Chi'chu
雞粥
CHICKEN CONGEE

To serve 4 to 6

PREPARE AHEAD: 1. Combine the long-grain and glutinous rice in a 2-quart saucepan, add enough cold water to cover and stir thoroughly. Pour off the rinse water.

2. Have the rice, stock, chicken, salt, kohlrabi and lettuce handy.

TO COOK: In a 4- to 5-quart heavy saucepan, bring the chicken stock to a boil over high heat. Stir in the rice, partially cover the pan, reduce the heat to low and simmer for 2 hours. Add the salt, then the chicken. Then ladle into individual soup bowls. Serve very hot and garnish the bowls with 1 or 2 tablespoons of shredded kohlrabi and lettuce.

¼ cup long-grain rice
2 tablespoons glutinous rice
2 quarts fresh or canned chicken stock, or 1 quart chicken broth and 1 quart water combined
1 cup cooked chicken, cut into ½-inch cubes, prepared according to the recipe for chicken stock in the *Recipe Booklet*
2 teaspoons salt
½ cup finely shredded preserved kohlrabi
1 cup finely shredded lettuce

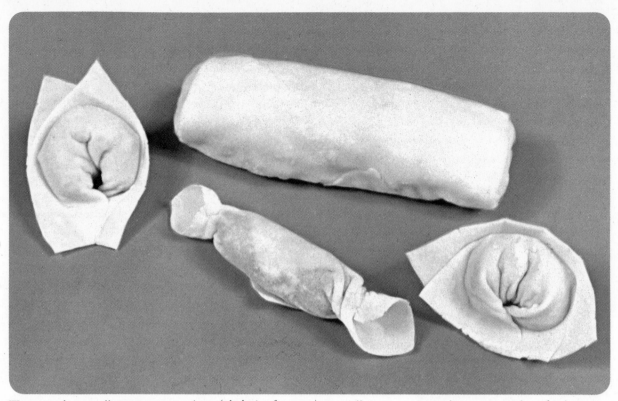

Wonton and egg-roll wrappers turn into *(clockwise from top)* egg roll, soup *wonton*, date *wonton*, deep-fried *wonton*.

Egg rolls take the large 7- to 8-inch square wrapper, sold ready-made in that size.

Wontons need 3½- to 4-inch squares; big wrappers must be cut into quarters.

Two Simple Wrappers Make a Variety of Shapes

Though the finished products are filled, shaped and cooked in different ways, both the egg-roll wrapper used for egg rolls and date *wontons*, and the soup and deep-fried *wonton* wrapper are made from easy-to-make, quite similar doughs. (However, both kinds of wrapper can be bought ready-made.) The egg-roll dough is a simple combination of flour, water and salt; for the *wonton* wrapper Chinese cooks add beaten egg to a flour, water and salt mix. Kneading then develops the gluten in the flour to make doughs that are elastic and manageable and at the same time stiff; it takes a good deal of energy to roll them out paper-thin. To compensate, perhaps, for the extra effort they require, both doughs can stand handling. As long as you do not let the dough dry out, you will not need to worry about overdoing the kneading or rolling, or even the folding and shaping shown in the pictures on the opposite page.

126

EGG ROLL
1 Place a cylinder of filling diagonally on a wrapper.

2 Fold one corner of the wrapper over the filling and tuck the point under it.

3 Fold up both ends of the wrapper; moisten the edges of the remaining flap.

4 Finish by rolling the enclosed filling in the rest of the wrapper.

DATE WONTON
1 Place a cylinder of filling diagonally on a wrapper.

2 Fold one corner of the wrapper over the filling and tuck the point under it.

3 Roll up the resulting tube until all the dough surrounds the filling.

4 Stick a finger into each end of the tube and give it a twist to seal the ends.

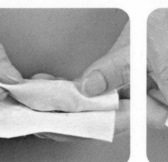

SOUP WONTON
1 Place a cylinder of filling straight across a wrapper.

2 Roll one side of the wrapper over the filling and tuck the edge under.

3 Roll a tube, leaving ½ inch of unrolled wrapper. Insert a finger in each end.

4 Pull ends around until they slightly overlap the tube. Pinch ends together.

DEEP-FRIED WONTON
1 Center a heaping spoonful of filling on a wrapper.

2 Fold one corner up over the filling at an angle to make two askew triangles.

3 Pull the bottom corners of the triangles gently down below their base.

4 Overlap the tips of the two corners slightly and pinch them together.

To make about 4 dozen *wonton*
  wrappers

4 cups sifted all-purpose flour
1 teaspoon salt
2 eggs, lightly beaten
1 cup cold water

To make about 4 dozen *wontons*

One recipe *wonton* wrappers, prepared
  according to the recipe above, or
  ½ pound ready-made *wonton*
  wrappers, or 1 pound ready-made
  egg-roll wrappers

THE FILLING
1 pound raw shrimp in their shells
2 tablespoons peanut oil, or flavorless
  vegetable oil
½ pound lean boneless pork, freshly
  ground
2 tablespoons soy sauce
1 tablespoon Chinese rice wine, or
  pale dry sherry
1 teaspoon salt
6 peeled and washed fresh water
  chestnuts, or drained canned water
  chestnuts, finely chopped
1 scallion, including the green top,
  finely chopped
1 teaspoon cornstarch dissolved in 1
  tablespoon cold chicken stock,
  fresh or canned, or cold water

3 cups peanut oil, or flavorless
  vegetable oil

Hün-t'un-pi 餛飩皮

WONTON WRAPPERS

1. Sift the flour and salt into a bowl, make a well in the center of the flour and pour into it the eggs and cold water. With your fingers, mix the ingredients until they can be gathered into a soft ball. Knead the dough in the bowl for 4 to 5 minutes, just until it is smooth but still soft.

2. Divide the dough into 4 equal-sized balls. On a lightly floured surface, roll out one ball at a time into 1/16-inch-thick sheets about 14 by 14 inches. For soup *wonton (page 107)* or deep-fried *wonton (below)*, cut the dough into 3½-inch squares with a sharp knife or pastry wheel. For steamed pork dumplings *(page 152)*, use a 3-inch cookie cutter or the rim of a glass to cut the dough into rounds. If the wrappers must rest for any length of time, cover them with a lightly dampened towel.

Yu-cha-hün-tün 油炸餛飩

DEEP-FRIED WONTON FILLED WITH PORK AND SHRIMP

PREPARE AHEAD: 1. Shell the shrimp. With a small, sharp knife, make an incision down their backs and lift out the black or white intestinal vein with the point of the knife. Chop the shrimp fine.

2. To prepare the filling: Set a 12-inch wok or 10-inch skillet over high heat for 30 seconds. Pour in the 2 tablespoons of oil, swirl it about in the pan and heat for another 30 seconds, turning the heat down if the oil begins to smoke. Add the pork and stir-fry for 1 minute, or until the meat loses its reddish color. Add the shrimp, soy sauce, wine, salt, water chestnuts and scallions, and stir-fry for another minute, or until the shrimp turn pink. Give the cornstarch mixture a stir to recombine it and pour it into the pan. Stir constantly until the liquid thickens, then transfer the contents of the pan to a bowl and cool to room temperature.

3. Cut homemade *wonton* wrappers or ready-made egg-roll wrappers into 3½-inch squares. Ready-made *wonton* wrappers are already cut.

4. To assemble the *wontons:* Place 1½ teaspoons of the filling in the center of each *wonton* wrapper. With a finger dipped in water, moisten the edges of the wrapper. Then bring one corner up over the filling to the opposite corner, but fold the wrapper at an angle so that two overlapping triangles are formed, with their points side by side and about ½ inch apart. Pull the two bottom corners of the folded triangle forward and below the folded edge so that they meet one another and slightly overlap, to create a kind of frame around the mound of the filling. Moisten one end with a finger dipped in water and pinch the two ends firmly together. As each *wonton* is finished, place it on a plate and cover it with a dry towel. If the *wontons* must wait longer than 30 minutes before cooking, cover them with plastic wrap and refrigerate.

TO COOK: Set a 12-inch wok or 10-inch skillet over high heat and pour 3 cups of oil into it. Heat the oil until a haze forms above it or it registers 375° on a deep-frying thermometer. Deep-fry the *wontons,* 8 or 10 at a time, for 2 minutes, or until they are crisp and golden. Transfer them to paper towels to drain while you fry the rest. Serve attractively arranged on a heated platter. Fried *wontons* can be kept warm for an hour or so in a 250° oven, or reheated for 5 minutes in a 450° oven.

Tsao-ni-hün-tün 棗泥餛飩

DEEP-FRIED WONTONS WITH DATE FILLING

To make about 4 dozen

One recipe egg-roll wrappers (*page 130*), or 1 pound ready-made egg-roll wrappers, cut into quarters

THE FILLING
4 eight-ounce packages pitted dates
2 cups finely chopped walnuts
3 tablespoons grated fresh orange rind
3 to 5 tablespoons orange juice or cold water (if needed)
3 cups peanut oil, or flavorless vegetable oil
Confectioners' sugar

PREPARE AHEAD: 1. To make the filling: With a cleaver or sharp knife, chop the pitted dates fine, adding a teaspoon or so of orange juice or water if they are too sticky to cut. Combine the dates, walnuts and grated rind in a small bowl. Knead the mixture with your fingers until it can be gathered into a ball. If the mixture is dry, moisten it with orange juice or water. Roll a tablespoon of filling between the palms of your hands to form cylinders 1 inch long and about ⅓ inch in diameter.

2. To assemble the *wontons:* Place a cylinder of filling diagonally across each wrapper, just below the center. With a finger dipped in water, moisten the lower point of the wrapper. Fold the point over the filling and tuck it underneath. Roll up the resulting tube until all the dough surrounds the filling. Stick a finger into each end of the tube and give it a twist to seal the ends.

TO COOK: Pour the oil into a 12-inch wok or deep-fryer and heat the oil until a haze forms above it or it reaches 375° on a deep-frying thermometer. Deep-fry the *wontons,* 8 or 10 at a time, turning them occasionally, for 2 to 3 minutes, or until they are golden brown and crisp. As they are finished cooking, transfer them to paper towels to drain and cool. Just before serving, sprinkle the *wontons* with confectioners' sugar.

Cha-shao-chao-mien 义燒炒麵

NOODLES WITH ROAST PORK AND CHINESE CABBAGE

4 dried Chinese mushrooms, 1 to 1½ inches in diameter
½ pound Chinese cabbage (celery cabbage or *bok choy*)
3 tablespoons peanut oil, or flavorless vegetable oil
½ cup whole canned bamboo shoots cut into 2-inch-long and ⅛-inch-wide shreds
½ pound roast pork, sliced ½ inch thick and cut into 2-inch-long and ⅛-inch-wide shreds (about 1½ cups), prepared according to recipe on page 193
1 tablespoon soy sauce
1 teaspoon salt
½ cup chicken stock, fresh or canned
2 teaspoons cornstarch dissolved in 2 tablespoons cold chicken stock, fresh or canned, or cold water
½ pound fresh Chinese egg noodles, or substitute other narrow egg noodles
1 scallion, including the green top, cut into 2 inch lengths and finely shredded

PREPARE AHEAD: 1. In a small bowl, cover the mushrooms with ½ cup of warm water and let them soak for 30 minutes. Discard the water. Cut away and discard the mushroom stems; cut each cap into ⅛-inch strips.

2. With a cleaver or sharp knife, trim the top leaves of the cabbage and the root ends. Separate the stalks and wash them under cold water. Cut each stalk, leaves and all, into strips about 2 inches long by ¼ wide.

3. Have the mushrooms, cabbage, oil, bamboo shoots, pork, soy sauce, salt, stock, cornstarch mixture and shredded scallions within easy reach.

TO COOK: Preheat the oven to 375°. In a 4-quart saucepan, bring 2 quarts of water to a boil over high heat. Drop in the noodles, bring to a boil again, and cook for 5 minutes, stirring occasionally. Drain the noodles, transfer them to a shallow baking dish and stir in 1 tablespoon of oil. Bake the noodles for 7 or 8 minutes, or until lightly browned, then turn them over and bake 7 or 8 minutes longer to brown the other side.

Meanwhile, prepare the sauce. Set a 12-inch wok or 10-inch skillet over high heat for 30 seconds. Pour in 2 tablespoons of oil, swirl it about in the pan for 30 seconds, turning the heat down to moderate if the oil smokes. Add the cabbage, mushrooms and bamboo shoots, and stir-fry for 2 minutes. Add the soy sauce and salt, mix well, then add the roast pork and stir-fry for 1 minute. Pour in the stock and bring to a boil. Give the cornstarch mixture a stir to recombine it, add it to the pan, and cook, stirring until the sauce thickens and clears. Turn off the heat and cover the pan.

When the noodles are ready, serve them at once from the baking dish. Transfer the pork and cabbage mixture to a heated bowl and serve topped with the shredded scallions. As a main course, this will serve 2 to 4.

Ch'un-chüan
EGG ROLLS WITH SHRIMP AND PORK

春 捲

THE FILLING

½ pound fresh bean sprouts or substitute a 1-pound can of bean sprouts

½ pound raw shrimp in their shells

3 tablespoons oil

½ pound lean boneless pork, finely ground

4 cups finely chopped celery

2 to 3 medium fresh mushrooms, cut in ¼-inch slices (about ½ cup)

1 tablespoon soy sauce

1 tablespoon Chinese rice wine, or pale dry sherry

2 teaspoons salt

½ teaspoon sugar

1 tablespoon cornstarch dissolved in 2 tablespoons cold chicken stock, fresh or canned, or cold water

THE WRAPPERS

2 cups flour

½ teaspoon salt

¾ cup cold water

1 egg, lightly beaten

Note: 1 pound ready-made egg-roll wrappers may be substituted for these homemade wrappers

3 cups peanut oil, or flavorless vegetable oil

PREPARE AHEAD: 1. Rinse the fresh bean sprouts in a pot of cold water and discard any husks that float to the surface. Drain and pat them dry with paper towels. To crisp canned bean sprouts, rinse them under running water and refrigerate them in a bowl of cold water for at least 2 hours. Drain and pat them dry before using.

2. Shell the shrimp. With a small, sharp knife, devein them by making a shallow incision down their backs and lifting out the black or white intestinal vein with the point of the knife. Using a cleaver or large knife, cut the shrimp into fine dice.

3. TO MAKE THE FILLING: Set a 12-inch wok or 10-inch skillet over high heat for 30 seconds. Pour in 1 tablespoon of oil, swirl it about in the pan and heat for another 30 seconds, turning the heat down to moderate if the oil begins to smoke. Add the pork and stir-fry for 2 minutes, or until it loses its reddish color. Then add the wine, soy sauce, sugar, shrimp and mushrooms, and stir-fry for another minute, or until the shrimp turn pink. Transfer the entire contents of the pan to a bowl and set aside.

Pour the remaining 2 tablespoons of oil into the same wok or skillet, swirl it about in the pan and heat for 30 seconds, turning the heat down to moderate if the oil begins to smoke. Add the celery and stir-fry for 5 minutes, then add the salt and bean sprouts, and mix thoroughly together. Return the pork and shrimp mixture to the pan, and stir until all the ingredients are well combined. Cook over moderate heat, stirring constantly, until the liquid starts to boil.

There should be about 2 or 3 tablespoons of liquid remaining in the pan. If there is more, spoon it out and discard it. Give the cornstarch mixture a quick stir to recombine it, and add it, stirring until the cooking liquids have thickened slightly and coated the mixture with a light glaze. Transfer the entire contents of the pan to a bowl and cool to room temperature before using.

4. TO MAKE THE WRAPPERS: Sift the flour and salt into a large mixing bowl. With a large spoon or your hands, gradually combine the flour and salt with the water, mixing until a stiff dough is formed. Knead the dough in the bowl for 5 minutes, or until it is smooth, then cover the bowl with a dampened cloth and let it rest for 30 minutes. Turn the dough out on a lightly floured surface and firmly roll it out until it is no more than 1/16 inch thick. With a cookie cutter, pastry wheel or sharp knife, cut the dough into 7-inch squares. When you have finished, there should be 16 squares.

TO ASSEMBLE: For each egg roll, shape about ¼ cup of filling with your hands into a cylinder about 4 inches long and an inch in diameter, and place it diagonally across the center of a wrapper. Lift the lower triangular flap over the filling and tuck the point under it, leaving the upper point of the wrapper exposed. Bring each of the two small end flaps, one at a time, up to the top of the enclosed filling and press the points firmly down. Brush the upper and exposed triangle of dough with lightly beaten egg and then roll the wrapper into a neat package. The beaten egg will seal the edges and keep the wrapper intact.

Place the filled egg rolls on a plate and cover them with a dry kitchen towel. If they must wait longer than about 30 minutes before being fried, cover them with plastic wrap and place them in the refrigerator.

TO COOK: Set a 12-inch wok or heavy deep-fryer over high heat, add 3 cups of oil and heat it until a haze forms above it or it reaches a temperature of 375° on a deep-frying thermometer. Place 5 or 6 egg rolls in the hot oil and deep-fry them for 3 to 4 minutes, or until they have become golden brown and are crisp. Transfer the egg rolls to a double thickness of paper towels and let the oil drain off while you deep-fry another batch of 5 or 6.

Serve the rolls as soon as possible, arranged attractively on a large heated platter. If necessary, the egg rolls can be kept warm for an hour or so in a preheated 250° oven, or they can be reheated for about 10 minutes in a 450° oven.

TO MAKE SPRING ROLLS: Substitute 1 pound fresh, ready-made spring-roll wrappers for the egg-roll wrappers. Prepare the filling according to the recipe already given, then assemble the rolls and deep-fry them as described above.

Because preparing spring-roll wrappers from scratch is so demanding and precise a culinary operation, even the fussiest Chinese cook prefers to use the ready-made variety.

Cha-chiang-mien   炸醬麵
BOILED EGG NOODLES WITH MEAT SAUCE

To serve 4

PREPARE AHEAD: 1. With a small, sharp knife, peel the cucumber. Then cut it in half and scoop out the seeds by running the tip of a teaspoon down the center of each half. Now cut the cucumber into ⅛-inch slices, and cut the slices into strips ⅛-inch wide and 2 inches long.

2. Arrange the cucumber, garlic and scallions side by side on a small serving plate.

3. Have the garnishes, and the oil, pork, wine, bean sauce, scallions, sugar, chicken stock and noodles within easy reach.

TO COOK: Set a 12-inch wok or 10-inch skillet over high heat for 30 seconds. Pour in 2 tablespoons of the oil, swirl it about in the pan and heat for another 30 seconds, turning the heat down to moderate if the oil begins to smoke. Add the ground pork and stir-fry for 2 to 3 minutes, or until it browns lightly. Add the wine, brown-bean sauce, chopped scallions and sugar, mix well, and pour in the chicken stock. Bring to a boil and cook rapidly over moderate heat for 8 to 10 minutes, stirring constantly, until all the stock has evaporated. Turn off the heat and cover the wok or skillet to keep the meat sauce warm.

In a 3- to 4-quart heavy saucepan, bring 2 quarts of water to a boil over high heat. Drop in the noodles and boil them vigorously, uncovered, for 5 minutes, stirring occasionally with a large fork to prevent them from sticking. Drain the noodles through a colander.

Serve the noodles immediately in the following fashion: Place them on a large, deep, heated platter or in a deep serving bowl and toss them about quickly with the remaining 1 tablespoon of oil. Ladle the meat sauce into a serving bowl, and pass the sauce and the cucumber, garlic and scallion garnishes separately.

GARNISHES
1 medium cucumber
1 tablespoon finely chopped garlic
3 scallions, including the green tops, cut in 2-inch lengths and finely shredded

3 tablespoons peanut oil, or flavorless vegetable oil
1 pound boneless pork shoulder, freshly ground
2 tablespoons Chinese rice wine, or pale dry sherry
¼ cup brown-bean sauce
2 scallions, including the green tops, finely chopped
1 teaspoon sugar
½ cup chicken stock, fresh or canned
1 pound fresh Chinese egg noodles, or substitute other narrow egg noodles

for example, the rice fields are sown, manured, weeded and harvested by machinery. But in China the ancient farming methods have not been altered to any great extent, and the production of the grain is still an arduous affair. Indeed, *The Growing of Grain* gives an account of 17th Century methods that are strikingly similar to today's. It directs that the rice seed be planted in wet fields shortly before the vernal equinox. Before planting, the seeds are wrapped in straw and soaked for several days until shoots appear; then, when they are set out, they must be kept submerged by flooding until the seedlings are three inches high. Even then the ground should be kept sopping wet until the young plants have gained another three inches. At that point, the field is drained and the plants are carefully thinned out and transplanted, though as the book cautions, "this should not be done . . . if the fields are suffering from drought or flood." If the plants are not transplanted, the farmer is warned, they will harden and develop sections in the stalks, and produce only a few grains. The importance of watering is stressed, and the reader is cautioned never to allow rice plants to go short of water for longer than 10 days at a stretch; periodically the rice bed must be flooded anew. When the plants have attained a height of 15 inches the land is drained, weeded by hand and cultivated with a hoe: then the flooding begins again and continues until the harvest. In addition to generally applicable methods, *The Growing of Grain* goes into detail about special procedures to be followed with particular varieties.

Three hundred years after this manual was written, much of the advice it offers is still valid for rice farmers not yet able to afford mechanization. Anyone who has walked in the Chinese countryside will remember the flat paddy swamps where the little fields are separated by low clay walls and all the levels of water are different. The irrigation system consists of complicated networks of runnels fed by buckets lifted by hand, or filled as they rotate in endless chains around a primitive pump. The squeak and thumping of this pump sounds all through the day as the young rice grows higher and higher, its delicate apple-green color darkening week by week. At transplanting season the farmers work in long lines, crouching in the damp. It is all hard, backbreaking work. The harvest does not see the end of the toil, for then the grain must be laboriously husked.

Always aware of the work that goes into its raising, the Chinese respect rice far too much ever to waste it. Children are taught to eat every bit served to them. For every grain left in the bowl, children are told, there will be a pockmark on the face of their future spouses, and the threat still means something in a country where smallpox has not been vanquished. Rice figures strongly in a variety of ritual acts. It is considered bad luck to upset a rice bowl. To insult a person in the worst way possible you pick up a bowl of his rice and spill it out on the ground. Quitting one's job is referred to as "breaking one's rice bowl." Rice is a symbol of life and fertility: it is from the East that we have inherited our custom of throwing rice grains at wedding couples. In some parts of China it is the practice to "present the New Year's rice"; that is, to place a wooden bowl of rice on the altar dedicated to the family ancestors. Rice serves as a thanksgiving offering for the gifts of the previous year and a petition for

VI

Gentle Teas and Strong Spirits

You can taste and feel, but not describe, the exquisite state of repose produced by tea, that precious drink which drives away the five causes of sorrow.

—EMPEROR CHIEN LUNG (1710-1799), MANCHU DYNASTY

Riches and poverty, long or short life,
By the Maker of Things are portioned and disposed;
But a cup of wine levels life and death
And a thousand things obstinately hard to prove.

—"DRINKING ALONE BY MOONLIGHT," LI PO, 701-762 A.D.

China and tea seem so inseparably associated that it is hard to imagine a time when there was no tea in China. But there was; and the date when this pleasant beverage came into use in Chinese households can be estimated with fairly good accuracy. Wine and even stronger spirits are another thing completely. The Chinese use and enjoyment of these drinks go so far back into the past that it is impossible to fix the year or even the century when a Chinese first tasted the intoxicating, aromatic liquid in a crock of rice that had been left outside to soak. Since we can talk about tea from a considerably more factual basis, I have chosen to start with it and then to move into the headier subject of alcohol.

One of the earliest by-products of the era of discovery by European explorers was the introduction of tea to Western tables. Like all new things, it excited both praise and condemnation.

"Among many other novelties," wrote an English medical man in 1722, "there is one which seems to be particularly the cause of the hypochondriac

Three itinerant food peddlers pause for tea, a drink the Chinese have long enjoyed at all times of the day. In this anonymous painting of the 17th or 18th Century a young servant fans the fire of a brazier. The tiered stands, loaded with the peddlers' stock in trade, are carried at the ends of long poles balanced on the men's shoulders.

disorders, and is generally known as thea, or tea. It is a drug which of late years has very much insinuated itself." (This was not exactly spot news. Almost half a century earlier another Englishman had spoken scathingly of men he knew "who call for tea, instead of pipes and a bottle after dinner—a base Indian practice. . . .")

In the centuries that have intervened since those angry words were written, tea and tobacco have exchanged places in terms of acceptance by medical authority. However, even when tea first arrived in the West in the 17th Century, it had its stout champions. Two Dutch physicians of the time, Nikolas Tulp and Cornelis Decker, thought it an excellent medicine for practically every complaint: in fact, Dr. Decker made his patients drink from 50 to 200 cups a day. By 1756, when Jonas Hanway, in his journal, alleged that tea was "pernicious to health, obstructing industry, and impoverishing the nation," he was pushing a hopeless cause. Westerners were too enthralled by the fragrant Eastern leaf.

Chinese legend has it that a long-ago emperor discovered the drink by accident one day while sipping boiled water in his garden. A leaf from a nearby tea bush fell into the cup, the emperor tasted it, he liked it immensely, and so the drink was born. According to another story it was in an army camp that the lucky accident occurred, when some tea leaves fell into a vat of boiling water and the soldiers discovered that this water had a new and pleasant taste. It does not matter exactly how the discovery came about: for thousands of years man has tried different herb beverages, possibly ever since he first learned to use fire, and tea is not the only one he experimented with. *Maté* in South America is another. The French use a variety of herb drinks called *tisanes* for medical purposes, and Americans have done the same with sassafras and other roots; but most of us have taken to tea. We each have our special ways of using it. The Chinese drink it straight without sugar, cream or lemon; the Moslems put in mint; the British, when faced with crises, rush to make a nice strong cup of "Indian" mixed with milk; the Irish like it so strong that—to use their own expression—"a rat couldn't sink its foot in it"; and the Australians probably brew it longer than anyone else. For all of us it is a refreshing, tasteful beverage that possesses no calories—unless you add cream and sugar—and no salt. Of course it contains caffeine, which is why it is stimulating, but the tannins in tea interact with the caffeine and somehow damp down its ferocity. A cup of tea before bedtime may disturb your sleep, but not quite as much as coffee.

None of us swallows as much tea as the Chinese appear to. Studies of tea appeared early. A book called *Ch'a Ching (The Tea Classic)*, seems to have been written by one Lu Yu in 780 A.D. Among many other bits of information, it asserted that regular cultivation of the tea plant for beverage purposes began in 350 A.D. But since a much older source, the official Chinese Dictionary of 350 A.D., had already accurately defined tea, it seems clear that Lu Yu erred, and that tea cultivation is older than he thought.

Even before it was extensively cultivated for use as an everyday drink the Chinese seem to have taken tea as a medicinal herb; it was recommended for such a purpose now and then during the First and Second Centuries. Lin Yutang, the modern Chinese scholar, has found in a Third

Century manuscript what he thinks is the earliest reference to tea as a drink: "When true tea is drunk, it keeps one awake"—which can be just as much a fact now as it was then. He has also found definite evidence that it was used as a beverage about 300 A.D., and further reference to tea in a story dated 307, at a time when many Chinese who were fleeing invaders from the north crossed the Yangtze river to the Wu region, now the Shanghai district. According to the record, one of these refugees was mocked by the natives because he had never heard of tea, a plant originally grown in the south. Archives of the period 317-322 mention tea being sold in the city streets, and literature shows that at that time it became an integral part of Chinese life, as it has remained ever since.

Tea used to be grown only in India and China. Later its culture spread to Indonesia, Japan, Korea and Ceylon. The Chinese tea leaf, which is all we are discussing here, was the first to be exported to the West. There, in spite of calamity howlers like Jonas Hanway, it became so popular that the previously waning fortunes of the British and Dutch East India companies came to depend chiefly on the fragrant plant *Thea sinensis*. All through the 17th Century thousands of people had invested in the companies in the happy expectation that their ships would bring home spices, jewels, silks and gold. None of these treasures ever materialized, and the stockholders faced ruin: it was tea and only tea that returned a profit. Between 1739 and 1785 it was the most valuable single commodity in the return cargoes of the company ships.

After the demise of the East India companies in the 19th Century, the trade in tea was taken over by individuals sailing the sleek, fast clipper ships, many of them American and many especially built for this profitable trade. One of the first of these vessels was the *Ann McKim,* a lavishly appointed vessel, described in a newspaper on June 3, 1833, thus: "Her fastenings are altogether copper, no iron having been used in her construction . . . her whole cost when completed will fall little if anything short of fifty thousand dollars." At 143 feet, she was the longest American merchant ship of her day. Another American clipper, the *Rainbow,* in 1851 made the trip from New York to Canton and return in the then record time of 180 days. British clippers were equally swift. With the allure of premium prices for the first tea cargo of the season lending additional fury to the customary drive of skippers, each year was marked by races between competing vessels to get to market first. The most famous tea race of all ended in a dead heat between two British ships, the *Ariel* and the *Taeping,* both arriving in London 99 days after leaving China.

Along with the drink, the British took over the southern Chinese name for the beverage, "tay," later altering the pronunciation to its present form. When first used in the West tea was so expensive that only the wealthiest could afford to drink it. Coffee and chocolate, introduced a little later, were also very costly, but tea must always have been more economical to use: one pound of it will make 200 cups, whereas a pound of coffee beans provides only 40 cups of liquid coffee.

Today, after more than 16 centuries, tea is more popular than ever, although fashions of preparing it have changed radically. Tea-drinkers East and West will hold forth on the only right and proper way to make it— *Continued on page 138*

Tea from Taiwan's Slopes

Tea is probably the most popular drink in the world. In China, where water usually should be boiled before drinking, tea is a healthier drink than plain water. However, both the taste and the stimulation of the beverage are prized in East and West alike. One of the first writers on tea, Lu Yu, wrote in the Eighth Century, "Tea tempers the spirits, calms and harmonizes the mind; it arouses thought and prevents drowsiness, lightens and refreshes the body, and clears the perceptive faculties." Sydney Smith, a 19th Century English divine and writer, expressed himself more simply: "Thank God for tea . . . I am glad I was not born before tea."

Picking shoots from a tea plant, a young woman on Taiwan carefully plucks the best part of the bush, the bud and two adjoining leaves that are used to make the island's delicate green tea. Some of the more than 300 native and crossbred varieties grown on Taiwan are shown on the facing page, ready for sale in their brightly decorated canisters and containers. In the background is a tea farm, its slopes contoured to hold natural moisture and to slow soil erosion, a serious threat to the relatively small amount of arable land on the densely populated island.

water over flame just on the boil but not boiling too long, teapot warmed by a preliminary application of hot water, leaves steeping just so long and no longer. The most particular tea-drinker today can hardly be more finicky than some of the long-dead Chinese who drew strict rules for its preparation. In *Through a Moon Gate* by L. Z. Yuan, the writer tells how Chien Lung, the famous 18th Century Emperor of the Ching Dynasty, demanded not only the best leaf but the best grade of water as well. "He once so liked the tea produced on the summit of the East Hill of Tung Ling, Kiangsu, that he stationed a company of soldiers around the tea shrubs to make sure that none of the leaves were stolen." And when touring the various provinces of his domain the Emperor listed the fountains he came upon and graded them according to the tea-making quality of their waters. He weighed samples from these different sources and concluded that the "lightest" was the best for brewing tea. He awarded first place to the Jade Fountain outside Peking because its water was the lightest—like that of melted snow, he declared.

Melted snow is cited with the same high approval by the anonymous author of the late-16th Century novel *Chin P'ing Mei,* in a passage where a character named Moon Lady goes into the snow-covered courtyard, sweeps a portion of snow from the path, and puts it into a tea kettle. With this snow she then makes tea with a special blend of "the noble Phoenix and the mild Lark's Tongue teas," and serves it to the company. Then poetic fancy takes over:

Shaking a large bamboo screen, two men sift tea leaves to grade them by size. Now, the tea has only to be blended and packaged before it is ready to be sold. On the opposite page are arranged two rows of tea leaves and two rows of tea brewed from them to show the range of colors produced by various kinds of tea. The top row holds cups of copper-colored leaves of black tea whose processing involves a fermentation step; below each is tea brewed with that particular kind of leaf. The leaves in the bottom row, surmounted by cups of the drink brewed from them, include, from left, two partially fermented oolongs, two scented pouchongs and three unfermented green varieties.

In the jasper crock
Light puffs of crystalline vapor;
From the golden bowls
A wild rare fragrance mounts.

Ts'ao Hsueh-Ch'in's *Dream of the Red Chamber*, published in the 18th Century (and thought by many critics to be China's greatest novel), gives us this passage about a nun offering tea to guests:

"The matriarch asked her what it was, and the nun answered that it was rainwater saved from the year before. . . . The nun then took Black Jade and Precious Virtue into another room to make some special tea for them. She poured the tea into two different cups . . . of the rare Sung period. Her own cup was of white jade. 'Is this last year's rainwater?' Black Jade asked. 'I did not think you were so ignorant,' the nun said, as if insulted. 'Can't you tell the difference? This water is from the snow I gathered from the plum trees five years ago in the Yuan Mu Hsiang Temple. It filled that blue jar there. . . . All this time it was buried under the earth and was opened only this last summer. How could you expect rainwater to possess such lightness and clarity?'"

An even taller story concerning the punctilio of tea-making tells about a general named Li Chi-ching, who encountered Lu Yu, the famous tea master and author of *Ch'a Ching*, near the place where the Nanling River runs into the Yangtze. The general suggested that since Nanling water

was supposed to be marvelous for making tea, and since the worthy master Lu was right there, they should have a tea party. "We should not miss an opportunity that may happen but once in a thousand years," the general observed, and sent some of his soldiers to the Nanling to fetch the water. When it arrived, Lu spilled some into a ladle and tasted it. "This is not Nanling water," he declared. He ordered that it should be poured into a basin. The jar was about half empty when he stopped the man who was pouring, tasted the remainder, and said, "This is true Nanling water." Then the story came out: the soldiers had filled their receptacle with Nanling water, but on the way back their boat rolled badly and half of the water was spilled, so they refilled the jar with Yangtze water. The most persnickety English tea snob could hardly outdo such sensitivity.

Although Chinese connoisseurs of tea do stand on ceremony when they serve the beverage, generally speaking, no special ritual is involved when Chinese drink tea. It is so much a part of the daily round that ceremony would be out of place. In drinking it the Chinese have a common-sense way of sucking in air at the same time, to cool the hot liquid. This is a noisy process, but the Chinese do not mind noise.

There is no hard-and-fast rule about tea at table. In the south tea is occasionally drunk with the meal, and in all provinces the host serves tea as a final courtesy when the party is over and it is time for the guests to go home, but the Chinese usually treat it rather as an in-between drink.

When I lived in China tea was brought out on every occasion, not just at social meetings but at hardware stores, the dentist's and everywhere else. If you are conjuring up visions of dainty porcelain cups and steaming teapot at such times, banish them. In China dainty porcelain was used only for special occasions; what I usually got in college classrooms or banks or bookshops was a cracked five-and-ten tumbler holding hot, reddish liquid in which sad-looking wilted leaves circled thickly before subsiding into a loose heap at the bottom. There was only one rule that prevailed regardless of the surroundings: tea was always served in glazed pottery or porcelain or glass—preferably without cracks. The wealthy might use the costliest cups, the esthetic the most beautiful, the workingmen serviceable mugs. But only a barbarian would stoop to metal.

The shrub, *Thea sinensis,* which is the source of so much pleasure, is an evergreen that can grow as high as 30 feet. When cultivated for its leaves, it is kept in bushy form by pruning it to no more than five feet high so that the pickers can reach every branch and the plant will expend its strength in producing leaves rather than height. It grows in warm climates on land otherwise poor for farming. While it does well enough on low land, tea flourishes at elevations of up to 6,000 feet. Planters prefer high land because the lower the elevation, the tougher the leaf tends to be. Large plantations are usually sited in hilly country. Besides, it is thought that leaf quality is improved by clouds, snow and misty atmosphere.

The methods of culture of the shrub vary from one country to another, but the Chinese farmer follows an old pattern, sowing his tea seed first in nursery beds and later transplanting the young plants. Finally they are set out in rows from three to six feet apart. The leaves are suitable for tea when the bushes are three years old. And after the first early spring harvest, the shrubs continue to be productive for 25 to 50 years. The finest sort of leaves come from the bud at the end of a stem with the two choice leaves nearest it. For medium grade the bud and first three leaves are plucked, and for coarse plucking the fourth and fifth leaves also are included. About 3,200 shoots make up a pound of the finished product, and a good picker can collect almost 10 times that much in a day.

Teas are graded for quality into the first two prime categories, a secondary category and several variations. The prime ones are green, or unfermented, tea, and black, or fermented, tea. In the secondary category is semifermented, or oolong, tea. The variations are scented or smoked. Both green tea and black (the Chinese with more accuracy call black tea "red") are derived from the same plant: the difference results from the treatment the leaf gets after it is picked. Those leaves destined to make black tea are fermented, whereas those for green tea, which is unfermented, are dried in the sun or in drying rooms. Oolong is fermented to less than half the extent of black.

To make black tea, the leaves are spread on a screen and are dried either by the sun or by a gentle current of hot air. Next they are carefully rolled to expose and oxidize the juice, then left to wilt on cool tables that may be made of metal, stone, glass or tile, then they are fired over charcoal. In every case they come out of the process a dark, coppery red.

For green tea the leaves are steamed to softness and rolled on mats. The process is repeated until they are crisp after rolling; then they are dried over charcoal. Both green and black tea leaves are sifted and sorted through meshes into different sizes and then packed according to several standards of size and grade. The smallest leaves are considered best because they have not grown large enough to develop tannic acid, which gives tea a bitter taste. Another grading divides leaves into leaf tea and broken tea, the latter made up of larger leaves broken into fragments and apt to be stronger and bitter. Yet another system reflects the size and appearance of the leaf from largest and most perfect on down: orange pekoe, pekoe souchong, fannings and dust are terms here employed.

Oolong, the semifermented tea, halfway between green and black, is produced mainly in Taiwan, though it is also prepared in a few places on the mainland. The name means "black dragon" and is said to have originated when a tea-picker noticed a very pleasant fragrance emanating from one particular plant. When he went to look at it closely he found coiled around it a beautiful black snake. Unlike most people I know, he did not scream and run away from the reptile—in fact, the legend does not go into detail about just what he did do with that snake but merely reports that he took the whole thing as a good omen, picked some of the shrub's leaves, and made himself a cup of tea, which proved to have a new, delicious flavor. In spite of the story I like oolong. An even less fermented Taiwanese tea is pouchong, generally called scented tea, because the leaves are mixed with jasmine and gardenia blossoms. Other scented teas include two green varieties, one perfumed with chrysanthemum, the other with narcissus, and two black teas redolent respectively of litchi and rose blossoms. Another well known variety is lapsang-souchong, a smoked black tea from Hunan, rich and heavy.

Epicures describe green tea as cool, refreshing and clean in flavor. It is said to aid digestion, and is served with highly flavored and fried food. Black tea's color (copper red) pleases the eye: it has a full-bodied flavor, is warming, and is usually served with sea food. Gourmets sometimes preserve choice black tea leaves in earthenware jars for a time to bring out their full pungency. Some of the descriptive names for certain varieties are extremely flowery: Dragon Well takes its name from a spring of the same name outside Hangchow in Chekiang, and is considered the best green tea in China. Cloud Mist is another green tea, and the name is self-explanatory: it grows high up on Kiangsi mountain cliffs, and the Chinese will assure you that monkeys are trained to pluck the leaves and bring them down to the workers. Iron Kuan Yin (Iron Goddess of Mercy), a black tea with stiff, shiny leaves (hence the appellation "iron"), is naturally fragrant and will keep for years where other teas tend to dry out and crumble into dust after a year or two.

The Chinese have many beliefs about the medicinal properties of these various leaves and mixtures. During hot days, for instance, people sip chrysanthemum tea on the theory that it thins the blood and keeps it cool. Once in Hong Kong I had a sudden chill with violent aching in the bones. My houseboy insisted that I go straight to bed, and brought me a large, steaming cup of some kind of tea that tasted nastier, I think, than any other drink I have ever had. He stood over me until I had swallowed

Making an exotic concentrated tea, this Taiwanese pours boiling water into a pot stuffed with the tea leaves called Iron Kuan Yin, after the Chinese goddess of mercy; while they steep, the pot is warmed in a bowl containing more boiling water. The resulting essence makes a bitter, highly stimulating tea popular in the southeastern part of the mainland. The "iron" in the name refers to the tea leaves' resistance to crumbling even after long storage. The rest of the name is fine poetic fancy.

it all. I sweated copiously all night, and next morning I felt perfectly well. I was surprised but he was not. Of course I asked what the medicine had been, but all he said was, "tea."

One form of tea that we in the West rarely see is brick tea, which has always been sold direct to Tibet and Russia. Brick tea was invented before modern methods of packaging came into use. Most of the tea plant goes into it—stalks, and leaves of any size, whole or broken. Some brick teas are merely sewn into cowhide bags in loose masses, but the better sort is pressed so tight that the result really deserves the name brick. When a purchaser needs tea he simply cuts off a hunk from his brick—like a tobacco-chewer cutting a plug—and boils it in water.

Sometimes Central Asians stew their brick tea with milk, salt and yak butter, and eat it as a vegetable. Tibetans simply melt yak butter in the brew, and the resultant mixture, though it sounds unappetizing to us, is said to be the most important part of their diet. An American journalist, James Burke, had butter-tea once, and was glad to get it. He had found it necessary to climb to a Himalayan border pass nearly 15,000 feet above sea level, coming straight up from Indian plains through mist and sleet without any preliminary training. Naturally he was exhausted and numb from cold when he got there. He stopped to rest at the top at the camp of a Tibetan. One of the men told an old woman to prepare tea for the visitor. She took an implement like an old-fashioned butter churn into which she poured a quart of dark, steaming tea that had been sitting in a pot by the fire. Then she brought out a ball of dirty, strong-smelling yak butter and cut off a quarter-pound hunk, which she dropped into the churn with the tea. She added salt. She bore up and down on the churn stick for a couple of minutes, poured the fluid into a wooden bowl, and served it.

"Oily globules floated on the tea surface, and anywhere else it would have been a nauseating concoction, both in sight and smell," wrote Burke. "But here in the rarefied cold of the Himalayas the strong salty flavor was strangely satisfying. And the effect was like a rich, hot soup—which is what the drink, with its nourishing fat content, amounts to, I suppose. After finishing two bowls, my numbness and exhaustion were gone and I was off down the steep trail like a mountain goat."

Now for the other kind of stimulant: Most Chinese alcoholic beverages are called wine, for purposes of simplicity, though none is made from grapes. Before Western customs came into fashion in the East, Chinese people drank alcohol only when they were eating. I hasten to add that this tradition did not prevent them from drinking copiously. A drunkard might be constrained to eat several snacks between lunch and dinner just to keep up appearances, and thus be able to drink as much as he wished. Though lip-service was paid to temperate drinking, in reality nobody was scandalized by tipsiness, perhaps because ordinary Chinese rice wine has a quick effect that wears off just as quickly. In the past, however, the official attitude toward wine has at times been severe. Within the 2,500 years that elapsed between the Chou Dynasty and the end of Mongol reign in 1368, laws against the manufacture, sale and consumption of wine were promulgated, enforced and then repealed—41 times.

Pious maxims, too, bear witness to prohibitionist sentiment: "Let those who desire to break off drinking habits observe when sober a drunken man," and "Medicine may heal imagined sickness but wine can never dispel real sorrow." However, for each of these there are plenty of sayings expressing exactly the opposite point of view. For instance: "Three cups of wine will settle everything and a drinking bout will dissipate a thousand cares," or "Wine doesn't intoxicate men; they intoxicate themselves." Some are simply observant, taking no sides: "The first glass, the man drinks the wine; the second glass, the wine drinks the wine; the third glass, the wine drinks the man."

It is clear from such maxims that the Chinese know all about alcohol. I numbered few teetotalers among my acquaintance in China, but on the other hand the Chinese I knew never gave American-style cocktail parties, the kind where people drink a good deal in a short time. The Chinese do not understand anyone who gives a party at which food is not the main consideration. As we know, Chinese love to talk about food, but once you have said a few words about rice wine or the powerful liquor called Kaoliang there is little left to discuss. And I doubt whether I ever met a solitary drinker there: one finds few solitaries at all where practically everything, of necessity, is done in public.

Mary Sia, who has written on Chinese life and culture, says the Chinese look down on solitary drinking with the same disdain as do Westerners. She also says that there has existed a kind of Chinese Alcoholics Anonymous called the *Li Men,* or Door of Reason Society, with chapters in most large Chinese cities. However, she herself is not opposed to liquor in moderation, and points to its honorable tradition as a part of social activities and family ceremonies.

Wine is drunk at weddings, not only by the guests but also at a ceremony during which little cups for the bride and groom are tied together. When the couple have sipped each from his own cup the wine from the two cups is mingled, the cups are exchanged, and the pair sip again. Marriage wine is usually made from rice, and this is the form of alcohol most commonly drunk in China.

There is a story—of course—about the discovery of rice wine, according to which a chef in the Imperial Palace, 3,500 years ago, put some rice to soak in an earthen crock. His attention was diverted and he forgot about it for several days. Then he remembered, and tasted the contents. He found the rice-water marvelous: he kept sipping it, and soon broke into song. When the rest of the kitchen staff saw his actions they told other palace people who told yet others, until the emperor himself heard the tale, and commanded that some of the mysterious rice-water be brought so that he could test it. He found it delicious, and gave a party for his officials at which it was served. A good time was had by all. Next morning, however, nobody turned up for the daily audience at which state affairs were supposed to be conducted. The emperor, pondering the wonderful new drink, decided that it must be treated with caution, and laid down certain rules for its use: it should be served in very small cups rather than the soup bowls they had rashly used at the party; it should never be taken on an empty stomach but always accompanied by food; and drinkers must indulge in a mild form of exercise apart from elbow-bending to keep their minds busy. I am not sure about that third rule, but the other two have been obeyed ever since.

Chinese poets have a reputation for being fond of drink: one might almost say that drunkenness is in the poetic tradition. Many of them have written eloquently about the delights of wine, and these writers used to be known as "Drunken Dragons." The Eighth Century poet Li Po was a Dragon of Dragons. In one of his poems to wine he wrote:

> *The rapture of drinking, and wine's dizzy joy,*
> *No man who is sober deserves.*

One night, full of alcoholic cheer, he fell overboard from a boat and drowned while trying to embrace the moon's reflection in a lotus pool.

An earlier Dragon was T'ao Ch'ien, who lived in the late Fourth Century. He could never get down to work until he had had a few cups. And the great Dragon, Confucius, seems to have been overcome by wine at least once, though he deprecated overindulgence in drinking as in everything: "There is no limit in wine-drinking, but one must not get drunk," he decreed. Wang Chi was known as the Five-Bottle Scholar, a nickname that suggests, but may not have limited his capacity. The poet Liu Lung never went anywhere without two servants in attendance, one to carry his bottle and the other with a shovel so that he could bury his master if the poet should suddenly die of drink. In an essay, the 17th Century writer Chang Chao, pretending to cheer up a depressed friend, wrote, "Wine is the best dispeller of sorrows. Its name is Uncle Joy, and it has been compared to liquid jade. I know you love to drink. . . ."

Rice wine is generally referred to as yellow wine, even though it is often colorless. The various types, although made in much the same way, take on slightly different tastes from a number of extra ingredients. One variety called Shantung comes from Peking, and there are many others. Shaohsing wine is considered the best. It is difficult to describe the taste of these liquors, which for foreigners take some getting used to, partly because they are always served warm; one English youth I knew described yellow wine as tasting exactly like kerosene. A better comparison, I think, is hot sherry. It took me some time but I now like rice wine very much and think that it has a sharp, clean taste. Rice wine is somewhat thicker than water, and the alcohol it contains is extremely volatile: when you gulp a cupful, fumes immediately ascend the inner passages of the nose, but before you have quite decided that this is unpleasant, elation takes over. The heat plus volatility enormously speeds the wine's effect—in other words, you could get drunk on it with lightning rapidity. Merrymaking Chinese exhibit a peculiar reaction, becoming quite red in the face, but since the intoxication that has come on so quickly departs with equal rapidity everyone is usually of normal hue by the time the goodnight tea is served. I have never seen anyone pass out on rice wine, but when Chinese take to foreign liquor things are different. At one Hong Kong party our Chinese host drank Western brandy throughout the meal, and by the end was stretched out insensible. Small wonder, since he had been playing guessing games all evening, the kind at which each player must pay a forfeit every time he loses by drinking a whole

At their wedding banquet, a young Taiwan businessman and his bride raise cups of rice wine in a traditional all-inclusive toast to thank the guests for coming. Then the newlyweds are expected to drink to the occupants of each table at the party. The Chinese, an extremely pragmatic people, often hire a young lady stand-in to drink in place of the bride, a wise precaution considering the potency of Chinese drinks.

145

cupful in one gulp. Our host had downed glassfuls instead of cupfuls.

Rice wines differ widely in quality. The differences arise out of varied manufacturing methods and also from age, purity of ingredients and so on. A good wine will age well, becoming darker yellow and having a thicker consistency. In *Musings of a Chinese Gourmet* Dr. F. T. Cheng speaks of rice wine very much as a Frenchman might chat of the wines of his country. He says that before World War II it was almost impossible to find good wine outside of private cellars in the port cities—especially Shanghai—in which foreigners congregated. The rich Chinese in those places, he explains, were corrupted by foreign ways and drank beer and whiskey and brandy rather than the honest wine of their fathers, whereas people who could not afford foreign drinks put up with bad wine because they did not know the difference. Nowadays Chinese living abroad get few chances to drink yellow wine, bad or good, although some is shipped to America from Taiwan. So limited is the quantity, however, that the custom of using rice wine for cooking has almost died out: the wine that does arrive is drunk at the table, while sherry goes into the food.

The Chinese equivalents of Western spirits are Kaoliang, a specialty of northern China made from sorghum grain, and liqueurs distilled for the most part from fruit juices. Kaoliang is very strong and comes in several forms, one flavored with rose petals. It is usually colorless. The taste is peculiar, with a tang that reminds me somehow of decaying vegetation, but after all, gin tastes strange too, and Kaoliang is no worse. Of the fruit distillations (usually artificially colored to match their names), there is one called "tiger tendon and quince white wine," which is colorless; others include plum wine, usually red; orange wine, tinted as you might suppose; and pear wine, which is yellowish. Then there is the famous Cantonese snake wine, of a virulent green color and very strong; it is indeed too strong, I used to think, to taste of anything but fire. Snake wine is usually drunk in the autumn, for many Chinese believe this is the time for reinvigorating their bodies with tonic food. To make it a large jar is filled with high-proof liqueur, and the snake, of as poisonous a species as can be obtained, is placed in the alcohol and left there sometimes for years, the longer the better. Dragon-and-Phoenix wine consists of this kind of snake meat and pheasant meat steeped in wine. Such beverages are often taken for the drinker's health, the recipe varied slightly, according to the complaint to be cured, by the addition of several sorts of herbs. Serpent's bile and gall bladder, brewed in like manner and soaked in wine, are supposed to be good for rheumatism and are also reputed to aid in rejuvenation.

For want of rice wine those foreign purists who like to stay close to original national customs in eating and drinking can swallow sherry with Chinese food. The next nearest thing is probably Chablis. But Chinese expatriates are not so particular. They cheerfully drink all sorts of foreign wines with their meals, and we may safely follow their example. If expense is no object champagne is always good, but there is no law whatever against other drinks, regardless of color or strength. Recently in a private house in London I had a very good Chinese dinner with red Burgundy to drink. I thought it was a fine combination, and that noted gourmet Dr. F. T. Cheng, a fellow guest, thought so too.

Dumpling Snacks

Some of the many varieties and shapes of *dim sum*—savory, nourishing snacks of minced meat or vegetables wrapped in dough—are shown on the opposite page in front of the stacked steamers in which they are usually cooked.
1 Flower rolls
2 Buns with date filling
3 Buns with roast pork filling
4 Pork dumplings, northern style
5 Crabmeat dumplings
6 Pork dumplings, Cantonese style
7 Shrimp dumplings

CHAPTER **VI** RECIPES

1 package or cake of dry or
   compressed active yeast
1 tablespoon sugar
¼ cup lukewarm water
1 cup milk, heated to lukewarm
4 cups sifted all-purpose flour

STEAMED BREAD DOUGH

1. Sprinkle the yeast and sugar into ¼ cup of lukewarm water. Be sure that the water is lukewarm (110° to 115°). If the water is too hot, it will kill the yeast; if it is too cool, the yeast will not be activated. Let the yeast and sugar stand 2 or 3 minutes, then stir together to dissolve them completely. Set the cup in a warm, draft-free place, perhaps a turned-off oven, for 3 to 5 minutes, or until the yeast bubbles up and the mixture almost doubles in volume. If doubling does not take place, discard the mixture and start again with fresh yeast and water.

2. Sift 4 cups of flour into a large mixing bowl. Gradually pour in the yeast mixture and the lukewarm milk, stirring first with a large wooden spoon, and then, when the mixture becomes too difficult to work, with your hands until all the ingredients are well combined and a firm dough is formed.

3. Place the dough on a lightly floured surface and knead it by pressing it down, pushing it forward, then turning it back on itself. Repeat this kneading process for about 5 minutes, sprinkling it with a little flour every now and then to prevent the dough from sticking to the board. Place the dough in a large bowl, cover the bowl with a lightly dampened

SHAPING FLOWER ROLLS
1 For each roll, pair two sliced rounds of dough, standing one on the other.

2 Push down firmly on each pair with a chopstick or blunt edge of a knife to press the rounds together.

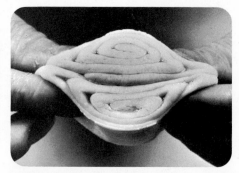

3 Pinch both ends of the rounds together and pull them slightly away from one another.

4 Draw the ends of the rounds backward around the main part of the roll until they meet behind it.

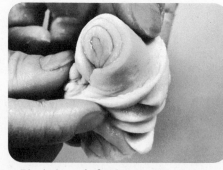

5 Pinch the ends firmly together with your thumb and forefinger to secure them and keep the roll in shape.

6 Stand the roll pinched side down. It will look like a flower with the oiled layers separated into petals.

towel and let it rest in the warm, draft-free place for 1½ to 2 hours, or until the dough doubles in bulk.

4. Punch the dough down with one blow of your fist to reduce it to its original volume. Cover with the towel and let it rise for another 20 to 30 minutes, or until it has again doubled in volume.

5. Turn the dough out on the floured board and knead it as described above for about 5 minutes until it is smooth and elastic. It is now ready to be made into flower rolls *(below)* and steamed buns *(pages 150-151)*.

Hua-chuän 花捲
STEAMED FLOWER ROLLS

To make 16 rolls

1 recipe steamed bread dough, prepared according to the directions opposite
2 tablespoons sesame-seed oil

PREPARE AHEAD: 1. Divide the dough into halves. On a large floured surface, roll out one half of the dough into a rectangle approximately 12 inches long, 8 inches wide and about ¼ inch thick. With a pastry brush, coat the surface of the dough lightly with the sesame-seed oil. Then lift up the long side of the dough and carefully roll it jelly-roll fashion into a long cylinder about 1½ inches in diameter. Roll out the other half of the dough similarly.

2. With a cleaver or sharp knife, slice each cylinder crosswise into rounds ¾ inch thick, and pair the rounds by placing one on top of another, rounded surfaces touching. With a chopstick or the blunt edge of a large knife blade, press down firmly on each pair to make the rounds adhere to each other.

Shape each roll in the following fashion: Holding the ends of the rounds together with your thumbs and forefingers, gently pull the ends away from the center of the bun and then draw the ends backward until they meet. Pinch the ends firmly together to secure them. During this process the oiled layers should separate into flowerlike petals.

3. Place the rolls an inch or two apart on one or two heatproof plates that are ½ inch smaller in diameter than the pot in which you plan to steam them. Cover the rolls with a dry kitchen towel and let them rise for about 30 minutes, or until the dough springs back slowly when lightly poked with a finger.

TO COOK: Pour enough boiling water into the lower part of a steamer to come to within an inch of the cooking rack (or use a steamer substitute as described on page 56). If you have steamer trays, arrange the rolls on two trays—leaving 1-inch spaces between the rolls—and steam them all at one time. Or, if you have a single steamer, or are using the steamer substitute, leave the rolls on the plates on which they rose and place the first plate directly on the rack in the steamer. Bring the water in the steamer to a boil over high heat, cover the pan tightly and steam for 8 minutes. Then transfer the rolls to a heated plate. If you are doing two batches, return the first batch of rolls to the steamer after the second batch is done, piling them on the rolls still in it, and reheat these for 3 or 4 minutes. The extra steaming will not harm the rolls.

Serve the finished rolls on the steaming plate, placed directly on top of a platter, or arranged attractively on a heated platter. Flower rolls are a traditional accompaniment to Szechwan duck *(page 52)* or Mongolian fire pot *(Recipe Booklet)*.

To make about 2 dozen buns

1 recipe steamed bread dough,
    prepared according to the recipe
    on page 148

THE FILLING
2 tablespoons peanut oil, or flavorless
    vegetable oil
1 pound roast pork, prepared
    according to the recipe on page
    193, and finely chopped
1 teaspoon sugar
2 tablespoons soy sauce
2 tablespoons cornstarch dissolved in
    3 tablespoons cold chicken stock,
    fresh or canned, or cold water

Ch'a-shao-pao 义燒色

STEAMED BUNS WITH ROAST PORK FILLING

PREPARE AHEAD: 1. To make the filling: Set a 12-inch wok or 10-inch skillet over high heat for about 30 seconds. Pour in 1 tablespoon of oil, swirl it about in the pan and heat for 30 seconds, turning heat down to moderate if the oil begins to smoke. Add the chopped pork and stir-fry for 1 minute, and then stir in the sugar and soy sauce. Give the cornstarch mixture a quick stir to recombine it and add it to the pan. Cook, stirring constantly, for another 10 seconds, or until the mixture thickens and the pork is covered with a clear glaze. Immediately transfer the entire contents of the pan to a bowl and cool to room temperature.

2. On a lightly floured surface, form the dough with your hands into a long, sausagelike roll 2 inches in diameter. With a sharp knife, slice the roll into 1-inch rounds. Flatten each round with the palm of your hand, then with a rolling pin, roll out each round into a disc 4 inches in diameter, turning it counterclockwise as you roll to help keep its circular shape.

3. Place 2 tablespoons of filling in the center of each round. With your fingers, gather the sides of the dough up around filling in loose folds meeting at the top. Then twist the top of the dough firmly closed.

4. Place the buns on 2-inch squares of wax paper, cover them with a dry kitchen towel and let the rolls rise again for 30 minutes, or until the dough springs back slowly when poked gently with a finger.

TO COOK: Pour enough boiling water into the lower part of a steamer to come within an inch of the cooking rack (or use a steamer substitute as described on page 56). If you have steamer trays, arrange the buns an inch apart on two trays and steam them all at one time. In single steamers, place half of the buns on the rack in the steamer, leaving 1-inch spaces between them. Over high heat, bring the water in the steamer to a boil, cover the pan tightly and steam for 10 minutes. Then transfer the buns to a heated plate. If you are doing two batches, return the first batch of buns to the steamer after the second batch is done, piling them on the buns still on the rack. Reheat together for 3 or 4 minutes. Arrange the buns on a heated platter and serve hot.

To make about 2 dozen buns

1 recipe steamed bread dough,
    prepared according to the recipe
    on page 148

THE FILLING
¼ cup lard
1 cup canned red-bean paste
½ pound pitted dates, finely
    chopped
Red food coloring (optional)

Tou-sha-pao 豆沙色

STEAMED BUNS WITH DATE FILLING

These buns are made in the same way as the roast pork steamed buns (*above*), except for the filling, which is prepared in the following fashion: Set a 12-inch wok or 10-inch skillet over moderate heat and add the ¼ cup of lard. When the lard is fully melted, add the canned bean paste and chopped dates, and cook, stirring constantly, for 8 to 10 minutes. Transfer the entire contents of the pan to a bowl and cool thoroughly. With the palms of your hands, roll the filling into balls about 1 inch in diameter. Fill the dough rounds and shape them into buns, as in roast pork buns. Roll the finished buns between the palms of your hands to make them smooth balls. Steam for 10 minutes and serve hot.

To distinguish the date buns from the pork-filled ones, try following the Chinese custom of dipping the tip of the handle end of a chopstick in red food coloring and stamping a dot on the top of the bun.

DATE-FILLED BUNS
1 For each bun, center a ball of filling on a dough round.

2 Gather the dough up around the filling by pleating along the edges.

3 Bring the pleats up to the top of the ball and twist them securely together.

4 Roll the bun between the palms of your hands to turn it into a smooth ball.

PORK-FILLED BUNS
1 For each bun, place spoon of filling on a dough round.

2 Gather the edges of the dough up around the filling in loose, natural folds.

3 Bring the folds up to the top of the ball and twist them securely together.

4 Set the bun aside with its twisted side up. It should look like the one above.

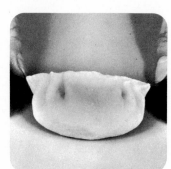

BOILED OR FRIED DUMPLINGS
1 For each dumpling, spoon filling on a dough round.

2 Fold the round in half across the filling and pinch it together at the center.

3 Make 3 or 4 pleats at each end to gather the dough around the filling.

4 Pinch along the top of the dumpling to seal the edges tightly together.

STEAMED PORK DUMPLINGS
1 For each dumpling, spoon filling on a round wrapper.

2 Gather the sides of the wrapper around the filling, letting them pleat naturally.

3 Squeeze the center of the now cylindrical dumpling to pack the filling tightly.

4 Tap the dumpling lightly to flatten its bottom and make it stand upright.

To make about 4 dozen dumplings

Wonton wrappers, prepared according to the recipe on page 128 and cut into 3-inch rounds, or substitute ½ pound ready-made *shao mai* wrappers

THE FILLING

2 stalks celery cabbage
1 pound boneless pork shoulder, finely ground
1 tablespoon Chinese rice wine, or pale dry sherry
1 tablespoon soy sauce
2 teaspoons salt
1 teaspoon sugar
¼ cup finely chopped canned bamboo shoots
1 tablespoon cornstarch

To make about 4 dozen dumplings

THE DOUGH

2 cups sifted all-purpose flour
¾ cup cold water

THE FILLING

½ pound Chinese cabbage (celery cabbage or *bok choy*)
1 pound lean boneless pork, finely ground
1 teaspoon finely chopped, peeled fresh ginger root
1 tablespoon Chinese rice wine, or pale dry sherry
1 tablespoon soy sauce
1 teaspoon salt
1 tablespoon sesame-seed oil
2 tablespoons peanut oil, or flavorless vegetable oil
1 cup chicken stock, fresh or canned
¼ cup soy sauce combined with 2 tablespoons white vinegar

Shao-mai
STEAMED PORK DUMPLINGS, CANTONESE STYLE

燒賣

PREPARE AHEAD: 1. With a cleaver or heavy, sharp knife, cut off the root ends and trim any wilted green tops from the cabbage stalks. Wash the stalks under cold running water, then drain them thoroughly and chop them into very fine dice. Place the chopped cabbage in a kitchen towel or double layer of cheesecloth and squeeze it firmly to extract as much of its moisture as possible.

2. In a bowl, combine the pork, wine, soy sauce, salt, sugar and cornstarch, and, with a large spoon, mix them thoroughly together. Stir in the cabbage and bamboo shoots.

3. To fill each dumpling, place a *wonton* or *sao mai* wrapper on the palm of your hand and cup it loosely. Place 1 tablespoonful of the filling in the cup. Then, with your other hand, gather the sides of the wrapper around the filling, letting the wrapper pleat naturally. Squeeze the middle gently to make sure the wrapper fits firmly against the filling and to give the cylinder a faintly wasp-waisted look. Tap the dumpling to flatten its bottom so that it can stand upright.

When all the dumplings are made, place them on a greased heatproof plate ½ inch smaller in diameter than the pot in which you plan to steam them. Cover with plastic wrap and refrigerate until you are ready to steam them—but no longer than 2 to 3 hours.

TO COOK: Pour enough boiling water into the lower part of a steamer to come to within an inch of the cooking rack (or use a steamer substitute as described on page 56). Place the plate of dumplings on the rack. Over high heat, bring the water in the steamer to a rolling boil. Cover the pan tightly and, over high heat, steam for 30 minutes.

If the dumplings must be made in 2 or more batches, keep the finished dumplings warm as you proceed with the rest by covering them with a saucepan lid. Or they may be reheated in the steamer for a minute or so before serving. In any case, during the steaming process, it is wise to keep a kettle of boiling water at hand if the water in the steamer boils away and needs replenishing.

Serve the dumplings on the steamer plate set directly on a platter or, with chopsticks, tongs or a slotted spoon, transfer the finished dumplings to a heated platter.

Chiao-tzŭ and Kuo-tioh
BOILED OR FRIED PORK DUMPLINGS, NORTHERN STYLE

餃子 鍋貼

PREPARE AHEAD: To make the filling: 1. With a cleaver or heavy, sharp knife, trim the wilted leaves and root ends from the cabbage, and separate the cabbage into stalks. Wash the stalks under cold running water, drain and chop them very fine. Then place the chopped cabbage in a kitchen towel or double layer of cheesecloth and squeeze it firmly to extract as much of its moisture as possible.

2. In a large bowl, combine the ground pork, chopped ginger root, wine, soy sauce, salt and sesame-seed oil, and then add the chopped cabbage. With your hands or a large spoon, mix all the ingredients together until they are thoroughly blended.

TO MAKE THE DOUGH: 1. Sift the flour into a mixing bowl and, with your hands or a large spoon, gradually combine it with the water, mixing until a stiff dough is formed. Knead the dough in the bowl for 5 minutes, or until it is smooth, then cover the bowl with a dampened cloth and let the dough rest for 30 minutes.

2. Turn the dough out on a lightly floured surface and knead it for another 2 or 3 minutes. Divide the dough into two parts, and, with your hands, firmly shape each piece into a sausagelike cylinder about 12 inches long and 1 inch in diameter.

3. With a cleaver or sharp knife, cut the rolls of dough crosswise into ½-inch slices. Lay the slices on a lightly floured surface and sprinkle their tops with a light dusting of flour. One at a time, press the slices with the palm of your hand to flatten them to about ¼ inch thickness. Then roll each slice with a rolling pin into a 3-inch-round shape about ⅛ inch thick, turning it an inch or so in a clockwise direction as you roll so that the circle keeps its shape. Arrange the rounds side by side on a lightly floured tray or cookie sheet. Cover with a dry kitchen towel.

TO ASSEMBLE: For each dumpling, place 2 teaspoonfuls of the filling in the center of a round of dough and shape the filling into a strip about 1½ inches long. Fold the round in half to make a half-moon shape and pinch the edges together at the center of the arc. With your fingers, make three or four small pleats in one side of the opening at each end of the arc to gather the dough around the filling. Pinch all along the top of the dumpling to seal pleated and smooth edges together. Transfer the finished dumpling to the floured tray or cookie sheet and keep it covered with the dry towel while you proceed with the rest.

TO BOIL: In a 4- to 5-quart pot, bring 2 quarts of water to a bubbling boil. Drop in the dumplings and turn them about in the water once with chopsticks or a large slotted spoon to prevent their sticking together. Cover the pot and cook over high heat only until the water comes to a boil. Immediately pour in 1 cup of cold water, re-cover the pot and bring the water in it to a boil again. Repeat this process twice more, adding 1 cup of cold water each time. Then remove the dumplings from the water with a bamboo strainer or slotted spoon.

Arrange the boiled dumplings on a heated platter and serve them at once. Serve the combined soy sauce and vinegar separately as a dip or sauce for the dumplings.

TO FRY: Set a 12-inch skillet over high heat for 30 seconds. Pour in 2 tablespoons of oil and swirl it about in the pan. Place the dumplings, sides just touching, pleated side up, in the pan. Cook over low heat for 2 minutes, or until the bottoms brown lightly. Add 1 cup of chicken stock, cover the pan tightly and cook over moderate heat for about 10 minutes, or until the liquid has been absorbed. Add the remaining 1 tablespoon of oil and gently swirl it about in the skillet. Let the dumplings fry uncovered for 2 minutes longer. With a spatula or large spoon, gently loosen the dumplings from the bottom of the skillet and transfer them browned side up to a heated platter.

Serve the fried dumplings as soon as they are finished. Accompany them with the soy sauce and vinegar, combined in a small bowl, to be used as a dip or sauce for the dumplings.

VII

Feasts
for Festivals

A cultured gentleman tries to avoid the following: incoherent and silly talk when drunk, putting things back on the plate, pouring wine back into the bottle, bringing too many attendants with him without consideration for the host.

—SHEN CHUNG-YING, "THE ART OF UNDERSTANDING," 17TH CENTURY

Sometimes I wonder which Chinese food I like the best, but I find it impossible to say. Appetite has a lot to do with it, of course. Perhaps the simple vegetarian dinner I ate high up in a mountain monastery would not have been as good as I thought it was if I had not been climbing all day beforehand. Then there was that party in a Chungking restaurant—was the wine we had that night really the best I had ever drunk? I thought it was. But more likely it was the cold, damp weather outside, and the knowledge of the muddy roads we had traveled to get there and the general insecurity of Chungking life that made the wine seem so warm and comforting. I am not saying anything new when I point out that circumstance has a lot to do with appetite; I merely want to show why it is that holidays in China are so deeply involved with eating. It is the food that makes the occasion in that country. Food means contentment, even happiness, and happiness in turn calls for food to emphasize it.

The Chinese, when I lived in Shanghai, punctuated the year with a large number of festivals and other observances. Most of them were based on events of importance to agriculture—seed time, harvest and so forth. Of all the regular festivals in China before the Communists gained power, New Year's took the lead, the Moon Festival coming second.

A puzzling fact to foreigners is that the Chinese New Year does not co-

These young Mongol aristocrats roast meat-filled buns—as modern children toast marshmallows—over a charcoal fire. After their conquest of China in the 13th Century the Mongols gradually adopted Chinese ways, including feasts and festivals beloved by people young and old.

incide with ours. The Chinese observe the lunar year, which is based on the waxing and waning of the moon. Because 12 such moon cycles take about 354 days rather than our 365, the Chinese New Year's Day wanders a bit when compared with the Western calendar. However, it always falls between our January 20 and February 20, at the inception of the second new moon after December 22, the winter solstice. That the exact date seemed always to be known used to amaze me, since in other respects the Chinese were often very inexact as to details. They managed without absolutes, moving cheerfully from one approximation to another. If I asked for an address, for instance, a Chinese might give me only the name of the street. When I persisted in asking for the number, he might answer, just to stop my worrying, "The number is something like six hundred." If it turned out to be five hundred and forty instead, or seven hundred, that was near enough, he thought. About the date of the New Year however, there was never any of this charming uncertainty.

Two weeks or so ahead of the old year's close, things would speed up. The stores and market stalls would display more goods than usual—clothes, toys and especially food and drink. With luck the proprietors would sell all the extra stock before they closed down over New Year's.

The butchers were especially confident of a flourishing business in pork, for New Year's without at least one of the traditional pork dishes was almost unthinkable; everybody in China thought it his right, or at least his children's right, to eat some of this meat at New Year's in whatever form, even if there was only enough to flavor the rice.

The festival was not all merrymaking. New Year's was the time when all debts were supposed to be paid. Despite the regular payment days during the year, New Year's was the big time to clear the books. For two weeks or so before the great day bills arrived in every mail, and among the population that did not depend on the written word there were scenes of frantic dunning, collections under protest, arguments, accusations, threats and brawls. Some people held out, refusing to pay until the very last minute. Others, who could not pay up, no matter what, simply went into hiding.

A more pleasant aspect of the season was that everyone who could possibly go home did so—"home" in this sense being the dwelling place of the head of the family. If the house was small or the relatives too many to sleep in it, the least that was expected was a call to pay one's respects.

With the visiting went feasting, an unending round of snacks and meals. The atmosphere was as festive as that of Christmas. I have been to many Chinese houses for New Year's festivities, but I remember best the first time I was invited for dinner with a family there. I found the living room adorned with special hangings, which, like the children's new toys, were decorated with symbols of the New Year, such as the peach of longevity and the carp that suggests the rewards for endeavor.

In the living room Grandfather, the head of the house, sat in state. Though he protested kindly that it was unnecessary, his children and grandchildren kowtowed to him, pressing their foreheads to the floor as they knelt in this most reverential of Chinese acts. One very small child was fat, and when he tried to bow he rolled over sideways. Everybody laughed, but his mother snatched him up and kissed him to stop his crying. The doorbell was kept ringing by family connections and friends who came to wish the family contentment and prosperity and long life, and then sat down to chat and luxuriate in idleness, sipping tea and nibbling at the snacks and sweets distributed here and there on little tables—bowls of lotus seeds, litchis and longans, trays of red jujubes and steamed rice cakes flavored with date or red-bean paste. Along one side of the room was the ancestral altar bearing fruit, bowls of rice and cups of wine for the dead, and burning joss sticks.

Dinner itself consisted of a variety of pork dishes—red-cooked pig's shank, steamed pork dumplings, crisp pork-skin cracklings and roast suckling pig—plus red-cooked carp and a number of side dishes of vegetables. After dinner, when the invited guests had gone, the head of the family would perform certain ceremonies, some seriously, some to humor the children. There were grave thanks and offerings to be made to three deities, the gods of earth, wealth and the afterworld. Pleas were also made to the god of the underworld on behalf of the shades of the family dead. Among the minor gods and patron saints who were honored the most important was Tsao Wang, the kitchen god, but this was done mostly for the sake of the children.

Tradition placed Tsao Wang in the house in person (actually in the form of a colored picture in a shrine), watching what went on from his vantage point on the kitchen wall. Contrary to what one might expect, Tsao Wang was not a critic of cooking, but a kind of heavenly monitor, a guardian of morals generally, who left the home once a year to make his report on the family's conduct to Heaven itself. He was usually depicted as a calm figure, splendidly garbed, with his horse at his side.

Seven nights before the end of the year the master of the house helped Tsao Wang prepare for his trip by burning incense that symbolized the provisions he would need on his trip, by setting out straw so that his horse would not go hungry, and by pouring out a bowl of water to assuage thirst. Then the god was taken down from the shrine and he, too, was put into the stove, horse and all—in other words, sent on his journey. A special kind of sticky sweetmeat was burned with him, or sometimes his lips were rubbed with honey just before he was consigned to the flames. The candy or honey was meant to flavor his report so that he would tell Heaven only sweet things about the family in his charge.

Everybody in the house was busy taking baths, getting haircuts and cleaning up generally. Masses of food had to be prepared in advance, because cooking would be impossible during the five days of the holiday, when nobody was supposed to use cutting implements such as knives or scissors or cleavers; moreover, with the shops closed for three days, nothing could be bought. Presents had to be readied and taken or sent, for New Year's is gift-giving time, as Christmas is with us. In the north presents tended generally to be useful things—servants were given new padded gowns to keep them warm during the bitter cold that follows the first of the year. But in the south, where the climate is kinder, gifts were more apt to be pleasant and frivolous—mainly baskets of food. My grocer and food merchant used to send me a basket with a duck, some good

Continued on page 160

Peking duck is a world-renowned delicacy created out of common ingredients plus as much as a full day of skillful and arduous work in the kitchen. The traditional version calls for the choicest fowl, brought to the exact degree of plumpness and tenderness through force-feeding, and readied for the table by a many-staged process. The birds are roasted in a mud-lined oven *(above)*, suspended from hooks to assure even heat on all sides. However, a simplified method *(page 166)* produces satisfactory results in modern home kitchens.

A festive party in Taiwan has just been served neatly sliced Peking duck. Meat and skin plus scallions and *hoisin* sauce are wrapped inside a pancake and eaten with gusto. The appearance of this major dish is the signal for a toast drunk in rice wine, and the playing of the finger game. Two players simultaneously fling out varying numbers of fingers and shout their guesses, often at the top of their voices, of the total number of outstretched fingers. If one guesses correctly, the loser must down a drink. A run of bad luck can have dire results.

brand of tea and a few other delicacies. Of course the very rich would give luxuries like silk or jewels to their intimates, but the most acceptable present was always some sort of choice food—a whole ham, prime live fowl or baskets of fruit. Children, however, also received "Lucky Money"— small sums in red envelopes lettered in gold.

In a country so largely agricultural it was natural that farming concerns should be much on the minds of the people. The first days of the New Year were devoted to animal "birthdays" in fixed order: the first day was dedicated to chickens, the second to dogs, the third to pigs, the fourth to ducks, the fifth to cattle and the sixth to horses. On the seventh, however, lesser animals were forgotten because it was the day dedicated to human beings, and the eighth day was given to honoring rice and some other cereals. The ninth belonged to fruit and vegetables. Wheat and barley claimed the tenth. During the eighth, ninth and tenth, the weather was anxiously forecast: Peasants were supposed to judge from these daily prophecies what sort of crops they could expect in the coming season.

New Year's was also the time when all family quarrels were supposed to be made up so that everybody could greet the New Year fair and square and clean-swept. Restored to amiability, the family took part in a ceremony to mark the new year. In old-fashioned houses it was quite elaborate. Everybody sat up to welcome the dawn of the new year's first day, passing the time with singing and lively talk. Incense and fragrant branches of fir, sesame and cypress were burned in the courtyard to discourage evil spirits; firecrackers were set off to frighten away any demons. A lamp was kept burning at Tsao Wang's empty shrine to help him find his way back, and in certain regions the doors were locked and sealed. Small children who weakened and fell asleep were put to bed until five in the morning, when everyone was called again. The master of the house then unlocked the doors and windows and removed the seals. This was the ceremony of Opening the Gate to Fortune. The master then lit incense at the main entrance, and burned a branch of sesame, some paper gods and an inscription of thanks to the deities. More firecrackers were popped. Then the men of the family bowed to the family gods and to the tablets bearing the ancestral names for the past three generations. They also paid their respects to the kitchen god. Sure enough, he had returned in the night all resplendent. The New Year's ceremonies were the responsibility of the men, not the women. After the high point of the festivities was reached the excitement began to taper off.

If New Year's was the man's festival, the Moon Festival was the woman's. It was held at harvesttime in the eighth month of the lunar year—September, more or less, in the Western calendar. For days ahead the shops were full of toys and cakes. Everybody fervently hoped that the festival would not be marred by cloudy weather, since the behavior of the elements was another omen for next year's crops and food supply. Since the Moon Festival usually took place in pleasant weather, people gave moon-viewing parties at which they gathered out of doors. At this time, too, those who had curios put them on exhibit, and children, in imitation, arranged their favorite toys to be admired by visitors.

I used to look forward enormously to the moon-viewing parties that

Opposite: At the climax of the bun festival in Cheung Chau, an island near Hong Kong, boys race up 60-foot "bun mountains" to seize the highest of the 30,000 sweet buns. Winners are supposed to have good luck in the coming year. The celebration takes place once a year as a kind of apology to the ghosts of fish and other animals killed for food. It features musicians, acrobats and clowns, as well as floats carrying silk-costumed children who pose in tableaux. After the parade, the presiding priests chant and invite the hungry spirits to the bun feast. Then the climbing race begins.

160

were especially popular among literary people. They loved to gather out of doors in the bright moonlight at this time, eating and drinking in agreeable company. They made punning jokes, composed poems and generally behaved in the tradition of that bibulous poet, Li Po. There was one party I attended in Hong Kong given by a young Englishman. He was trying to steep himself in the ways of the country and had planned everything carefully. We were to have an elaborate dinner of many courses in his courtyard, but we nearly had nothing at all because of one shocking breach of etiquette—*the wine was cold*. Of course the Chinese were too courteous to say anything, but we foreigners were not so tender of his feelings and soon told him what we thought of the arrangement. After that, everything—dinner, poetry, even conversation—was suspended while we waited glumly for the wine to be warmed. In time it arrived in a proper state, merriment was restored, and all went well, but it changed forever my mental picture of the lives of ancient Chinese poets. I know now that they did *not* compose their poems all alone among the trees and mountains and silences of nature—they simply could not have been out of touch with stoves and servants to keep their wine at the right temperature.

At the Moon Festival, you gave paper lanterns in certain symbolic shapes to your friends; a carp (for success through endeavor) to the scholar, a butterfly (for longevity), or a round and moon-shaped lantern. But the essential Moon Festival gift was a box of four moon cakes.

Moon cakes, unlike most Chinese dainties, are sweet, especially in the south, where sugar is plentiful. However they were not a regional specialty but were found everywhere in China, varying slightly as to size and ingredients. They were always baked of "moon-colored," or gray, flour. When finished they looked something like deep, covered pies, but were as heavy as the fruitcakes made at Christmastime in the West. The usual constituents, besides the flour, included lard, spices, eggs, orange peel, citron, almonds, other nuts and fruits as available, and a lot of sugar. The women of the family piled these moon cakes on the altar table in pyramids, and they also made similar pyramids of round fruits that suggested the moon—apples, peaches, pomegranates, grapes or melons.

Although moon cakes are very good in themselves, the Chinese have an extra reason for eating them. In the 14th Century, when the country was ruled by tyrannical Mongols, the Chinese nobles who lived in Peking had very hard lives. Even in the privacy of their homes they dared not complain, since the Mongols planted spies in every noble household to sniff out incipient rebellion. Then one year noble womenfolk devised a clever way to outwit their rulers. As the Moon Festival approached, these brave ladies inserted messages into their moon cakes before baking them, and then sent the cakes as ordinary presents to all the people who could be depended on to join in an uprising. But on the designated night every would-be rebel knew where to be to carry out the plan, and the exact time to strike. Armed with makeshift weapons like clubs and kitchen cleavers, the conspirators successfully overthrew the unsuspecting Peking garrison and started the great war that rid the whole country of the tyrants. So proud were Chinese women of their moon cakes that many always baked them at home instead of buying them from confectioners.

The Chinese I knew never waited for a major festival if they felt like giving a banquet; I never did find out what the first such affair I attended was celebrating. My hosts, Mr. and Mrs. Lu, received their guests in a living room which opened onto a dining room, and I could see a big, round table ready for dinner. A manservant brought me a cup of tea. It was delicious tea of an unfamiliar flavor, served in porcelain as thin as an egg shell. Mrs. Lu presented me to the guests of honor, a Dr. Liang and his wife, before she slipped away for the anxious housewife's last look around. Then she came back and nodded to her husband, who said to the Liangs, "Well, shall we have some dinner?" To my surprise—for he had spoken perfectly plainly—neither of the Liangs seemed to have heard him, but merely stood there. Mr. Lu said, more pressingly, "Shall we eat?" and this time the couple evidently got the message, because they bowed and started forward toward the dining room, only to pause again at the door to hang back as if shy, and implore others to precede them. All this, of course, was manners. After protesting briefly, the Liangs surrendered and walked into the dining room followed by the rest of us.

When Mrs. Lu told us where our places were, there was more bashful jockeying, but finally we were arranged around the table with Mr. Lu and his wife sitting with their backs to the serving room—so that they would get most of the noise in the kitchen—and the Liangs opposite. We were 10, the customary number for a group seated at one table. In the center of the table the cold dishes were waiting, the food arranged in elaborate patterns of blended or contrasting colors, very pretty.

"I apologize for the poor meal you are going to have," said Mr. Lu. Mrs. Lu did not take this amiss, of course, but smiled in conventional agreement, and Dr. Liang assured his hosts that they should not be so modest, as all the world knew their hospitality, which was of the very best. The rest of us murmured agreement, while a servant filled the little wine cups. Mr. Lu raised his cup to Dr. Liang in the first toast, and the gentlemen emptied their cups together. Then Mr. Lu toasted the whole company and we toasted him back. He gestured with his chopsticks toward the cold dishes and said, "Please don't be shy. Serve yourselves," and the banquet was well away. This first course consisted of roast pork, mushrooms, abalone, white chicken, cucumber salad, chicken livers, ham and jellied fish. (Eight is the customary number for the cold plates.) The mushrooms were of that enormous flat, black kind that is a specialty of China, cut to look like the petals of some huge flower. The chicken livers, which I ate first, were juicier than I expected, very flavorful because of subtle spicing.

The next dish was the conventional shark's fin soup, brought in a tureen that was set down where Mr. Lu could easily reach it to fill all our bowls with a ladle. It was to be the only time he served the company like that, and was a gesture of hospitality to start us off. We were expected to help ourselves during the rest of the meal. After the soup, we were served a very decorative dish Mrs. Lu called chicken in snow, the chicken cut very fine and served in a surrounding ring of fluffy meringue of egg white, decorated with delicately crisscrossed shreds of ham and green vegetable. The chicken seemed as light as the meringue, so that one was left with the erroneous sensation of not having eaten much.

In the meantime drinking continued, everyone toasting others as they liked. The toaster usually said, in Chinese, *"Kan-pei!"* ("bottoms up!"), which was a challenge to the other man to empty his cup in one gulp, afterward turning it over to show the challenger that he was not cheating. I say "he" because ladylike ladies in China did not do so much drinking.

Occasionally we took time out while the servant changed our plates for clean ones, and handed us all hot steamed towels to wipe our faces and hands, and then the servant collected the towels on a tray. This little ceremony was repeated several times more during the meal—after the next course, which was lobster in spicy sauce, for example. The lobster was followed by scallops with water chestnuts and snow peas, crisp and cooling after the spicy sauce, and after the scallops came "phoenix-tailed" shrimp with the shell of the tail left on. This tail shell, a bright red from cooking, stuck out conveniently from the rest of the shrimp, which had been deep-fried and coated in batter to crumble in the mouth. We ate the shrimp with our fingers, and again used those welcome hot towels. I was beginning to slow down, having eaten too heartily of the earlier dishes. I realized that I had to learn to pace myself.

The gentlemen were playing the finger-guessing game that makes Chinese parties so noisy. The challenger suddenly puts out one fist over the table—really, he throws it out, extending some of the fingers as he does so and shouting any number up to 10. Simultaneously the challenged man flings out his fist and shouts the number of his fingers, trying by guess to hit on the correct number that with his adversary's adds up to 10. If he has been right, the challenger must drink. Of course, it is possible to play it the other way around, with the winner drinking and the loser refraining, but the main idea is to drink. It was fortunate for me that women are not expected to play the game, because it was all I could do to manage the number of cups that came my way.

Imperceptibly, what with all the noise and merrymaking, drinking ceased, and the wine flush in the men's cheeks faded. Everyone was able to do justice to the next course, which was Peking duck with all its trimmings: meat, skin and scallion brushes rolled together in a pancake with dark, sweet bean sauce.

Banquets traditionally include a fish served whole toward the end (to take advantage of the pun on the Chinese word for fish, which sounds much the same as "more"; thus the host wishes his guests more than enough money throughout his life. The Lu's gave us a crispy sweet-and-sour sea bass with its head pointing, as it should, toward Dr. Liang, the guest of honor. It was followed by icicle-radish balls with dried scallops, tart and freshening. At the end, there was an eight-treasure rice pudding, made of glutinous rice steamed with sugar and oil and red-bean paste. A great variety of fruits—dates, dried plums, lotus seeds, raisins, orange peel, citron and possibly others, and walnuts and almonds, were embedded on the surface in a flower pattern, and the same fruits and nuts made up a layer near the bottom of this exceedingly pretty cold dish. Unfortunately none of us had room to eat much of it, but that was as it should be, a compliment to the dinner. I had begun to learn that there is a good deal of one-upmanship in Chinese entertaining.

Opposite: Moon cakes and rice wine mark the Moon Festival, a major Chinese holiday that falls at the eighth full moon of the Lunar Year, in the early fall. The patterned moon cakes are bought at bakeries and given as presents. Fireworks are not prescribed for this festival, but are used here to symbolize the moon, which is contemplatively viewed by banqueting celebrants who sip wine and recite their own poems and those of classic Chinese poets.

Pei-ching-k'ao-ya

北京烤鴨

PEKING DUCK

A 5-pound duck
6 cups water
¼ cup honey
4 slices peeled fresh ginger root,
    about 1 inch in diameter and ⅛
    inch thick
2 scallions, including the green tops,
    cut into 2-inch lengths

THE SAUCE
¼ cup *hoisin* sauce
1 tablespoon water
1 teaspoon sesame-seed oil
2 teaspoons sugar

12 scallions
Mandarin pancakes, prepared
    according to the recipe on page
    172 and reheated

PREPARE AHEAD: 1. Wash the duck under cold water, then pat dry inside and out with paper towels. Tie one end of a 20-inch length of white cord around the neck skin. If the skin has been cut away, loop the cord under the wings. Suspend the bird from the string in a cool, airy place for 3 hours to dry the skin, or train a fan on it for 2 hours.

2. In a 12-inch wok or large flameproof casserole, combine 6 cups water, ¼ cup honey, ginger root and cut scallions, and bring to a boil over high heat. Holding the duck by its string, lower it into the boiling liquid. With string in one hand and a spoon in the other, turn the duck from side to side until all of its skin is moistened with the liquid. Remove the duck (discarding the liquid) and hang it again in the cool place, setting a bowl beneath it to catch any drippings; the duck will dry in 1 hour with the fan trained upon it or 2 to 3 hours without it.

3. Make the sauce by combining *hoisin* sauce, water, sesame-seed oil and sugar in a small pan, and stirring until sugar dissolves. Bring to a boil, then reduce heat to its lowest point and simmer uncovered for 3 minutes. Pour into a small bowl, cool and reserve until ready to use.

4. To make scallion brushes, cut scallions down to 3-inch lengths and trim off roots. Standing each scallion on end, make four intersecting cuts 1 inch deep into its stalk. Repeat at other end. Place scallions in ice water and refrigerate until cut parts curl into brushlike fans *(page 69)*.

TO COOK: Preheat oven to 375°. Untie the duck and cut off any loose neck skin. Place duck, breast side up, on a rack and set in a roasting pan just large enough to hold the bird. Roast the duck in the middle of the oven for one hour. Then lower the heat to 300°, turn the duck on its breast and roast for 30 minutes longer. Now raise the heat to 375°, return the duck to its original position and roast for a final half hour. Transfer the duck to a carving board.

With a small, sharp knife and your fingers, remove the crisp skin from the breast, sides and back of duck. Cut skin into 2-by-3-inch rectangles and arrange them in a single layer on a heated platter. Cut the wings and drumsticks from the duck, and cut all the meat away from breast and carcass. Slice meat into pieces 2½ inches long and ½ inch wide, and arrange them with the wings and drumsticks on another heated platter.

To serve, place the platters of duck, the heated pancakes, the bowl of sauce and the scallion brushes in the center of the table. Traditionally, each guest spreads a pancake flat on his plate, dips a scallion in the sauce and brushes the pancake with it. The scallion is placed in the middle of the pancake with a piece of duck skin and a piece of meat on top. The pancake is folded over the scallion and duck, and tucked under. One end of the package is then folded over about 1 inch to enclose the filling, and the whole rolled into a cylinder that can be picked up with the fingers and eaten. As a main course, Peking duck will serve 6. As part of a Chinese meal *(page 200)*, it will serve 8 to 12. If you plan to serve more than 6, increase the number of pancakes and scallion brushes.

A duck farmer escorts his flock into the sunset—and the restaurant kitchen,
there to be transformed into Peking duck. In this dish, skin and meat are served
in separate plates, accompanied by scallion brushes, *hoisin* sauce and thin pancakes.

Pa-pao-ya
EIGHT-JEWEL DUCK

八寶鴨

1 cup glutinous rice

2 dried Chinese mushrooms, 1 to 1½ inches in diameter

10 or 12 dried shrimp

A 4- to 5-pound duck

1 cup quartered, canned whole water-pack French or Italian chestnuts

2 tablespoons peanut oil, or flavorless vegetable oil

¼ pound lean, boneless pork, finely ground

½ teaspoon sugar

1 tablespoon Chinese rice wine, or pale dry sherry

2 tablespoons soy sauce

¼ cup canned whole gingko nuts

3 peeled and washed fresh water chestnuts or drained canned water chestnuts, sliced ⅛ inch thick

A ¼-inch-thick slice of cooked Smithfield ham, cut into ¼-inch dice

2 teaspoons salt

Fresh Chinese parsley sprigs (*cilantro*), or substitute fresh curly or flat-leaf parsley

PREPARE AHEAD: 1. In a bowl, cover the rice with cold water and soak for 2 hours. Then pour enough boiling water into the lower part of a steamer to come within an inch of the cooking rack (or use a steamer substitute as described on page 56). Line the rack with a double thickness of paper towels. Now drain the rice and spread it evenly over the lined rack. Over high heat, bring the water in the steamer to a rolling boil. Cover the pan tightly and steam the rice for 30 minutes, or until the rice is tender. Keep a kettle of boiling water on the stove to replenish the water in the steamer if necessary. Remove the rice from the pot, place it in a bowl and cover it with aluminum foil to keep warm.

2. In a small bowl, cover the dried shrimp with ¼ cup of warm water and allow them to soak for at least 30 minutes. Do not drain the shrimp or discard the water.

3. In a small bowl, cover the mushrooms with ½ cup of warm water and let them soak for at least 30 minutes. Then remove them with a slotted spoon and discard the water. With a cleaver or large, sharp knife, cut away and discard the tough stems of the mushrooms and chop the caps fine.

4. Meanwhile, bone the duck, following the directions and diagrams on the opposite page.

5. Have the above ingredients, and the oil, pork, sugar, wine, soy sauce, gingko nuts, water chestnuts, ham, salt and parsley sprigs—plus trussing pins or clips or a large needle and strong thread for closing the cavities of the duck—within easy reach.

TO COOK: Set a 12-inch wok or 10-inch skillet over high heat for 30 seconds. Pour in the 2 tablespoons of oil, swirl it about in the pan and heat for another 30 seconds, turning the heat down to moderate if the oil begins to smoke. Add the pork and stir-fry for 2 or 3 minutes until the pork loses its reddish color. Stir in the wine and soy sauce, then add the mushrooms, gingko nuts, water chestnuts, rice, ham, shrimp and soaking water. Mix them together thoroughly and gently fold in the chestnuts, being careful not to let the chestnuts crumble. Transfer the entire contents of this stuffing mixture from the pan to a bowl and cool to room temperature.

Preheat the oven to 400°. Rub the inside surfaces of the duck with the 2 teaspoons of salt, then—with clips, trussing pins or needle and strong thread—close up the neck opening very securely. Pack the stuffing loosely into the cavity of the duck and close up the tail opening in exactly the same fashion as you already closed the neck. Pat, shape and mold the body of the duck back into its original shape and place it, breast side up, on a rack set in a deep roasting pan. Add about 1 inch of water to the pan. Roast in the center of the oven for 30 minutes, reduce the heat to 350° and roast the duck for 1½ hours longer.

When the duck is done, remove its clips, trussing pins or thread. Place the duck on a heated serving platter. Decorate the platter with fresh parsley sprigs and serve at once. At the table, carve the duck into 8 portions by first cutting it in half lengthwise and then making 3 evenly spaced crosswise cuts.

1 Pull the neck skin taut and cut it off to within an inch or so of the body, using kitchen scissors as shown or a sharp, heavy knife.

Eight Steps to Bone an Eight-Jewel Duck

Allow 30 minutes to bone a duck, although chances are you'll finish in less time. If frozen, be sure the duck is thoroughly defrosted. Remove neck, giblets and any loose fat; wipe the duck completely dry inside and out with paper towels. For boning, use any kitchen scissors or knife with which you are familiar so long as it is relatively heavy, has a sharp point and finely honed cutting edge.

2 Fold remaining neck skin as far back as it will go and, with tiny snips or cuts, free meat around the neck cavity from the carcass.

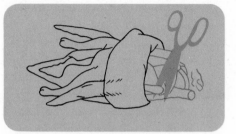

3 Wiggle each wing to find the joint where it meets the carcass, then cut through the joint to detach the wing. Leave the wing itself intact.

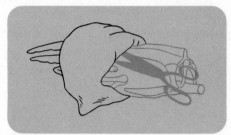

4 Continue to free the meat from the carcass with tiny snips or cuts, turning the duck over and rolling the skin back as you work.

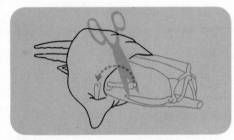

5 Free the meat around each thigh and cut the joint to detach the drumstick from the thigh. Leave the thigh bones on the carcass.

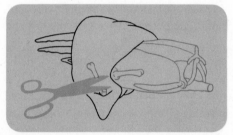

6 Free the meat halfway down the length of the drumstick bone, then cut off and remove the exposed half of the bone. Leave the bottom intact.

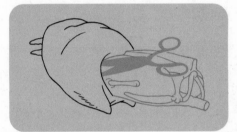

7 Cut the meat away from the rest of the carcass, always cutting as close to the bones as you can. Try never to pierce the duck's skin.

8 Cut through the joint where the tail bone is attached to the backbone of the duck, leaving the tail with the skin and meat. Then turn the skin of the now boned duck right side out again. It should look like the one pictured at right. The Chinese keep the wing bones and the tips of the drumsticks intact to make the finished eight-jewel duck—after it has been stuffed and roasted—look like a whole bird. In thrifty Chinese style, you can use the carcass, other bones and giblets for duck stock (following the chicken stock recipe in the Recipe Booklet), and render the fat.

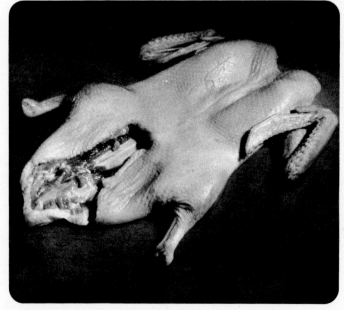

169

To serve 6 to 8

1 cup shelled pecans
½ cup sugar
1 cup peanut oil, or flavorless
    vegetable oil
1 pound fresh chestnuts
2 tablespoons brown sugar
½ cup water
½ pint heavy cream
2 tablespoons white sugar

4 pork kidneys
½ pound fresh or thoroughly
    defrosted frozen sea scallops
¼ cup peanut oil, or flavorless
    vegetable oil
1 tablespoon Chinese rice wine, or
    pale dry sherry
1 teaspoon finely chopped, peeled
    fresh ginger root
1 scallion, including the green top,
    finely chopped
2 tablespoons soy sauce
½ teaspoon salt
1 teaspoon sugar
1 teaspoon cornstarch dissolved in 1
    tablespoon chicken stock, fresh or
    canned, or cold water

Li-tzŭ-tan-kao

栗子蛋糕

PEKING DUST

PREPARE AHEAD: 1. In a small saucepan, combine the pecans with 2 cups of water. Bring to a boil over high heat, reduce the heat to moderate and simmer uncovered for 1 minute. Remove the pan from the heat and pour off all the water. Add the sugar to the pan and stir until the pecans are evenly coated. With a spoon, spread the pecans out on a sheet of wax paper and let them dry for 30 minutes. Set a 12-inch wok or 10-inch skillet over high heat and pour in 1 cup of oil. Heat the oil until a haze forms above it or it registers 375° on a deep-frying thermometer. Fry the pecans for 1 or 2 minutes, turning and separating them with a slotted spoon until the sugar coats the nuts with a rich brown glaze. Transfer the nuts to a large greased platter and spread them apart in a single layer to cool to room temperature.

2. Shell the chestnuts in the following fashion: Preheat the oven to 425°. With a small, sharp knife, cut a crisscross on the top of each chestnut. Spread the nuts out in a single layer in a shallow baking pan and pour in about ¼ cup of water—just enough to film the bottom of the pan. Roast the chestnuts for 10 minutes, or until they pop open. Turn off the oven and remove half the nuts from the pan. While the chestnuts are still hot, remove their shells and inner brown membranes with a small, sharp knife. Then peel the hot chestnuts similarly.

TO ASSEMBLE: In a heavy 3-quart saucepan, combine the brown sugar and ½ cup cold water. Add the shelled chestnuts, and turn them about with a spoon to coat them evenly with the sugar and water. Bring to a simmer over moderate heat, cover the pan and reduce the heat to the lowest possible point. Cook the chestnuts undisturbed for 45 minutes, or until tender; the liquid will cook away, leaving them quite dry. Uncover the pan, turn off the heat and let the chestnuts cool to room temperature.

Purée the chestnuts in a food mill set over a mixing bowl. If the purée seems coarse—it should be as fine as granulated sugar—press it through the mill a second time. With a whisk, or rotary or electric beater, whip the cream and white sugar together in a large bowl until the cream is stiff enough to form firm unwavering peaks when the whisk or beater is lifted out of the bowl. Spoon the whipped cream into a cone-shaped mound on a chilled serving platter. A few tablespoons at a time, sprinkle the chestnut purée over the cream, masking it completely. Arrange the glazed pecans side by side in a ring around the edge of the platter. Serve the finished dessert at once.

Hsien-kan-pei-yao-hua

鮮干貝腰花

STIR-FRIED SEA SCALLOPS AND PORK KIDNEYS

PREPARE AHEAD: 1. Peel off the thin outer membrane covering the kidneys, if the butcher has not already removed it, with a cleaver or sharp knife. Split the kidneys in half lengthwise and cut away the small knobs of fat and any tough membrane surrounding them. Place the kidney halves flat side down on a chopping board and score their surfaces diagonally to create a crisscross pattern, cutting about two thirds of the way down into them and spacing the cuts about ¼ inch apart. Then cut the kidneys crosswise into 1-inch slices, and cut the slices into strips about 2 inches long.

2. Wash the scallops under cold running water, pat them dry with paper towels and cut them horizontally into slices ¼ inch thick.

3. Have the above ingredients, and the oil, wine, ginger, scallions, soy sauce, salt, sugar and the cornstarch mixture within easy reach.

TO COOK: Set a 12-inch wok or 10-inch skillet over high heat for 30 seconds. Pour in 2 tablespoons of oil, swirl it about in the pan and heat for another 30 seconds, turning the heat down to moderate if the oil begins to smoke. Add the scallops and stir-fry for only 1 minute, or until they turn white but not too firm. Immediately pour in the wine and add the salt, stir well, and, with a large spoon, transfer the scallops to a plate. Pour the remaining 2 tablespoons of oil into the pan, heat for about 30 seconds, and add the ginger and scallions. Stir for a few seconds and drop in the kidneys. Stir-fry over high heat for 2 minutes, or until their edges begin to curl. Then add the soy sauce and sugar. Return the scallops and their accumulated juices to the pan, and mix with the kidneys for a few seconds. Give the cornstarch mixture a quick stir to recombine it and add it to the pan. When the kidneys and scallops are coated with a light, clear glaze—this will take no more than a few seconds—transfer the entire contents of the pan to a heated platter and serve at once. As a main course this will serve 4. As part of a Chinese meal *(page 200)*, it will serve 6 to 8.

White slices of scallops alternate with dark pieces of scored pork kidney, to achieve a contrast in color and a balance of flavor.

1 Cover one oiled circle of dough with second circle.

2 Roll joined layers of dough into a thin sheet.

3 Heat the pancake in a pan until brown flecks appear.

4 Peel apart; serve with Peking duck or *mu-hsü* pork.

Po-ping
薄餅

MANDARIN PANCAKES

To make 2 dozen pancakes

2 cups sifted all-purpose flour
¾ cup boiling water
1 to 2 tablespoons sesame-seed oil

Sift flour into a mixing bowl, make a well in the center and pour into it the ¾ cup of boiling water. With a wooden spoon, gradually mix flour and water together until a soft dough is formed; on a lightly floured surface, knead it gently for 10 minutes, or until smooth and elastic. Cover with a damp kitchen towel and let it rest for 15 minutes. On a lightly floured surface, roll dough into a circle about ¼ inch thick. With a 2½-inch cookie cutter or a glass, cut as many circles of dough as you can. Knead scraps together, roll out again and cut more circles. Arrange circles side by side, brush half of them lightly with sesame-seed oil and, sandwich-wise, place the unoiled ones on top. With a rolling pin, flatten each pair into a 6-inch circle, rotating the sandwich an inch or so in a clockwise direction as you roll so that the circle keeps its shape, and turning it once to roll both sides. Cover the pancakes with a dry towel.

Set a heavy 8-inch skillet over high heat for 30 seconds. Reduce heat to moderate and cook the pancakes, one at a time, in the ungreased pan, turning them over as they puff up and little bubbles appear on the surface. Regulate the heat so that the pancakes become specked with brown after cooking about 1 minute on each side. As each pancake is finished, gently separate the halves and stack them on a plate. Serve them at once or wrap them in foil and refrigerate for later use. Or they may be wrapped and frozen, if you like. Reheat them (frozen pancakes need not be defrosted first) either by steaming them in a steamer for 10 minutes, or warming them, still wrapped in their foil, in a preheated 350° oven for about 10 minutes. Serve with Peking duck *(page 166)* and soft-fried shredded pork and eggs *(Recipe Booklet)*.

To serve 8

2 cups glutinous rice
¼ cup lard
½ pound pitted dates, finely
   chopped, plus 8 whole pitted dates,
   cut in half
1 cup canned red-bean paste
20 dried jujubes
2 tablespoons sugar
2 tablespoons melted lard
Red and green candied cherries

SYRUP
¼ cup sugar
1 cup cold water
1 teaspoon almond extract
1 tablespoon cornstarch dissolved in
   3 tablespoons cold water

Pa-pao-fan
八寶飯

EIGHT-TREASURE-RICE PUDDING

This dessert is known as eight-treasure or eight-precious or even eight-jewel pudding because in China the design on the top of it was made with 8 different kinds of dried and candied fruits or nuts—such as dried lotus seeds, candied green or red plums, seeded dragon's eye nuts, watermelon seeds, preserved dates, dried jujubes, candied orange peel, candied red or green cherries, and blanched walnuts. The version described here is simply decorated with pitted dates, dried jujubes and candied cherries.

PREPARE AHEAD: 1. In a large bowl, cover the rice with cold water and soak for 2 hours.

2. In a 12-inch wok or 10-inch skillet, melt the ¼ cup of lard over moderate heat. Add the chopped dates and red-bean paste, and cook over low heat, stirring frequently, for 20 minutes, or until the mixture begins to come away from the sides of the pan. Remove from the pan to a small bowl and cool to room temperature.

3. Combine the jujubes and 2 cups cold water in a 2-quart saucepan. Over high heat, bring the water to a boil, then reduce the heat to low and simmer the jujubes, covered, for about 10 minutes. Drain the jujubes through a sieve, and, when they are cool enough to handle, cut them in half and remove and discard the pits.

4. Have the rice, date and bean-paste mixture, jujubes, cherries, sugar, water, almond extract and cornstarch all within easy reach.

TO COOK: Pour enough boiling water into the lower part of a steamer to come within an inch of the cooking rack (or use a steamer substitute as described on page 56). Line the rack with a double layer of paper towels. Drain the rice and spread it evenly over the lined rack. Over high heat, bring the water in the steamer to a rolling boil, cover the pan tightly and steam the rice for 30 minutes, or until the rice is thoroughly cooked, replenishing the water if it boils away.

Transfer the rice to a bowl, and stir into it the 2 tablespoons of sugar and 2 tablespoons of melted lard. Spoon half the rice into a shallow heat-proof bowl (about 6 inches across and 3 inches deep). On top, place the red-bean-paste mixture, spreading it to within ½ inch of the sides of the bowl. Place the remaining rice over it, spreading it out evenly to the edges of the bowl and pressing down on it lightly with the palm of your hand. Put an inverted dinner plate over the top of the bowl, and, grasping the edges of both the plate and the bowl, turn them over together. Lift the bowl up gently to unmold the pudding. Now decorate the sides and top of the pudding with the jujubes, halved dates and candied cherries. Any sort of design you devise would be proper. In the picture on page 174, the bottom edge of the pudding is decorated with a row of date halves spaced about an inch apart; the top edge is rimmed with jujubes, laid side by side; the top of the pudding is ornamented with flowers and leaves made of cherries.

When the decoration is complete, gently spread a long piece of plastic wrap over it to hold the fruit in place, invert the bowl again and carefully set it over the top of the pudding. Grasping the edges of the bowl and plate together, turn the bowl over and remove the plate. Bring the water in the steamer to a boil again, place the bowl on the rack and cover the pan tightly. Steam the pudding for an hour, replenishing the water when it boils away. Have a kettle of boiling water handy.

TO SERVE: A few minutes before the pudding is done, make the syrup by combining the ¼ cup of sugar with the cup of water in a small saucepan and boiling it until the sugar dissolves. Add the almond extract, give the cornstarch mixture a quick stir to recombine it and stir it into the syrup. Cook, stirring, for a few seconds until the syrup thickens slightly and becomes clear. Now remove the pudding from the steamer and place a circular serving plate over it. Grasping bowl and plate securely, turn them over. The pudding should slide out easily. Carefully peel off the plastic wrap. Pour the hot syrup over the pudding and serve at once.

The Chinese customarily eat desserts at banquets and as snacks, but seldom at family meals. Pictured here are three delectable sweets *(from top to bottom)*, Peking dust, eight-treasure rice pudding and spun apple. Their lovely appearance, reminiscent of the delicacy of the ivory figurines *(top left)*, illustrates the Chinese desire for beauty as well as flavor in their food.

Pa-ssŭ-ping-kuo
SPUN APPLES

拔絲蘋果

To make 16 spun apple slices

1 cup all-purpose flour
1 egg, lightly beaten and combined
    with ½ cup plus 2 tablespoons of
    cold water
2 medium-sized firm apples
3 cups plus 1 tablespoon peanut oil,
    or flavorless vegetable oil
1 cup sugar
¼ cup cold water
1 tablespoon black sesame seeds

PREPARE AHEAD: Pour the 1 cup of flour into a good-sized bowl and then, little by little, pour the beaten egg and water mixture into the flour, stirring constantly with a large spoon. Stir until you have formed a fairly smooth batter.

2. With a small, sharp knife, cut the apples into quarters. Peel off the skin and cut away the cores. Then cut the quarters into eighths.

3. Arrange your ingredients—the batter, the apples, the oil, the sugar, the water and the sesame seeds—within easy reach and set out a large serving plate lightly greased with oil and a large bowl containing one quart of water plus a dozen ice cubes.

TO COOK: In a 2- to 3-quart saucepan, heat the 3 cups of oil until a haze forms above it or it reaches a temperature of 375° on a deep-frying thermometer. At the same time, in a 12-inch wok or 10-inch skillet, heat the 1 tablespoon of oil with the sugar and water. Bring the sugar and water to a boil over high heat, stirring only until the sugar dissolves. Cook this mixture briskly without stirring until the syrup registers 300° on a candy thermometer or reaches the hard crack stage; that is to say, when a very small amount of the syrup dropped into ice water instantly forms a hard mass. Stir in the black sesame seeds and turn the heat down to its lowest point.

Now proceed to make the spun apples in the following fashion: Drop 8 of the apple wedges into the batter, stirring them about to coat them thoroughly. With chopsticks, tongs or a slotted spoon, transfer the wedges to the heated oil and deep-fry them for 1 minute, or until they turn light amber. Immediately, lift them out of the oil and put them into the skillet of hot syrup. Stir the wedges to coat them thoroughly with syrup, then— still using chopsticks, tongs or a slotted spoon—drop them one at a time into the bowl of ice water. The syrup coating will harden instantly and enclose each piece of apple in a clear, brilliant glaze. Transfer the finished spun apples to the lightly greased serving plate and make the second batch in precisely the same manner. Serve the spun apples as soon as you possibly can. The delicate candy glaze will soften if they are allowed to stand for long.

1 To make spun apples, batter-coated pieces of the fruit are deep-fried in hot oil until a light golden brown.

2 Add the apple and black sesame seeds to heated syrup, and stir rapidly to get a complete coating.

3 A piece is partly shelled to show the crunchy apple inside the crust. This dish requires accurate timing.

VIII

A Cuisine for All Continents

*I*n the Eastern kitchen the meat is sliced and ready—
Pounded beef and boiled pork and mutton.
The Master of the Feast hands round the wine. . . .

The fire glows and the smoke puffs and curls;
From the incense-burner rises a delicate fragrance.
The clear wine has made our cheeks red;
Round the table joy and peace prevail.
May those who shared in this day's delight
Through countless autumns enjoy like felicity.

—*"THE GOLDEN PALACE," ANON., C. FIRST CENTURY A.D.*

The fire pot is a do-it-yourself stove in which diners cook various combinations of food in a broth heated by a charcoal fire at the base of the circular chimney. Shown here is a chrysanthemum fire pot *(page 190)*, which includes *(clockwise from chimney)* pork, shrimp, spinach, beef, chicken and *bok choy*. Raw foods in the bowls are, from left to right, chicken, beef, clams and pork.

I remember the time when an old China hand returned to Shanghai from six months' leave in America in a state of high exasperation, and told me he couldn't understand his friends back in his home town.

"Does the same thing happen to you when you get back there?" he demanded. "Do people drag you practically right off the plane to a Chinese restaurant? They did that to me—they always do. Even people I've just met; the minute they hear I live in China, off we have to go to a Chinese restaurant. Wouldn't you think they'd realize it's the last thing I'd want to do, eat second-rate Chinese food after years of the very best?"

"Of course they take you to Chinese restaurants," I said, since the same had happened to me. "They want you to do the ordering. They don't know how, and it's a good chance to learn."

It is true that ordering a Chinese meal in America can be pretty difficult. The more modern restaurant proprietors have been making things a little easier in recent years by printing descriptions of the dishes in English, but even with this help it is still not simple to select an interesting meal. Chinese restaurateurs just have not appreciated the depth of Western ignorance about Oriental food. They generally have not realized that Westerners are used to one big dish, not several little ones. They find it hard to believe that customers could not know that while it is all right to have meat and fish and perhaps more meat and fish all at once, it is not a good idea to have both noodles and rice in one meal.

Two dishes that Westerners do know and repeatedly order are chop suey and chow mein. This is a great pity, for while chow mein can be good enough, there is little one can say in favor of chop suey, a dish unknown in China. One explanation of its origin is that the dish was born when the famous 19th Century diplomat Li Hung Chang, traveling in the West as the Chinese emperor's emissary, got indigestion from rich foreign food at banquets he had to attend. He had so agonizing an attack of biliousness following a hard week's banqueting in the United States that his aide Lo Feng-luh suggested a bland diet. Between them the gentlemen thought up the plainest possible dish—a concoction of celery and other vegetables sautéed with a little pork. Thus was chop suey born.

According to another theory we can blame chop suey on America's first transcontinental railways. To work on the building of these, indentured laborers were brought in by the thousands from southern China. Their American contractors learned that the coolies would toil patiently all day long, but had to have the rice they were used to. The Americans knew nothing about Chinese food, so they drafted cooks from the ranks of the coolies themselves—self-made cooks whose highest talents could achieve nothing better than a sloppy stew ladled over rice. When the railways were finished and the workers were shipped home, some of the Chinese elected to remain in the States. Among those who stayed were cooks from the old railway gangs, and they now set up in business for themselves, catering to other Chinese in humble sheds that were the first chop suey joints. When Westerners found that the food was cheap they too became customers, always asking for chop suey because that's all there was.

That other standby of Chinese restaurants in the United States, chow mein, is something else again. It had an honorable origin in China, where it is often eaten as a snack or light meal. When well prepared, it can be very good. (I still remember the chicken chow mein I ate on my first date, hundreds of years ago in St. Louis, in a Chinese restaurant where we were awed and delighted by lovely hanging lamps with red silk panels that gave out little illumination, and a romantic table of black wood inlaid with bits of abalone shell or possibly genuine mother-of-pearl. All the mysterious East was ours in Missouri, and chow mein too.)

Even after the old railway cooks died off, their successors continued to cook chop suey and chow mein for Americans. But under the pressure of criticism from their Chinese customers, the quality improved. The years passed and some of these restaurants expanded into prosperous establishments that served really good food to the Chinese, while patiently ladling out coolie food for Americans. But even some of the Americans were learning. A few daring souls sampled egg foo yung and spring rolls, and told their friends about them. Others, who had actually been to China, knew which places in Chinatown had the best cooks. Then, in the early years of this century, Chinese began to study abroad both in the United States and in England. These young people came from far more prosperous backgrounds than had the railway laborers and they wanted better food. Restaurants expanded to meet their needs—far more quickly in France than in North America. While Americans still floundered in the chop suey stage, a few excellent Chinese restaurants flourished in Paris.

The first Chinese in America came mostly from southern China, so the cooks of early days knew only southern-style cooking. Subsequent immigrants, too, were largely southerners. Thus Chinese restaurant cooking in America, even at its best, was for a long time limited to the style of South China. In saying this I mean no disrespect to the southern cuisine, which is one of the best China has to offer; I am merely stating a historical fact, which explains why it was the southern school of cookery that first spread over the world outside China.

The restaurant situation changed radically in the course of the Second World War. When China joined the Allies and declared war on the Axis, her diplomatic missions abroad had to be enlarged; in addition representatives were sent to many of the large cities of America, Free Europe and South America. The members of these missions often took their families with them, and in some cases the family cooks went too. Thus, for the first time numbers of people from provinces other than Kwangtung and Kwangsi went abroad, taking their regional cuisines with them. A lot of these people had to stay on after the war, and then the revolution in China left them—and their cooks—stranded where they were. Inevitably, some of the cooks opened restaurants for which we in the West are the gainers.

Today, in many large American cities, the discriminating diner can often have his choice of three of the great Chinese regional cuisines—Cantonese, northern and Szechwan. Among the many specialties of these regions, formerly unknown outside China, the fire pot may be the most unusual. Although this originated in the north, I first tasted it when Cantonese friends invited me to a chrysanthemum fire pot meal *(page 190)*. In the middle of the table stood the fire pot, an odd-looking vessel pierced in its middle by a thick metal cylinder whose base was filled with burning charcoal *(see picture, page 176)*. Bubbling chicken broth half filled the basin around the chimney and the heated cylinder. All around the fire pot lay a number of different uncooked foods. There was sliced white chicken meat, pork, beef, shrimp, sole, oysters, calf's liver, celery cabbage, bean curd and many other things. We chose the ingredient we wished first to eat—the hostess advised us to use the meat first, as it helps enrich the broth that way—and then, holding a piece in chopsticks, each of us dipped our food into the broth, held it there a minute or two, and then doused it in sauce. (We even mixed the sauce to our own taste.) When the cooked tidbit had been cooled by the sauce, it was ready to eat. It was absolutely delicious, this Chinese version of the chafing dish.

Later I discovered that there are several variations on this technique. In Shanghai they have a version called ten-varieties hot pot *(page 194)*,

Chinese women—a rare presence in the days of exclusionary immigration laws—grace a room of a turn-of-the-century San Francisco Chinatown restaurant. This lounge was a place where Chinese relaxed and gossiped before or after dinner among familiar flowers and plants, musical instruments and scrolls with lines of poetry—all nostalgic reminders of their distant homeland.

where meat, fish, shrimp balls and vegetables are cooked in advance and the guests pick the stuff out of the boiling broth just before eating it. In Peking I found myself liking the Mongolian fire pot *(Recipe Booklet)* best of all, but I knew it would never do for South China, where lamb, its main ingredient, has never been a favorite.

While the do-it-yourself fire pot meals are admittedly among the most exotic of the Chinese dishes to have reached the United States in the years since World War II, a great many other dishes, formerly to be had only in mainland China, are now regularly available in Chinese restaurants that have sprung up all over the world. Considering the remoteness of some of these eating places, it is amazing that the level of the cooking they offer is, generally speaking, so high.

Another interesting sidelight on Chinese restaurants abroad is that wherever they may be, in England or the United States or France or Germany or elsewhere, they seem to take on a little of the character of the country—although not enough to blur the Chinese style of the food. A Chinese restaurant I used to visit in Montmartre looked rather like any moderate-priced French café. In another quarter of Paris were more luxurious Chinese restaurants with decorations that recalled the Paris of the 1890s, all red plush and discreetly shaded lamps, patronized by well-dressed peo-

ple who made a lot of fuss about the wine. Both types of restaurant were un-mistakably French, and—basically—just as unmistakably Chinese.

However, you can never tell from the décor what kind of service you will get. In London, where Chinese restaurants have proliferated almost as rapidly as they have in New York, I often passed one in the West End but never felt tempted to try it out, because I was put off by what I could see of the interior. It looked like a teashop, one of those places la-dies go into for their elevenses and eat little cakes and drink strong India tea after a hard morning's shopping. But not long ago, at a dinner at an-other Chinese restaurant where we had one of the best meals I've ever eaten in London, a Japanese neighbor paused over his sautéed mushroom to say, "Yes, this is a good place, but I know a better one." You can imag-ine my surprise when he went on to name my refined teashop.

A Japanese should know what he's talking about when Chinese res-taurants are the subject, because Japan has the best Chinese food of any country outside China. Even before World War II Chinese cooking was ex-tremely popular among those Japanese city-dwellers who had a chance to sample it; since the war its popularity has had an enormous upsurge, and today the best hotels feature excellent Chinese food. A good indication of its prestige is that Japanese tycoons frequently favor Chinese restaurants

American women gather for a meal at the Far East Restaurant in New York's Chinatown sometime around 1905. For many years Americans visiting cities with large Chinese communities looked upon a sightseeing tour of Chinatown as an adventure whose thrills were heightened by shrewd guides with stops to view "dens of iniquity" and other staged excitements.

181

when they wish to give impressive luncheons for potential customers.

Australia, many of whose people have become familiar with the Far Eastern scene through business and sometimes through war, offers plenty of Chinese cooking, especially in places like the Campbell Street section of Sydney. I knew more than one Chinese in Shanghai and Canton whose relatives ran restaurants in Australia: it was so common a circumstance that I sometimes thought of Australia almost as an outgrowth of China.

I cannot speak from personal experience of Chinese restaurants in most of the Near East, except Turkey, where the influence of China is easily seen. This is not too surprising when you remember that Turkey was at the western end of the old silk caravan route from China. I remember eating in one Istanbul restaurant in a rundown district. It was located in a basement, put on no airs whatever, and served a simple, good and inexpensive meal that was just like the food one could get at any unpresuming café in a Chinese city. There are lots more frills and much higher prices at the Istanbul Hilton, where good Chinese dishes are also available. In between these extremes, of course, are all gradations of service and cost. In Ankara a few years ago I heard that a Chinese restaurant had just opened, the town's first, and of course I went to try it out. Like many eating houses in Turkey it was a roomy place set up in the plainest possible surroundings. Strictly speaking it was not Chinese after all, but Chinese-Turkestan, run by a Turkestani woman who had fled from the Communists during the revolution. "I got on my horse and escaped," she said, and then added, with the national pride that survived centuries of Chinese rule, "Chinese can't ride; they're hopeless with horses." Her food also defied Chinese influence in that it was highly peppered—much the way Western cuisines cooked in China used to be—and the main dish was a kind of minced meat on rice.

Somehow you do not expect to come upon Chinese food in Africa. It is there, though. East Africans like highly flavored, peppered food, and rice is their staple anyway. In Kenya the Pagoda Restaurant has long been a landmark of Nairobi. Romantically decorated with lanterns that light up at night, its popular bar off the main dining room even has plenty of rice wine. The Chinese proprietor and his assistants supervise African waiters in white uniform. The food served at authentic Chinese tables is excellent. Sooner or later everybody in Nairobi eats at the Pagoda —Africans, Europeans and Asians (as East Africa's Indians are called), and even Chinese. In Rhodesia's capital, Salisbury, the Bamboo Chinese Restaurant, though plain in appearance outside, is even more ornately decorated inside than the Pagoda, with a ceiling especially imported from the Far East, which is said to have cost thousands of dollars. There, too, the food is excellent, with plenty of variety. Another Chinese restaurant in Salisbury is the noisy and somewhat more showy Golden Dragon, whose decor includes giant plastic prawns and dusty lanterns. Sometimes an amateur rock-and-roll band adds to the din.

There is a fascinating Chinese restaurant in Addis Ababa called the China Bar, spacious and lavishly decorated and a favorite with Ethiopian women, who are themselves very decorative in their long white dresses and embroidered shawls, American tourists, Ethiopian men-about-town in smart Western suits, Africans from all over the continent—and Chinese. The Chinese owners take the orders, writing in Chinese, English and Amharic, and direct the Ethiopian waiters. The food is very good. Another Addis Ababa Chinese restaurant is the Hong Kong, decorated on the exterior to look like a pagoda but whose plain interior is not unlike that of a Horn & Hardart Automat.

In the Western Hemisphere, Latin American historians dispute as to when the Chinese first arrived. Coolies were imported for labor from 1850 to 1874 just as they were on the west coast of the United States. In North America, Canada has in recent years gained excellent Chinese restaurants as an aftermath of the revolution, but the first Chinese in Canada were drawn to British Columbia during the Gold Rush of the 1850s.

When I consider the remote corners of the world to which Chinese cooking has spread, it is my inescapable conclusion that Chinese cooking, rather than French, is now the truly international cuisine. Chinese cooking can adapt itself to every purse, from the poorest to that of the richest epicure. Long before we of the West knew of it, Chinese cooking had taken hold in Thailand, where it still exercises a very strong influence. Many Indonesian dishes are a blend of Chinese and Indian cuisines. The food of Vietnam is primarily Chinese in its nature. Chinese settlers sailed to Malaya 2,000 years ago and though the population is now chiefly Malay the food has never ceased to be more Chinese than anything else: in Singapore, where a major percentage of the population is Chinese, the cooks, in the Chinese tradition, have adapted the native foodstuffs but use them in their own inimitable way. Burma and Cambodia, like so much of the Far East, bow to China in the kitchen.

When I say that Chinese is the most international cuisine of the world, I do not mean that it will ever usurp the unique position of French cookery. I cannot imagine a time when Chinese names will push good old kitchen French off our Western menu-cards. But in numberless places a long way from France, where it is impossible to get a truly French dish, and where the local cookery is dreadful, we still, in all probability, can find some Chinese restaurant and eat well. Before the Chinese cook works his magic the vegetables may be old and the meat tough, but he will surmount those difficulties and the customer will enjoy his meal.

Besides, it is a healthy cuisine, being low in calories and fat content. In affluent Western societies those who can afford to are prone to eat too much, especially of fatty foods. But even in affluent societies, unfortunately, there are poor people who suffer from malnutrition. Chinese cooking avoids the faults of overrich food, and its cheap but nutritious ingredients can supply a healthy diet for poor people. Many dietitians call it the best-balanced diet in the world. A most revealing demonstration of its healthful quality took place early in World War II. When the Japanese occupied Hong Kong they imprisoned the foreign residents of the city and put them on a starvation diet of two meals a day, consisting of a little rice and a smaller amount of thin stew made of vegetables and fish or, very infrequently, a bit of meat. We were all sure that some of the older people, especially those in bad health, would never survive. They had lived well, and more than a few had drunk or worried themselves into stomach ulcers or heart conditions. Many were overweight. One man in particular looked unlikely to last a week in camp—and yet, after two months of the diet there, he was practically cured. The same can be said of many other prisoners. Before this period, one of the foods ulcer patients were especially warned to avoid was rice. Since the experience of the prison camps, however, doctors often recommend a rice diet to such sufferers.

All this talk about restaurant food should not mislead the housewife. Though Chinese are fond of eating out, home cooking is not the same thing as restaurant cooking in China any more than it is in the West. A restaurant chef must cook in large quantities. He knows that certain advantages of home cooking—individual seasoning, swift service from kitchen to table—must be sacrificed to his necessity to purvey a lot of food to many people, some of them in a hurry. It is tempting for a chef to be careless if he is catering to unwary foreigners, and some Chinese restaurants, even those with good reputations, are guilty of the common faults of restaurant cooking: too much oil because there is too much food cooking all at once in the wok, and overlavish use of monosodium glutamate to bring up the flavor of tired vegetables.

Another problem that plagues restaurateurs is that while the Chinese are very appreciative of really good chefs, sadly there are never enough superchefs to supply the needs of the good Chinese restaurants. While this may be true to a greater or lesser degree of other national cuisines, the situation is particularly difficult for the Chinese because the mother country is no longer supplying as many young cooks as it once did. Nowadays in China the emphasis is placed on economics and politics, even on the village level. Within a dozen years after the Communist takeover Peggy Durdin, a writer who grew up in China, was lamenting the official stance against culinary traditions in a *New York Times* article entitled "Mao's 'Great Crime' against Cuisine."

Communists, said Mrs. Durdin, having destroyed the art of conversation through spies, and having forced everyone to write poems of dubious literary value if great patriotic fervor, had turned their efforts to destroying "one of the greatest pleasures of every Chinese—food. . . ." The Communists, she continued, had abolished individual kitchens in rural areas and organized instead a system of groups that ate in what she called the world's largest and worst chain of government-run cafeterias. Such a system, especially with the shortages of food that have occurred periodically in China, would be fatal to any cuisine, but twice as quickly lethal in China, where good cooking calls for long preparation. Moreover, China never trained many cooks in the skills necessary to cater for such large numbers and there were far from enough large stoves or utensils. The news from the mainland at that time indicated great shortages of meat, fish and fruit, and frequently no fresh or even pickled vegetables. Sometimes even soy sauce was lacking. Rice and wheat were frequently in short supply and had to be supplemented with husks, sweet potatoes and coarse beans. Vegetable oil was practically unobtainable. As a result, reported Mrs. Durdin, Chinese food was often dull, tasteless, monotonous or simply badly cooked. "The Chinese Communist press . . . ran a story . . . highly commending a commune cook because she had evolved *thirty* ways to

184

A Chinese market in New York City presents exotic foods arranged on shelves and counters or hung from racks overhead.

cook the sweet potato, thus eliminating the need for any other dishes."

What a change from the food she enjoyed in her childhood, Mrs. Durdin recalled—the eight-jewel roast duck of Shanghai, stuffed with rice and eight other ingredients, or Hangchow's beggars' chicken, "a fattened fowl salt-spiced, wrapped in great fragrant leaves, enveloped in a thick coat of mud, baked very slowly, carried from the kitchen in a great shovel and broken open by the chef in the customer's presence." In the north, she remembered, the dishes of the poor, though simpler, were often as good as those of the rich, cooked as carefully, and eaten with as much enjoyment. In closing, Mrs. Durdin made the gloomy prognostication that in another 15 or 20 years China might well have forgotten its own dishes and all that would remain of the world's best cooking would be found "in the 'chop suey' restaurants of New York and San Francisco, where the food always becomes less and less Chinese, and the cooks themselves will hardly recollect the origin of the tasteless, hybrid and homeless dishes they are cooking."

Mrs. Durdin's grim appraisal of Chinese cooking both inside and outside China was written in 1961, before political unrest in mainland China threatened to eradicate the last traces of the ancient tradition of fine eating. In following years Mao's Red Guards, that bullying crowd of schoolchildren, turned their attention to the restaurants of Peking after having burned priceless ancient scrolls and destroyed old bronzes snatched from the city's museums. Since, according to the Red Guards, the restaurants encouraged the public to indulge in the capitalist vice of eating good food, it was necessary to burn the menu-cards, substitute standardized lists of commune food, and decree that all proprietors thenceforth must serve only the plainest meals. And yet the classic Chinese cuisine somehow survived in its native land, a happy outcome that became clear following the warming of relations among the onetime cold warriors. Sumptuous banquets lavished on distinguished visitors displayed Chinese cooking at its best and removed any fear that a glorious tradition can ever be totally submerged.

During times of both turmoil and tranquillity in the homeland, devoted people outside China have been doing their utmost to maintain the highest standards of Chinese cooking, and Chinese restaurants are no longer chop suey places. I recently had dinner at the New York restaurant run by Emily Kwoh. Also present was Grace Chu. These two are among the outstanding experts on Chinese food in America. I asked Mrs. Chu if she thinks the Chinese dishes in America are really the same as they used to be at home.

"Of course not," she said, "and cooking is bound to change even more. It's not that the technique deteriorates, but we have to use substitutes for many of the ingredients we can't get. However, that doesn't necessarily mean that the dishes will be less good. One of the important things about Chinese cuisine is that it can adapt itself. It has always adapted itself to the stresses and strains that happen in a long history."

"Still, the danger is certainly with us," said Emily Kwoh. "One's got to watch out, constantly. And some of the best recipes will be lost when the chefs who guard them die, unless other people are trained in the same techniques. For a while at first I was very gloomy about all this—I thought possibly our people living abroad might lose interest in cooking,

and get careless, and let it be lost, but I don't think that way any more. The cooking today is good—outside of China, I mean. It's going down on the mainland, naturally, but it's being kept alive outside, especially in Taiwan. I'm beginning to think, though, that we ought to consolidate while there is still time: the people with quality restaurants ought to get together to maintain a kind of pool of knowledge." Emily continued, "The best of Chinese cooking of all regions must be preserved. If I'd been asked ten years ago I might have said it would be impossible to do, because only the expatriate Chinese would be interested and they aren't numerous enough to swing it. Nowadays, Americans too would understand what we're after. Lots of Americans know how to eat. Our chefs are cooking for educated palates."

She left the table to greet an incoming party and find them a table. The room was very full. But, looking around, I reflected that there wasn't likely to be one order for chop suey in the lot.

Marchers in a Chinese New Year's Eve parade frolic through the heart of New York's Chinatown on a night also marked by one of the year's most elaborate feasts. Symbolic figures (like the one near the banner of a local club), designed to ward off evil, highlight the procession.

Hsing-jen-ping
ALMOND COOKIES

杏仁餅

To make 8 dozen cookies

½ pound lard
¾ cup sugar
2 eggs
1 tablespoon almond extract
4 drops yellow food coloring
2½ cups unsifted flour
½ teaspoon baking soda
¼ teaspoon salt
½ cup blanched almonds, split in half
1 egg, lightly beaten

PREPARE AHEAD: In a large mixing bowl, cream the lard and sugar by beating them together with a large spoon until light and fluffy. Beat in the eggs, one at a time, then add the almond extract and food coloring. Combine the flour, baking soda and salt and sift them into the bowl. With your fingers, mix the ingredients together until a fairly firm dough is formed. Divide the dough in half and shape it into two fat cylinders, then roll them on a lightly floured surface with the palms of your hands until each cylinder is about 12 inches long and 1½ inches in diameter. Wrap in wax paper and refrigerate for at least 3 hours.

TO COOK: Preheat the oven to 375°. With a cleaver or sharp knife, cut the chilled dough crosswise into slices ¼ inch thick. Lay a dozen or so of the circles side by side and 1 inch apart on an ungreased cookie sheet, and press an almond half gently but firmly in the center of each. Brush the cookies with a thin film of beaten egg and bake in the center of the oven for about 10 minutes, or until they are golden brown. With a spatula, transfer the cookies to a rack to cool.

K'ao-pai-ku
BARBECUED SPARERIBS

烤排骨

2 pounds spareribs in one piece

MARINADE
¼ cup soy sauce
2 tablespoons honey
2 tablespoons *hoisin* sauce
2 tablespoons white vinegar
1 tablespoon Chinese rice wine, or pale dry sherry
1 teaspoon finely chopped garlic
1 teaspoon sugar
2 tablespoons chicken stock, fresh or canned
Canned plum sauce

PREPARE AHEAD: 1. With a cleaver or large, sharp knife, trim any excess fat from the spareribs. If the breastbone is still attached, use a cleaver to chop it away from the ribs and discard it. Place the spareribs in a long, shallow dish, large enough to hold them comfortably.

2. In a small bowl, combine the soy sauce, honey, *hoisin* sauce, vinegar, wine, garlic, sugar and chicken stock. Stir until they are well mixed. Pour the sauce over the spareribs, baste them thoroughly and let them marinate for 3 hours at room temperature (6 hours if refrigerated), turning them over in the marinade and basting them every hour or so.

TO COOK: Preheat the oven to 375°. To catch the drippings of the spareribs as they roast, and to prevent the oven from smoking as well, fill a large shallow roasting pan or baking dish with water and place it on the lowest rack of the oven. Insert the curved tips of two or three S-shaped hooks—such as curtain hooks or 5-inch lengths of heavy-duty wire or even unpainted coat hangers bent into shape—at each end of the spareribs. As if hanging a hammock, use the curved ends of the hooks to suspend the ribs from the uppermost rack of the oven directly above the pan of water. Roast the ribs undisturbed for 45 minutes. Then raise the oven heat to 450° and roast about 15 minutes longer, or until the spareribs are crisp and a deep, golden brown.

To serve, place the ribs on a chopping board and, with a cleaver, separate the strip into individual ribs. If the ribs are large, chop them each in half crosswise. Serve hot or cold with plum sauce. As a main course, this will serve 4 to 6. As part of an elaborate Chinese meal *(page 200)*, it will serve 6 to 8.

Barbecued ribs are crisp and succulent when seasoned the Chinese way and cooked suspended from a rack in the oven by S-shaped lengths of wire.

Hsi-mi-chü-keng 西米橘羹

HOT ORANGE PUDDING

To serve 4 to 6

PREPARE AHEAD: 1. In a small bowl, cover the tapioca with ½ cup of cold water and let it soak for at least 4 hours.

2. With a small knife, peel the orange and remove the white membrane clinging to each section. Break the orange meat into small pieces.

3. Have the tapioca, orange and sugar within easy reach.

TO COOK: In a 2-quart saucepan, combine 2 cups of cold water with the sugar. Bring to a boil over high heat, stirring until the sugar dissolves. Drain the tapioca and pour it into the pan slowly, stirring constantly. Cook over moderate heat, stirring, for 2 minutes until the pudding thickens. Stir in the orange and bring to a boil again. Serve at once.

½ cup pearl tapioca
1 large orange
2½ cups cold water
¼ cup sugar

189

4 ounces cellophane noodles

1 whole chicken breast, about ¾
    pound

½ pound lean, boneless pork

½ pound top sirloin of beef

½ pound calf's liver or chicken livers

½ pound raw shrimp in their shells
    (about 30-36 to a pound)

½ pound fillet of sole or pike

1 dozen small oysters, or small hard-
    shell clams, shucked

1 pound celery cabbage

½ pound fresh, crisp spinach leaves

2 three-inch squares fresh bean curd,
    about ½ inch thick, cut into ½-
    inch-wide slices

¼ cup soy sauce

2 tablespoons sesame-seed oil

2 tablespoons Chinese rice wine, or
    pale dry sherry

3 eggs, lightly beaten

8 cups chicken stock, fresh or canned

Chu-hua-kuo 菊花鍋

CHRYSANTHEMUM FIRE POT

PREPARE AHEAD: 1. Place the pork, beef, calf's liver or chicken livers and sole or pike in your freezer for about 30 minutes, or only long enough to firm the meat for easier slicing. Then, with a cleaver or sharp knife, cut the pork, beef, liver and fish horizontally into the thinnest possible slices. To make fairly uniform pieces that will be easy to handle with chopsticks, cut the slices into strips 3 inches long and 1 inch wide.

2. Bone, skin and slice the chicken breast in the following fashion: Lay the whole chicken breast on its side on a chopping board. Holding the breast firmly in place, cut it lengthwise along the curved breastbone with a cleaver or sharp knife. Carefully cut away all the meat from one side of the breastbone. Then grasp the meat in one hand and pull it off the bones and away from the skin—using the cleaver to free the meat if necessary. Turn the breast over and repeat on the other side. Remove each tube-shaped fillet from the boned breast meat, and pull out and discard the white tendons. Freeze the chicken for 30 minutes to firm it. Then lay the breast meat and fillets flat, and cut them horizontally into paper-thin slices. Then cut the slices crosswise into pieces 3 inches wide and 1 inch long.

3. In a large, flat pan or dish, cover the cellophane noodles with 2 cups of warm water and soak them for 30 minutes. Then drain the noodles and cut them into 6-inch lengths.

4. Shell the shrimp. With a small, sharp knife, make a shallow incision down their backs and lift out the black or white intestinal vein with the point of the knife. Slice the shrimp in half, lengthwise.

5. With a cleaver or sharp knife, cut away any wilted leaves from the cabbage and separate it into stalks. Wash the stalks under cold water and cut each stalk into 1-by-3-inch pieces. Blanch the cabbage by dropping the pieces into a pot of boiling water. Immediately turn off the heat. Let the cabbage pieces rest in the water for 3 minutes, then drain and pat them dry.

6. Trim the spinach leaves of their stalks and wash the leaves thoroughly.

7. Arrange each kind of meat, fish or seafood, and the noodles and vegetables in overlapping layers on plates or in separate rows on 2 large platters.

8. Mix the soy sauce, sesame-seed oil and wine in a small bowl, and stir in the eggs. Mix thoroughly, then ladle a tablespoon of the sauce into each of 6 individual soup bowls, and pour the rest into a serving bowl.

9. Have the above ingredients and the chicken stock within easy reach.

TO COOK: If you have a fire pot, preheat the broiler to its highest point. Arrange 20 charcoal briquets side by side in a baking pan lined with heavy aluminum foil and place it under the broiler. Heat for 10 to 15 minutes until a white ash forms on the briquets. With tongs, transfer the briquets to the funnel of the fire pot. Lay an asbestos mat in the center of the dining table and carefully set the fire pot on it.

If you do not have a fire pot, substitute an electric casserole set at 300°. In a 3- to 4-quart saucepan, bring the chicken stock to a bubbling boil, then pour it into the fire pot (or electric casserole). Keep the stock simmering throughout the meal. Arrange the plates or platters of uncooked food around the fire pot and give each guest a bowl of sauce. Place the extra sauce in its bowl on the table. Traditionally, each guest picks up a piece of food from the platters with chopsticks and transfers it to a wire strainer to cook in the simmering stock. When cooked to taste, it is plucked out of the strainer with chopsticks, dipped into sauce and eaten. The strainer may be eliminated and the food held in the stock with chopsticks. Or long-handled forks with heatproof handles may be used—fondue forks if available. When all the meat, fish and seafood have been consumed, a little of the stock (now a rich, highly flavored broth) is ladled into each guest's bowl and drunk as a soup. The noodles and vegetables are then dropped into the stock remaining in the fire pot, cooked for a minute or so, and ladled with the broth into the bowls to be eaten as a last course.

Yen-wo-t'ang
BIRD'S NEST SOUP

燕窩湯

To serve 6

1 cup loosely packed dried bird's nest
1 whole chicken breast, about ¾ pound
¼ cup cold water
1 teaspoon cornstarch
1 teaspoon salt
2 egg whites
1 quart chicken stock, fresh or canned
⅛ teaspoon ground white pepper
2 tablespoons cornstarch dissolved in 3 tablespoons cold chicken stock, or cold water
A ⅛-inch-thick slice cooked Smithfield ham, minced

PREPARE AHEAD: 1. Place the bird's nest in a medium-sized bowl, add enough warm water to cover and soak the nest for 3 hours. Then, with a pair of tweezers, carefully remove any protruding feathers. Wash the nest thoroughly under running water. Place the bird's nest in a small saucepan, cover it with cold water and bring to a boil over high heat. Boil it uncovered for 5 minutes, then drain and discard the water.

2. Make chicken velvet (*photographs of the process, page 41*) in the following fashion: Lay the whole unsplit chicken breast on its side on a chopping board. Holding the breast firmly in place with one hand, cut it lengthwise along the curved breastbone with a cleaver or sharp knife. Carefully cut away all the meat from the bones, following the side of the breastbone and the outside of the ribs. Then grasp the meat in one hand and pull it off the bones and away from the skin—using the cleaver to free the meat if necessary. Turn the breast over and repeat on the other side. Remove each tube-shaped fillet from the rest of the breast meat, and pull out and discard the white tendons in each fillet. Slice the fillets lengthwise into thin strips. Holding the front of one main breast section, scrape the meat away from its membrane with repeated light strokes of the cleaver. Repeat with the other side of the breast.

Combine the breast meat with the fillets and then mince finely, adding about ¼ cup of water—a little at a time—as you work. Place the minced chicken in a mixing bowl, sprinkle it with the cornstarch and salt, and stir together gently but thoroughly with your hand or a large spoon. In a separate bowl, beat the egg whites with a fork or whisk until they are frothy, then pour them into the chicken mixture and mix thoroughly. The finished chicken velvet should be light and fluffy.

3. Have the bird's nest, chicken velvet, chicken stock, white pepper, cornstarch mixture and ham within easy reach.

TO COOK: In a 3- to 4-quart saucepan, bring the chicken stock to a boil over high heat. Drop in the bird's nest, bring to a boil again, then reduce the heat to low and simmer covered for 5 minutes. Add 1 teaspoon of salt and the white pepper. Give the cornstarch mixture a quick stir to recombine it and add it to the pan, stirring constantly and gently until the mixture thickens. Add the chicken velvet, stir once or twice to disperse it evenly through the soup and remove the pan from the heat. Pour the soup into a tureen, sprinkle the top with ham and serve at once.

A hollowed-out melon filled with Chinese fruits colorfully mixes litchis, kumquats and loquats with melon balls.

Shih-chin-kuo-pin 什錦菓品

WATERMELON SHELLS FILLED WITH FRUIT

To serve 6 to 8

1 medium-sized, firm ripe watermelon
   (about 10 pounds)
24 canned litchis, drained
8 canned loquats, drained
8 preserved kumquats, drained
8 canned water-pack kumquats,
   drained

Using a cleaver or large, sharp knife, cut the melon in half crosswise. Scoop out most of the melon pulp with a large spoon, leaving a shell of pulp about ½ inch thick inside each half. Carefully remove and discard all the watermelon seeds. If desired, cut a design in the outer rind *(opposite)* with a sharp knife or scallop the top edges of each melon half.

Cut the melon pulp into 1-inch cubes or, with a melon baller, shape it into balls. In a large bowl, combine the melon cubes or balls with the litchis, loquats and kumquats. Spoon the fruit into the two melon shells, dividing the fruit evenly between them. Chill thoroughly before serving.

NOTE: Other fruits—such as cantaloupe or honeydew melon balls, orange sections or apple wedges—may be added to the mixture in the melon shells, or substituted for the fruits listed above if these are not readily available.

Ch'a-shao 义燒

ROAST PORK STRIPS

2 pounds boneless pork, preferably
   butt
2 tablespoons chicken stock, fresh or
   canned
2 tablespoons soy sauce
1 tablespoon brown-bean sauce,
   mashed
1 tablespoon Chinese rice wine, or
   pale dry sherry
1½ tablespoons sugar
¾ teaspoon salt
1 teaspoon finely chopped garlic
2 to 3 drops red food coloring

PREPARE AHEAD: 1. With a cleaver or a large, sharp knife, cut the pork butt into 1½- to 2-inch-wide strips. Lay the strips flat and cut them in half lengthwise. Depending on the original size of the butt, you should have from 6 to 8 long, thick strips. Lay the strips flat in one or two layers in a large, shallow dish or pan long enough to hold them easily.

2. In a small bowl, combine the chicken stock, soy sauce, brown-bean sauce, sugar, wine, salt, garlic and food coloring. Stir until the ingredients are well mixed. Pour the sauce over the pork strips, baste them thoroughly and let them marinate for at least 3 hours at room temperature or for at least 6 hours in the refrigerator. Turn the strips over in the marinade every hour or so.

TO COOK: Preheat the oven to 350°. To catch the drippings of the pork strips as they roast and to prevent the oven from smoking as well, fill a large, shallow roasting pan with water and place it on the lowest rack of the oven. Insert one curved tip of an S-shaped hook at the end of each strip of pork. (Any hook will do: a curtain hook, S-hook, even a 5- or 6-inch length of heavy-duty wire or unpainted wire coat hanger bent into that shape.) Hang the hooks from the uppermost rack of the oven, directly above the pan of water. Roast the pork undisturbed for 45 minutes. Then increase the oven heat to 450° and roast for 15 minutes longer, or until the pork strips are crisp and a rich, golden brown. Remove the pork from the oven, take out the hooks and cut the strips crosswise into paper-thin slices. Serve the sliced pork hot, arranged in overlapping layers, on a heated platter. As a main course, this will serve 4 to 6. As part of a Chinese meal *(page 200)*, it will serve 8 to 10.

If you like, the pork may be cooled to room temperature, or wrapped in aluminum foil and chilled in the refrigerator, and then presented as a cold meat course or as part of a Chinese cold plate. Leftover roast pork can be wrapped tightly and stored in the refrigerator or freezer for use in such recipes as steamed buns with pork filling *(page 150)* or ten-varieties hot pot *(page 194)*.

To serve 6 to 8

8 dried Chinese mushrooms, 1 to 1½
 inches in diameter
2 ounces cellophane noodles
½ pound Chinese cabbage, celery
 cabbage or *bok choy*
1 pound fresh spinach leaves, washed
 and torn into small pieces
12 bamboo shoot slices (⅛ inch
 thick) cut into tree shapes
 according to directions on page 69
2 slices (⅛ inch thick) cooked
 Smithfield ham, cut into 2½-by-1-
 inch pieces
12 shrimp balls, prepared according
 to the recipe on page 54
12 slices (2½-by-1-by-⅛-inch) star
 anise beef, prepared according to
 the recipe on page 46
12 slices (2½-by-1-by-⅛-inch) roast
 pork, prepared according to the
 recipe on page 193
12 slices (½ inch thick) egg pancake
 with pork filling, prepared
 according to the recipe on page 86
6 cups chicken stock, fresh or canned
¼ cup soy sauce
1 tablespoon sesame-seed oil

Shih-chin-nuan-kuo
什錦煖鍋
TEN-VARIETIES HOT POT

PREPARE AHEAD: 1. In a small bowl, soak the mushrooms in ½ cup of warm water for 30 minutes. Discard the water. With a cleaver or knife, cut away and discard the tough stems of the mushrooms, and cut each cap in half.

2. In another bowl, soak the noodles in 2 cups of warm water for 30 minutes. Drain, discard the water and cut the noodles into 4-inch lengths.

3. With a cleaver or sharp knife, trim any wilted green leaves and the root ends off the cabbage. Separate the stalks, wash them under cold water and cut them lengthwise into strips 3 inches long by 1 inch wide. Blanch the strips in 2 quarts of boiling water for 1 minute, then drain them thoroughly.

4. In a large bowl, combine the soy sauce and sesame-seed oil, and mix thoroughly. Then ladle the sauce into 6 or 8 individual soup bowls.

5. Have the above ingredients, spinach, bamboo shoots, ham, shrimp balls, beef, pork, egg pancake slices and chicken stock within easy reach.

TO COOK: Prepare the fire pot as described in the recipe for the chrysanthemum fire pot *(page 190)*, or substitute a chafing dish, fondue pot or electric casserole.

Place the cabbage, spinach and noodles in the fire pot or whatever utensil you are using, in one layer, and on top of them arrange the ham, shrimp balls, beef, mushrooms, pancake slices, pork and bamboo shoots. Pour the stock in along the side of the pot, trying not to disturb the pattern of the food. Bring to a boil, cover the pot and cook for 10 minutes.

Give each guest a bowl of dipping sauce and either chopsticks, a long heatproof-handled fork or a fondue fork, and let them help themselves from the pot. When all the food is consumed, ladle the remaining stock into soup bowls and serve it as a final course.

1 pound lean spareribs
1 large clove garlic, crushed and
 peeled
1 tablespoon peanut oil, or flavorless
 vegetable oil
1 tablespoon soy sauce
1 teaspoon sugar
1 tablespoon fermented black beans,
 chopped
½ cup cold water
1 teaspoon cornstarch dissolved in 1
 tablespoon cold chicken stock,
 fresh or canned, or cold water

Tou-sh'ih-pai-ku
豆豉排骨
BRAISED SPARERIBS WITH FERMENTED BLACK BEANS

PREPARE AHEAD: 1. With a cleaver or large, sharp knife, separate the spareribs and chop them crosswise into 1½-inch lengths.

2. Have the spareribs, and the oil, garlic, soy sauce, sugar, fermented black beans and ½ cup of water within easy reach.

TO COOK: Set a 12-inch wok or 10-inch skillet over high heat for 30 seconds. Pour in the oil, swirl it about in the pan and heat for another 30 seconds, turning the heat down if the oil begins to smoke. Add the spareribs and stir-fry them for 3 to 4 minutes until lightly browned on both sides. Add the garlic, soy sauce, sugar, black beans and water, and stir to coat the spareribs with the mixture. Bring to a boil, cover the pan and reduce the heat to low. Simmer for about an hour, turning the meat occasionally.

To serve, arrange the spareribs on a heated platter. Skim and discard the surface fat from the sauce and remove the garlic. Give the cornstarch mixture a quick stir to recombine it and pour it into the pan. Cook, stirring, for a few seconds until the sauce thickens and clears. Then pour it over the ribs and serve at once. As a main course, this will serve 2. As part of a Chinese meal *(page 200)*, it will serve 4 to 6.

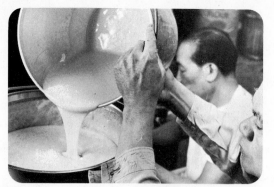

1 Batter, consisting mainly of wheat flour, brown sugar, water and eggs, is poured into a vat.

2 Batter drops onto conveyor-belt griddles, and is stamped into cookie shape by a round mold.

Shaping a fortune cookie, a baker sits near a cooling rack, a tray of fortunes (some are shown on the next pages) and finished cookies.

3 After being quick-baked while moving, the cookie is returned to receive the printed fortune.

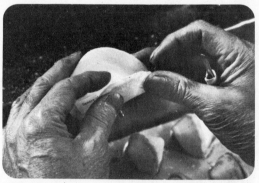

4 With dexterous movements, a baker folds the still-hot cookie before it can cool and harden.

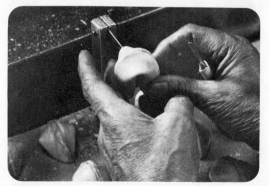

5 The fortune cookie is bent into its finished shape over a small metal arm.

195

The sayings found in fortune cookies range from the banal to the serious to the unintentionally funny.

A Guide to Ingredients in Chinese Cooking

Most of the ingredients called for in this book's recipes can be found at any grocery store or supermarket. The exceptions are listed and described on these pages—and may require a visit or letter to a Chinese market. Some Chinese foods can be approximated by more familiar ingredients—but substitutes may change the character of a dish somewhat. If an ingredient is not available, the best course is often to omit it from the recipe. To make your shopping easier, the name of each food is spelled out in Chinese characters above its English translation. Many Chinese markets do their own packaging, usually in small plastic bags to encourage experimentation. By shopping around, one can find a large selection packaged in a variety of sizes.

罐 頭 筍

BAMBOO SHOOTS: Ivory-colored, conical-shaped shoots of tropical bamboo, usually about 3 inches across and 4 inches long. Sold canned in Oriental specialty stores. (Can sizes range from 4 ounces up.) Large wedges packed in water are best. After opening, drain and store in fresh water in a covered jar in the refrigerator, changing the water daily. Can be kept for about 10 days. Kohlrabi or celery hearts will approximate the texture but not the flavor.

豆 腐

BEAN CURD, FRESH: Square, custardlike cakes of pressed puréed soybeans. Sold by the cake, usually ½ to ¾ inch thick and 3 inches square, in Oriental specialty stores. Drain and store in fresh water in a covered jar in the refrigerator for up to 2 weeks, changing the water daily. No substitute.

二 竹

BEAN-CURD SKIN: Thin, stiff sheets of dried bean curd. Sold by weight in Chinese specialty stores (5 to 6 sheets weigh about 1 ounce). Needs no refrigeration. No substitute.

綠 豆 芽

BEAN SPROUTS: Young sprouts of the mung bean, 1½ to 2 inches long. Sold fresh by weight and in 4- to 8-ounce cans. The fresh ones have parchmentlike husks that must be removed before using. Refrigerate fresh sprouts in water in a covered jar for up to 2 weeks. After opening canned sprouts, drain and store in fresh water in a covered jar in the refrigerator—they will keep for 2 to 3 days. No substitute.

燕 窩

BIRD'S NEST: Fragments of a translucent, gelatinous material with which Asian swiftlets coat their nests. Available in Chinese specialty stores, usually in 4- to 8-ounce packages. Needs no refrigeration. No substitute.

豆 豉

BLACK BEANS, FERMENTED: Strongly flavored, preserved black soybeans. Sold in 3- to 4-ounce cans and 3- to 4-ounce plastic bags in Chinese specialty shops. After opening, store up to 6 months, refrigerated, in tightly covered container or plastic bag. Add a few drops of peanut oil or flavorless vegetable oil or water if they seem to be drying out. Substitute additional quantity of soy sauce or salt.

白 菜

BOK CHOY: A variety of Chinese cabbage that grows somewhat like celery but has 12- to 16-inch-long smooth white stalks and large dark-green leaves. Sold fresh by the bunch or weight in Oriental specialty stores. Refrigerate in plastic bag for about a week. Substitute celery cabbage or romaine lettuce.

原 晒 豉

BROWN-BEAN SAUCE: Thick sauce made from fermented yellow beans, flour and salt. Sold in cans of 1 pound or more in Chinese specialty stores. After opening, it keeps for months refrigerated in a covered jar. Substitute additional salt.

天 津 白 菜

CELERY CABBAGE: A variety of Chinese cabbage that grows like celery but has crisp, tightly packed, yellow-white stalks 14 to 16 inches long and 4 to 5 inches wide. Sold fresh by the bunch or weight in Oriental specialty stores and some vegetable stores and supermarkets. Store, refrigerated, for about 2 weeks. Substitute savoy cabbage.

粉 絲

CELLOPHANE NOODLES (BEAN THREAD): Thin, translucent noodles made from ground mung beans. Dried in looped skeins and sold in 2- to 6-ounce packages in Chinese specialty stores. Wrap to store. No substitute.

芫 茜

CHINESE PARSLEY (FRESH CORIANDER OR CILANTRO): Aromatic herb with flat leaves and stronger flavor than curly parsley. Sold fresh by the bunch in Chinese, Italian and Latin American grocery stores and some vegetable stores. Store in plastic bag in refrigerator for a week. Substitute flat-leaf Italian parsley for appearance but not flavor.

雲 耳

CLOUD EAR: Small, crinkly, gelatinous dried fungus, about 1 inch long. Sold by weight in Chinese specialty shops. Store in a covered jar. No substitute.

蘇 梅 醬

DUCK SAUCE (PLUM SAUCE): Reddish-brown condiment with sweet and pungent flavor made from plums, apricots, chili, vinegar and sugar. Sold in 1-pound cans and 4- to 12-ounce bottles in Chinese specialty stores and in gourmet shops. After opening, can be kept, refrigerated, for months. The canned variety should be transferred to a covered jar. No substitute.

蛋 麵

EGG NOODLES, CHINESE: Long, thin noodles no more than ⅛ inch wide made of flour, eggs and water. Sold, by the pound, fresh or dried, in Chinese specialty stores. Fresh ones may be stored in plastic bags in the freezer for months or in the refrigerator for 1 week. Substitute any other narrow egg noodle.

五 香 粉

FIVE-SPICE POWDER: A combination of five ground spices (anise seed, fennel, clove, cinnamon and Szechwan pepper) sold ready-mixed by weight in Chinese specialty stores. Store at room temperature in tightly covered container. Substitute allspice.

薑

GINGER ROOT, FRESH: Gnarled brown root, about 3 inches long. Sold by weight in Oriental and Puerto Rican specialty shops. Whole ginger root will keep for a few weeks wrapped in paper toweling in the refrigerator. Peeled, sliced fresh ginger root may be placed in a jar of dry sherry and refrigerated for several months. Peeled, sliced ginger root in brine is available in cans and may be substituted.

海 鮮 醬

HOISIN SAUCE: Sweet, brownish-red sauce made from soybeans, flour, sugar, water, spices, garlic and chili, for use in cooking. Sold in 1-pound cans and up. After opening, can be stored for several months in the refrigerator in tightly covered container. No substitute.

白 蘿 蔔

ICICLE RADISH: White, crisp-textured radish about 2 to 4 inches in diameter and 6 to 10 inches long. Available only in Oriental specialty shops. Can be stored in vegetable section of refrigerator for about a week. Substitute the small white radishes sold in supermarkets and vegetable stores. These are sometimes also called icicle radishes but are not the same variety as the Chinese vegetable.

紅 棗

JUJUBES (RED DATES): Small, red dried fruit with puckered skin and a sweet, subtle prunelike flavor. Sold by weight in Chinese specialty stores. Must be covered with boiling water and soaked 1 to 2 hours before using. Store in covered container. Substitute prunes, not California dates.

金 橘

KUMQUATS: Yellow-orange citrus fruit, about 1 to 1½ inches long, with a tart orange flavor. Sometimes available fresh in midwinter or early spring, but usually sold in cans and jars of various sizes, often preserved in rich syrup. Found in Chinese specialty shops, gourmet food stores and many supermarkets. After opening canned kumquats, store in their own syrup in a tightly covered jar in the refrigerator. No substitute.

荔 枝

LITCHIS: Small, oval fruit with rough red skin, white pulp and large pit. Sold fresh in July in Chinese specialty stores; or in 1-pound cans or dried in 10-ounce packets in Chinese stores and gourmet shops. After opening, refrigerate the canned variety in its own syrup in a tightly covered jar. No substitute.

枇 杷

LOQUATS: Small, yellow-orange pitted fruit the size of an apricot with peach flavor. Sold pitted and preserved in 14-ounce cans in Chinese specialty stores. After opening, store in own syrup in a covered jar in the refrigerator. Substitute canned apricots or peaches.

藕

LOTUS ROOT: Long, potatolike root. Sold fresh in sections about 2 to 3 inches in diameter and 4 to 6 inches long, canned in various sizes, and dried in 4-ounce boxes in Chinese specialty stores. Each has a different texture and flavor, and they cannot be used interchangeably. Store the fresh or canned roots in the refrigerator. No substitute.

冬 菇

MUSHROOMS, CHINESE DRIED:

Strongly-flavored dried mushrooms from ¾ to 2 inches in diameter. Sold by weight or already packaged in Oriental specialty shops. Can be stored indefinitely, at room temperature in a covered jar. No substitute. (European dried mushrooms have a different taste.)

酸 菜

MUSTARD GREENS, PICKLED: Green, cabbagelike vegetable packed in brine. Sold in 16-ounce jars, 16-ounce cans and from barrels in Chinese specialty stores. Store in the refrigerator. Substitute rinsed sauerkraut.

蠔 油

OYSTER SAUCE: Thick, brown sauce with a rich flavor, made from oysters, soy sauce and brine. Sold in 6- or 12-ounce bottles in Oriental specialty shops. It will keep indefinitely. No substitute.

紅 豆 沙

RED-BEAN PASTE: Thick, sweet paste made from red soybeans. Available in cans in Oriental specialty shops. It will keep for months refrigerated in a covered jar. No substitute.

糯 米

RICE, GLUTINOUS: A variety of short-grain rice which becomes sticky when cooked. Sold by weight in Chinese specialty stores. Store in a covered container. No substitute.

米 粉

RICE STICK NOODLES: Thin, brittle white noodles, dried in 8-inch looped skeins. Sold in 8- to 16-ounce packages in Chinese specialty stores. Will keep indefinitely. No substitute.

鹹 蛋

SALTED EGGS: Duck eggs soaked in brine for a month or more. Sold individually in Chinese specialty stores only. The yolks are sold separately in packets. Store in refrigerator. No substitute.

芝 蔴

SESAME SEEDS: Tiny, flat seeds, either black or white. Sold by weight in Oriental specialty stores, in Middle Eastern and Italian stores, and gourmet food shops. Store in a covered container. No substitute.

蔴 油

SESAME-SEED OIL: Strong, faintly nutty-flavored oil made from roasted sesame seeds. Sold in bottles in Oriental specialty stores. It will keep indefinitely. No substitute. Do not confuse it with the mild sesame-seed oil sometimes sold in supermarkets.

魚 翅

SHARK'S FIN: Long threads of dried cartilage from the fins of sharks. Sold by weight and in 6- or 8-ounce boxes in Chinese specialty stores. It will keep indefinitely. No substitute.

蝦 米

SHRIMP, DRIED: Tiny shelled and dried shrimp with a sharp, salty flavor. Sold by weight in Chinese specialty shops. Store in a jar. No substitute.

火 腿

SMITHFIELD HAM: Cured smoked ham with a strong, distinctive flavor, sold already cooked. Not Chinese, but close in taste to Chinese ham. Available by weight or by the slice in Chinese specialty stores, gourmet shops and some supermarkets. Will keep for several weeks tightly wrapped in foil or plastic in refrigerator. Substitute Italian *prosciutto* or Westphalian ham.

雪 豆

SNOW PEAS: Flat, pale-green peas eaten pods and all. Sold fresh by weight in Oriental specialty stores and also available frozen in 10-ounce boxes in supermarkets. Store fresh ones in plastic bag in refrigerator; use as soon as possible.

醬 油

SOY SAUCE: Pungent, salty, brown liquid made from fermented soybeans, wheat, yeast and salt. The imported Chinese and Japanese sauces are best and are available in various-sized bottles in supermarkets as well as Oriental specialty stores.

八 角

STAR ANISE: Dry, brown, licorice-flavored spice that looks like an 8-pointed star about an inch across. Sold whole (though often the sections break apart) by weight in Chinese specialty stores. Store indefinitely in tightly covered containers. Substitute anise extract, but use it very sparingly.

花 椒

SZECHWAN PEPPER (FAGARA): Speckled brown peppercorns with a mildly hot flavor and a pleasant scent. Sold whole, not ground, by weight in Chinese specialty shops. It will keep indefinitely in tightly covered containers. No substitute.

西 米 粉

TAPIOCA FLOUR: Waxy-textured flour made from the same cassava root that is the basis of tapioca. Sold in 1-pound plastic bags in Oriental and health-food shops.

Store like regular wheat flour. No substitute.

皮 蛋

THOUSAND-YEAR EGGS: Duck eggs that have been coated with a paste of ashes, lime and salt, and buried for several months. Sold individually in Chinese specialty stores. Will keep for about a month. No substitute.

金 針

TIGER LILY BUDS, DRIED: Pale-gold lily buds about 2 to 3 inches long. Sold by weight in Chinese specialty shops. Store in a covered container. No substitute.

麵 筋

VEGETABLE STEAK: A vegetarian food that looks like a small beefsteak but is made from wheat gluten. Sold in cans in Oriental and health-food stores. No substitute.

馬 蹄

WATER CHESTNUTS: Walnut-sized bulbs with tough, brown skins and crisp, white meat. Sold fresh by weight in Chinese specialty shops and in various-sized cans whole, sliced or diced, in supermarkets as well. Store fresh ones refrigerated for several days. After opening canned ones, drain and refrigerate in water in a covered jar for about a month, changing the water daily. No substitute.

澄 粉

WHEAT STARCH: Wheat flour with the gluten extracted. Sold in 1-pound sacks in Chinese specialty shops. Store like regular flour. No substitute.

冬 瓜

WINTER MELON: Round, green-skinned melons of varying sizes. The pulp is translucent and white. Its flavor most resembles zucchini or other soft-skinned squash. Sold fresh in slices by weight in Chinese specialty stores. Keep in refrigerator for 3 to 5 days with cut surfaces covered with plastic wrap. Substitute zucchini or cucumber.

Mail-Order Sources

The following stores, grouped by city, accept mail orders for Chinese foods. All carry canned and dried ingredients; a few will ship the fresh ones. Some can supply utensils. Because policies differ and managements change, it is best to check the stores nearest you to determine what they have in stock and how best to buy it.

East

Eastern Trading Co.
2801 Broadway
New York, N.Y. 10025

Yuet Hing Market Inc.
23 Pell Street
New York, N.Y. 10013

Legal Sea Foods Market
237 Hampshire Street
Cambridge, Mass. 02139

(Despite its name, Legal Sea Foods carries a full line of canned, dried and fresh Chinese foods.)

Wing Wing Imported Groceries
79 Harrison Avenue
Boston, Mass. 02111

Midwest

Kam Shing Co.
2246 South Wentworth Street
Chicago, Ill. 60616

Shiroma
1058 West Argyle Street
Chicago, Ill. 60640

Star Market
3349 North Clark Street
Chicago, Ill. 60657

West

Wing Chong Lung Co.
922 South San Pedro Street
Los Angeles, Calif. 90015

Shing Chong & Co.
800 Grant Avenue
San Francisco, Calif. 94108

Manley Produce
1101 Grant Avenue
San Francisco, Calif. 94133

South

Oriental Import-Export Co.
2009 Polk Street
Houston, Texas 77002

Canada

Leong Jung Co.
999 Clark St.
Montreal 128, Quebec

How to Use Chinese Recipes

When a hostess begins planning a menu based on one of the traditional Western cuisines, she may have a few problems arising out of seasonal availability of certain ingredients. But, generally speaking, she is on familiar ground, and she can proceed with confidence in her selection of appetizer, soup, entrée, vegetables, salad and dessert. Chinese meals are a special problem because the categories are different.

Anyone who has ever puzzled over the "long menu" in a Chinese restaurant knows how bewildering it can be first to decide how many dishes to sample, and then to try to achieve the balance of tastes and textures that is the hallmark of fine Chinese eating. If a few points are remembered, making up a memorable menu is not nearly the task it may seem to be at first glance, and the results are bound to enhance the reputation of the ingenious hostess.

Basic Rules of Chinese Meal Planning

In the first place, a Chinese meal is rather like a buffet, at which a guest eats little bits of this and that rather than a large portion of just one food. Chinese dishes are not served in individual portions, but are platters shared by all those who sit at the table. Everyone can—indeed he is expected to—eat from all the dishes presented.

A properly planned dinner includes at least one fowl, one fish and one meat dish—and these are complemented with appropriate vegetables. The Chinese set off spicy dishes with bland ones, delicate flavors with robust, and soft-textured foods are complemented by something crisp.

Concerned as they are with the appearance of food, the Chinese try to include both pale and richly colored dishes, and make a point of serving some bright-green vegetables for contrast.

While the Chinese serve many dishes at a meal, they do not—except at elaborate banquet-style dinners—present a menu in courses. Cold foods, meant to be nibbled like hors d'oeuvre, are sometimes placed on the table before the guests are seated. Otherwise, all the dishes are brought to the table at one time and eaten together. Hot tidbits like shrimp toast are classic banquet fare, brought to the table throughout the meal.

Although they are famous for excellent soups, the Chinese serve them in what may seem surprising ways. In some cases, soups appear early in the meal, but the light broths might be sipped throughout, and both the broths and richer, cornstarch-thickened soups like velvet corn or sour-and-hot soup may be presented separately in the middle of a dinner. The heavy, full-meal soups like *wonton* and Chinese noodle soup are most often eaten as lunches or snacks, though sometimes they become a part of the menu for a special occasion such as a birthday banquet.

You will find a number of so-called salads in this book, but the Chinese do not have a word for salad in the familiar sense of raw greens tossed with dressing. In China uncooked vegetables rarely appear at the table. Cold cooked vegetable dishes, dressed with soy sauce, wine and seasonings—and equivalent to the Western salad in many ways—are sometimes part of the main meal, but they also may be a feature of the cold hors d'oeuvre plate.

Desserts as such are practically unknown in China, though some hosts serve fresh fruit after a meal. The sweets included in this book would be more likely to appear between courses at a Chinese banquet.

Experimenting with Chinese Dishes

Since a full meal requires such a careful balance of foods—and the preparation of many new dishes at once—it may be easiest to start out by using the recipes in this book for simple substitutions in Western-style meals. A Chinese vegetable might be sampled one day, a chicken dish the next, while you stick to the sequence of courses you are used to. In this way you can perfect Chinese cooking techniques one at a time and gradually get acquainted with the special tastes of Chinese foods and seasonings.

In many cases, one Chinese preparation can replace several Western ones, for among their dishes are numerous combinations of meat or seafood and vegetables—equivalents to our stews and casseroles. One authority distinguishes between the "light meat dishes," which are more vegetable than meat, and the "heavy meat dishes," in which the proportions are reversed. If you plan to serve chicken with bean sprouts, bear in mind that it will take the place of both a chicken and vegetable dish in your menu.

The number of guests that a dish will serve depends on whether you are planning it as part of a Western meal or using it in a fully Chinese menu. The Western-style helpings would probably be larger and the dish would serve fewer guests than it might in a Chinese dinner. Some of the recipes in this book—such as those that make six pancakes, or for a duck traditionally carved into eight sections—are described as serving a definite number. For vegetables, a good rule of thumb is that one pound will serve four.

The number of dishes you can serve easily is also influenced by the way they must be cooked. One of the most frequently used of Chinese techniques is the stir-fry method—constant lifting and turning of small pieces of food to cook them quickly. This is simple enough to master, but stir-fried dishes, like other short-order foods, are meant to be brought to the table the minute they are done and served piping hot. And only one pound of meat can be stir-fried at one time. When you plan your menus, keep this in mind. In all likelihood, one modest stir-fried dish per meal will be all you can handle at first.

Planning an All-Chinese Meal

After a few successful experiments with several different recipes, your understanding of Chinese methods will have grown sufficiently so that you are ready to undertake a full Chinese meal. The easiest way to do this is to plan to serve only two or three Chinese dishes—maybe a soup and two main courses—together with the traditional rice and tea, and fresh fruit for dessert. If the quantities in a recipe seem small, you may double them if you remember the limitations on stir-frying; when you double a stir-fry recipe, you must make it in two batches using separate woks or skillets.

With a little practice, you will quickly gain the confidence to try full-scale dinners. Here are six family menus to start with. They include foods that are stir-fried or deep-fried, thus requiring last-minute attention, as well as others that can be finished earlier and kept warm in their pots. They combine a variety of basic foods (meat, poultry, fish or seafood), of tastes, of textures, of colors in typical Chinese style. As a concession to Western tastes, these menus do include desserts; if you like, you can prove yourself an old China hand by omitting the sweets.

Six Family Menus
(for four persons)

1
Stir-fried fish fillets *(Recipe Booklet)*
White-cut chicken and ham in green paradise *(page 84)*
Braised star anise beef, hot or cold *(page 46)*
Fresh asparagus salad *(page 46)*
Rice *(page 125)*
Almond float *(Recipe Booklet)*
Tea *(Recipe Booklet)*

2
Winter melon soup *(page 107)*
Stir-fried shrimp with peas *(page 51)*
Braised soy sauce chicken *(page 85)*
Cucumber salad with spicy dressing *(page 83)*
Rice *(page 125)*
Hot orange pudding *(page 189)*
Tea *(Recipe Booklet)*

3
Deep-fried phoenix-tailed shrimp *(Recipe Booklet)*
Stir-fried chicken with fresh mushrooms *(Recipe Booklet)*
Braised spareribs with fermented black beans *(page 194)*
Creamed Chinese cabbage *(Recipe Booklet)*
Rice *(page 125)*
Peking dust *(page 170)*
Tea *(Recipe Booklet)*

4
Sour-and-hot soup *(page 108)*
Steamed sea bass with fermented black beans *(page 104)*
Red-cooked pork shoulder *(Recipe Booklet)*
Stir-fried string beans with water chestnuts *(page 80)*
Rice *(page 125)*
Deep-fried *wontons* with date filling *(page 128)*
Tea *(Recipe Booklet)*

5
Lobster Cantonese *(Recipe Booklet)*
Roast pork *(page 193)*
Drunk chicken *(Recipe Booklet)*
Celery and dried-shrimp salad *(page 80)*
Rice *(page 125)*
Almond cookies *(page 188)*
Tea *(Recipe Booklet)*

6
Deep-fried *wontons* filled with pork and shrimp *(page 128)*
Squirrel fish *(page 106)*
Pepper steak *(page 54)*
Lion's head *(Recipe Booklet)*
Rice *(page 125)*
Melon filled with Chinese fruits *(page 193)*
Tea *(Recipe Booklet)*

Recipe Index

General Index

Credits and Acknowledgments

The sources for the illustrations in this book are shown below. Credits for the pictures from left to right are separated by commas, from top to bottom by dashes.

All photographs in this book are by Michael Rougier except: 4—Mary Ellen Mark—courtesy Grace Chu, Jim Hip Bok. 9—T. Tanuma. 12,13—Base map by Frederick Wong; typography by Lothar Roth. 14,15—Emil Schulthess from Black Star. 18,19—T. Tanuma. 26—Ivan Massar from Black Star. 33—Ralph Herrmanns. 38 through 41—Walter Daran. 44—Charles Phillips. 47—Drawing by Matt Greene. 50—Charles Phillips. 55—Top left and center left Charles Phillips. 56—Drawing by Matt Greene, Charles Phillips. 57—Bill Helms. 62,63—Bill Helms. 68,69—Charles Phillips. 75—Bill Helms. 76,77—Ralph Herrmanns. 88—John R. Freeman courtesy The British Museum. 106—Left (1-4) Charles Phillips, right (5) David Arnold. 110—John R. Freeman courtesy The British Museum. 118,119—John R. Freeman courtesy The British Museum. 122,123—Ralph Herrmanns. 126,127—Charles Phillips. 132—Raymond Schwartz courtesy the Freer Gallery of Art, Washington D.C. 148—Charles Phillips. 151—Charles Phillips. 154—T. Tanuma. 161—Larry Burrows. 165—Bill Helms. 169—Drawings and photograph by Matt Greene. 171—Bill Helms. 172—Charles Phillips. 175—Charles Phillips. 180—San Francisco Public Library. 181—Brown Brothers. 185—Lee Boltin. 187—Richard Meek. 195—Charles Phillips. 196,197—Richard Jeffery.

For their help in the preparation of this book the editors would like to thank the following: *in Hong Kong*, May Chang; *in Taiwan*, Lawrence K. Chang, Lillian Kiang; *in New York City*, David Arnold; Bibi and Haber Oriental Art, Inc.; The China Institute; Chueng Lam Dong, Yuen S. Chin and Richard F. Lee of Jen Gen, Inc.; Copeland and Thompson, Inc.; Frances Dominis; Eden & Co.; Charles R. Gracie & Co.; Gunn and Latchford, Inc.; Georg Jensen, Inc.; Keikos Gift Shop; Diane Kelly; G. Malina, Inc.; Mi-Sin Gift Shop; Mon Fong Wo Co.; Oriental Export & Import Co.; Quong Yuen Shing & Co.; Benny Seto, Pagoda Restaurant; Sherrill Imports Inc.; Margaret Spader; J. T. Tai & Co.; Wing On Wo & Co.; Wo Fat Company; George Young, The Chinese Benevolent Association.

Sources consulted in the production of this book include: *Land Utilization in China* by John Lossing Buck; *Chinese Creeds and Customs* by V. R. Burkhardt; *With the Empress Dowager* by Katharine A. Carl; *Peking* by Nigel Cameron and Brian Brake; *How to Cook and Eat in Chinese* by Buwei Yang Chao; *The Joyce Chen Cookbook* by Joyce Chen; *Musings of a Chinese Gourmet* by F. T. Cheng; *The Pleasures of Chinese Cooking* by Grace Zía Chu; *Court Dishes of China* by Su Chung (Lucille Davis); *A History of Chinese Literature* by Herbert A. Giles; *China Only Yesterday* and *China to Me* by Emily Hahn; *The Joy of Chinese Cooking* by Doreen Yen Hung Feng; *The Fine Art of Chinese Cooking* by Lee Su Jan; *Twilight in the Forbidden City* by Reginald F. Johnston; *The Tea Cookbook* by William I. Kaufman; *Food for the Emperor* by John D. Keys; *The Chinese in American Life* by S. W. Kung; *Harem Favorites of an Illustrious Celestial* by Howard Levy; *Ancient China* by Edward H. Schafer and the Editors of TIME-LIFE BOOKS; *The Gay Genius, The Importance of Understanding* and *My Country and My People* by Lin Yutang; *Two Years in the Forbidden City* by Princess Der Ling; *Mrs. Ma's Chinese Cookbook* by Nancy Chih Ma; *The Travels of Marco Polo*, William Marsden, tr.; *The Thousand Recipe Chinese Cookbook* by Gloria Bley Miller; *The Art of Chinese Cooking* by Mimi Ouei; *Mary Sia's Chinese Cookbook* by Mary Sia; *The Romance of Tea* by William Ukers; *The Yellow Emperor's Classic of Internal Medicine*, I. Veith, tr.; *The Life and Times of Li Po, The Life and Times of Po Chu-i* and *Translations from the Chinese*, Arthur Waley, tr.; *A Chinese Village* by Martin C. Yang.